Fabulous
FAT-FREE
COOKING

Fabulous FAT-FREE COOKING

MORE THAN 225 DISHES—All Delicious,
All Nutritious, All with Less Than 1 Gram of Fat!

LYNN FISCHER
Author of Lowfat Cooking for Dummies

RODALE

Printed in the United States of America on acid-free ∞, recycled paper ♻

Interior and Cover Designer: Debra Sfetsios
Cover Photographer: Angelo Caggiano
Front Cover Recipe: Mahimahi with Shrimp and Tropical Salsa (page 122)

Library of Congress Cataloging-in-Publication Data

Fischer, Lynn.
    Fabulous fat-free cooking : more than 225 dishes—all delicious, all nutritious, all with less then 1 gram of fat! / by Lynn Fischer.
       p.   cm.
    Includes index.
    ISBN 0–87596–383–8 hardcover
    1. Cookery.   2. Low-fat diet—Recipes.   I. Title.
TX714.F57   1997
641.5'638—dc21   97–872

    ISBN 1–57954–242–5 paperback

Distributed to the book trade by St. Martin's Press

    6 8 10 9 7 5   hardcover

2 4 6 8 10 9 7 5 3 1   paperback

Visit us on the Web at www.rodalecookbooks.com, or call us toll-free at (800) 848-4735.

RODALE

WE INSPIRE AND ENABLE PEOPLE TO IMPROVE
THEIR LIVES AND THE WORLD AROUND THEM

To **Chris**

In all Rodale Press cookbooks, our mission is to provide delicious and nutritious low-fat recipes. Our recipes also meet the standards of the Rodale Test Kitchen for dependability, ease, practicality, and, most of all, great taste. To give us your comments, call (800) 848-4735.

Contents

Foreword

In 1961, a committee of scientists reviewed the research from around the world on the relationship between heart disease and food. The evidence of a link between diet and heart disease was so strong that in that same year, the American Heart Association issued a warning to the public: Continued consumption of diets high in animal fats is related to the rapidly rising rate of heart attacks among our citizens.

Fortunately, the American public responded to the lifesaving message. In the intervening years, we have reduced our intake of both cholesterol and saturated fat. It is virtually certain that the decline in deaths from heart disease that began in 1965 is directly attributable to changes in our diet.

As a result of the reduction in heart attacks and stroke, Americans are now living longer than ever. More important, we are living healthier than ever.

One of the approaches to reducing the intake of saturated fats has been to warn against the overconsumption of dairy fats, eggs, and fatty meats. A very important supplementary approach, however, is to recommend nutritious, low-fat foods that can displace those dishes that contain the undesirable fats.

In this book, Lynn Fischer provides a very positive message by making fruits, vegetables, and grains more attractive. We can actually enjoy the dietary changes that are recommended by the American Heart Association and by the healthy eating plan outlined in the U.S. Department of Agriculture's Food Guide Pyramid.

Most of us have probably no more than 20 entrées that comprise our regular eating plan. If we identify the dishes that are high in saturated fat and replace them with recipes from this cookbook, we can dramatically improve the health benefits of our diet while increasing our culinary satisfaction.

Eating good food is one of the great pleasures of life. Lynn Fischer has made it possible for us to increase our pleasure while we improve our health.

W. Virgil Brown, M.D.
Professor of Internal Medicine, Emory University School of Medicine
President of the American Heart Association (1991–1992)

Acknowledgments

There are lots of people to give a nod to and thank publicly when you write a cookbook, because you can't do it alone. My thanks are both professional and personal.

Two food companies helped with a few of the recipes in this book. The White Lily Foods Company developed several dessert recipes. I asked them to participate because of their technical expertise in reducing the fat in cakes and cookies. I learned from them that soft-wheat flour, which has less gluten, doesn't need as much fat to tenderize it as all-purpose flour does. I thank Lloyd Montgomery, Steve Queisser, and especially Belinda Ellis.

Thanks to the Borden company for developing a scrumptious rice pudding recipe with their fat-free sweetened condensed skim milk.

Other talented people who tested or developed recipes were gifted dessert cook Beatrice Ojakangas; Susan McQuillan; Jenna Holst; Andrea Goodman, my former assistant who's such a sweetheart; Rita Calvert, our very talented tester and stylist for nearly all my 200-plus TV shows and food writer for the *Baltimore Sun*; and Leela Berman Greenblat, new mama and prop stylist for my shows.

I especially thank Gail Ross, my literary agent, adviser, lawyer, and friend, who has assisted me with contracts and contacts for nine years. Gail looks out for my best interests, and I greatly admire, respect, and care about her even more today than when I first met her.

My former assistant, Marty Cavendish, was of great help with the beginning of the book, but, darn, I lost her when she was named director of Washington's Women in Film and Video, where I sit on the board of directors.

Chris Loudon is a registered dietitian and the most pleasant, uncomplaining, on-time, always-accurate associate, who is one of the few in the food business who understands low-fat and fat-free cooking. Chris did all the nutritional analyses for this book and analyzes recipes for my television shows, too.

Finally, I thank several at Rodale Press. Tom Ney, food editor for *Prevention* magazine. Gentle managing editor for cookbooks Jean Rogers, for asking me if I would do this book in the first place. Also office manager Roberta Mulliner, who guided me around, literally. JoAnn Brader, manager of the Rodale Test Kitchen, and her helpful staff. Her kind and supportive words came at the right time (cookbooks are tough—good cookbooks are really tough).

I especially thank Sharon Sanders, cooking editor at Rodale Books, with whom I worked most closely and who really knows food and cooking. She has been my toughest, most talented, hardest working, and most demanding editor, but also the one from whom I learned the most. Her skills helped me make every one of these recipes really fabulous.

Thanks to family and friends, because they are so special, and their support and friendship are important. My sweet friend, mentor, and special joy is Virginia Von Fremd (world's best speech coach, too). My dearest friend, Beth Mendelson, jet-setting producer. My tallest friend, Kathy McClain, television station general manager. My lawyer friend, Pat Mahoney. My oldest friends, Jean and Bob Morressy. Susie Hart Wydler, Terry Frantz McKenzie, and my skiing buddies, Jennifer Douglas and Stanford Adelstein. Special friends Bob Furman, Lil Smith, Randy Feldman, Phil Beuth of ABC, Dr. Manuel Trujillo, Karl Viehe, Arna Vodenos, Denise Barta, Linda Ringe and Bob Franken, and Andrea and Marty Kalin all seem to be there when I need words of encouragement, to gossip, to go over a situation or problem—whatever. I adore and lean on them all and try to be there for them, too.

With family, I thank niece Susie Fischer McGarry and her husband, Mark McGarry, who always put me up in St. Petersburg, Florida. My brother Tom Connor and his wife, Mary, in Naples, Florida, and brother Bob Connor in Oakland, California, all of whom put me up when I visit and are always there by phone to offer counsel and support. I thank my sister Ann and her husband, Bill Taylor, who do the same in Oakland and brother Jim Connor and his wife, Trudy, in Troy, Michigan. My pop, Addison Connor, in Naples, who is 91 this year and has hung up his Rollerblades. My daughter, Lisa Jehle, and grandchild Wolf, both in Topanga. My son, Cary Bialac, in Austin. The whole big Gillette family—and especially Christopher Gillette, who's such a doll and is always there for me.

Introduction

I have an appreciation of people and a curiosity
about health, so I wasn't surprised when a sociologist told me that food habits are the most difficult habits to change. Even when we move to a new country and quickly change our style of dress, our language, and even our lifestyle, our food preferences linger.

Because change is difficult, I know why lowering the fat content of familiar foods can be upsetting for some. But we can change. In fact, for some of us, change isn't an option if we want to regain our health. I contend that if the food tastes and looks good, we will incorporate it into our lives and we will learn to love it. It can be done.

I've changed, and I've seen others change, too.

I began reducing the fat in my recipes decades ago. As a newlywed in the early 1970s, I faced a hefty healthy-cooking challenge. My husband, though only in his thirties, was diagnosed with dangerously high cholesterol, caused by too much total fat, saturated fat, and cholesterol in his diet. He eliminated egg yolks, butter, and cheese. He switched from whole milk to low-fat milk. But his cholesterol stayed at a badly elevated 286.

I felt I could improve it more. I attended classes at Eastern Virginia Medical School in Norfolk and buttonholed doctors for information. On Saturdays I scoured the Himmelfarb Health Sciences Library at George Washington University School of Medicine and Health Sciences in Washington, D.C., for every heart and cardiology journal available.

In the kitchen, however, I was on my own. Because I couldn't find anyone who was writing about or teaching low-fat cooking techniques, I improvised. I started to prepare extremely low cholesterol, low fat dishes (surreptitiously at first, because they had to look and taste like the fattier foods that my husband loved).

I served smaller meat portions, but he didn't notice the difference, because the dinner plates looked so abundant. I said I was conserving financially. We were actually eating more food.

A typical meal was cod fillet with a low-fat white lemon sauce speckled with fresh parsley. On the side was a fluffy mound of rice tossed with scallions, a bit of margarine, soy sauce, and ginger. Two or more vegetables, flavored with margarine, rounded out the dinner. In the 1970s, it was considered a pretty healthy meal.

From meat loaf to muffins, hash browns to hollandaise, cream sauces to casseroles, I learned to make low-fat food taste luscious and look lush.

My husband's cholesterol dropped 100 points to 186, and he got back down to his college weight of 186 pounds. Inspired by these improvements, and with a surge in energy, he began to exercise daily. This raised his levels of HDL, the good type of cholesterol that helps transport the bad cholesterol (LDL) from the body.

I also began to reap the rewards of a more healthful lifestyle. Our medical bills dropped. I noticed that I, too, had more energy. Best of all, we had a peace of mind that's gained when you take charge of your health.

An unexpected divorce and the economic climate took me to Washington, D.C. With my newly acquired medical knowledge, I became the television medical anchor for WTTG, part of the Fox Network. In 1989, I co-wrote *The Fischer/Brown Low Cholesterol Gourmet* with W. Virgil Brown, M.D.

With my subsequent books and

television cooking shows on the Discovery Channel and Public Broadcasting System, I've been privileged to bring my message of healthy eating to many more thousands. Allow me to share one more personal story.

Mark White is the talented director of all 230 episodes of my television shows. When I first started working with Mark in the early 1990s, he tipped the scales at 300 pounds. A lifelong struggle with weight, combined with a sedentary job and insufficient exercise, had brought him to his all-time high.

As we taped more and more shows, Mark developed what he called a heightened awareness of low-fat eating. But it was my low-fat apple crumble that really spurred Mark to make a positive change in his life.

Mark is an admitted sweets lover, and his mother was a caterer, so he knows delicious food when he tastes it. One bite of the apple crumble, and he was hooked.

As Mark sampled more of my dishes, he learned that he could feel satisfied without feeling bloated. He made the effort to revamp his eating habits, exercise more, and drink more water. He now weighs 200 pounds and feels better than he has in years.

Mark doesn't diet anymore; he just eats sensibly. But his "sensibly" is nearly fat-free. He eats about 3,000 calories a day, composed primarily of low-fat and fat-free foods.

Because of business travel, Mark must dine frequently in restaurants. So he relies on fat-free meals at home to keep his weight in check.

When I get impatient with slow set changes during program tapings, Mark says, "Be patient, Lynn. It doesn't happen by itself." I can share the same sentiment with all of you struggling with dietary change.

People always ask me if I really do eat this way. Of course I do. How else would I summon the energy to write six cookbooks, create two television cooking shows, launch a radio show, conduct seminars, give speeches and cooking classes, assemble a cookware catalog, create *Lynn Fischer's Healthy Indulgences* CD-ROM, enjoy a fulfilling personal life, and serve on the boards of several associations and charitable organizations?

Eating this way, I am convinced, gives me energy and vitality. I am confident that you will accomplish more in your life when you aim toward good health. I believe that this book can help you achieve your goal. Stay well.

Why **Fat-Free?**

Fat! Can't live with it. But we can't live without it.

Fat is essential for human life. Dietary fat
enables our bodies to absorb vitamins A, D, E, and
K. These vitamins help maintain vision, the skeletal
system, and neurological and vascular health.
Without fat to cushion body blows, our organs would
be black and blue. Fat regulates our body temperature, conditions our hair, softens our skin, and
soothes our nerves with a protective covering.

But if fat is so good, why is everyone saying that it's so bad?

Ever hear about too much of a good thing?

Overfed and Undernourished

America's natural abundance provides us with amber waves of grain (good sources of complex carbohydrates and fiber), but it also puts heavy cream, butter, full-fat cheeses, bacon, well-marbled steaks, greasy burgers, pork spareribs, french fries, and plump chickens on our tables. The buttercream frosting on the cake is a food industry adept at stirring lots of hidden fat into processed foods.

The uninvited guests at this feast are heart disease, some cancers, diabetes, and obesity—all life threatening and all directly linked to a diet that's too high in fat. Health experts agree that most Americans should reduce their intake of fat, particularly the saturated fat found primarily in animal foods such as red meat, poultry with skin, cheese, and butter as well as in tropical plant oils such as coconut and palm.

Most Americans eat a diet that gets about 37 percent of calories from fat. About 15 to 17 percent of that is saturated fat. But the U.S. Department of Agriculture (USDA), the American Heart Association, and other health authorities recommend that for the general population, no more than 30 percent of calories should come from fat. Of the total calories consumed, no more than 10 percent should come from saturated fat.

Some health experts recommend the total elimination of saturated fat from the diet—to be replaced by monounsaturated oils, like olive and canola, and polyunsaturated oils, like corn, safflower, and soybean. These monounsaturates and polyunsaturates have been found to lower total blood cholesterol when substituted for saturated fat in the diet.

Of course, all oils are a concentrated source of calories, containing approximately 120 calories and 14 grams of fat in each tablespoon. Even healthy individuals at normal weight are advised to eat fats sparingly.

Zeroing In on Fat

No one can, or should, eat a totally fat-free diet. In fact, it would be impossible.

Every food contains some fat as part of its natural composition—some less, some more. Four ounces of apple has 0.4 gram of fat, compared with an equal amount of Fuerte avocado, which has 10 grams. Three ounces of broiled haddock contain a mere 0.8 gram, while the same amount of broiled prime rib of beef contains 30 grams. One cup of skim milk has only 0.4 gram of fat, but 1 cup of heavy whipping cream has 88 grams.

Even the fat-free recipes in this book—which all contain *less than 1 gram of fat per serving*—contain trace amounts of fat.

So it comes down to choices. You have the power to make the right food choices to maximize your health.

My goal in creating these fat-free dishes is not to convince anyone to subscribe to a totally fat-free diet. Rather, I want to provide some truly delicious tools—more than 225 of them—to help you bring your total fat consumption way, way down.

How Much Fat Is Right for You?

That's a hard call. The American Heart Association recommends that fat intake for the general population go no lower than 15 percent of calories. Other health experts recommend a fat intake as low as 10 percent of total calories for individuals with coronary heart disease or risk

factors for heart disease, such as high cholesterol or obesity.

Dean Ornish, M.D., president and director of the Preventive Medicine Research Institute in Sausalito, California, describes his "reversal diet" in his book *Dr. Dean Ornish's Program for Reversing Heart Disease*. Dr. Ornish recommends an intake of no more than 10 percent of calories from fat to reverse the effects of arterial blockage.

The American Heart Association acknowledges that very low fat diets have been tested with favorable results in studies of persons at high risk, but such diets have not been demonstrated to be of value for the general population.

Consult your doctor to determine your individual dietary needs. Then compute your ideal calorie intake and set up a fat budget based on the percentage of calories from fat that you should consume.

If you're a healthy individual who needs to shed a few pounds, your doctor may recommend 25 percent or less calories from fat, combined with an exercise program, to trim your weight. If you're recovering from coronary heart disease, 10 percent of calories from fat may be the percentage recommended by your doctor.

Flexible Fat-Spending Account

Like shoe size, bank account, and IQ, each person's fat budget is an individual matter. To determine yours, consult your doctor or a registered dietitian about your ideal weight, calorie needs, and the recommended percentage of calories from fat that you should be eating.

Those people recovering from coronary heart disease may be advised to get only 10 percent of their calories from fat.

Persons advised to reduce their body weight may be directed to eat 25 percent of calories from fat (a good reduction from the typical 37 percent that most Americans consume).

Consult the chart to find your ideal weight, calorie intake, and recommended percentage of fat.

To factor in activity level, for every 100 calories that you burn while exercising, you can add 3 grams of fat to your daily budget.

Men

Ideal Weight	Fat Grams per Day at 25% of Calories	Fat Grams per Day at 10% of Calories	Total Calories
130	50	20	1,800
140	56	22	2,000
150	58	23	2,100
160	63	25	2,250
170	67	27	2,400
180	72	29	2,600
190	75	30	2,700
200	78	31	2,800
210	82	33	2,950
220	86	34	3,100
230	90	36	3,250
240	94	38	3,400

Women

Ideal Weight	Fat Grams per Day at 25% of Calories	Fat Grams per Day at 10% of Calories	Total Calories
90	31	12	1,100
100	36	14	1,300
110	39	16	1,400
120	42	17	1,500
130	47	19	1,700
140	50	20	1,800
150	53	21	1,900
160	56	22	2,000
170	61	24	2,200
180	64	26	2,300

Using Fat-Free Recipes

After you determine how much fat is right for you, you can step into the kitchen to incorporate my fat-free recipes into your meals.

Those of you who have been advised to dramatically reduce total dietary fat can create entire meals from the recipes in this book. My menu chapter provides a start, but you can create dozens of other meals from these recipes, following your own taste buds. The meals in the menu chapter average about 5 percent of calories from fat. The overwhelming majority of these recipes contain no added fat. I guarantee that you won't miss it a bit.

Those of you who have been advised by your doctor to lose a few pounds will find these fat-free recipes an invaluable aid to reducing the total fat in your eating plan.

When you work within your personal fat budget, it's easy to average your fat intake over several days or even a week. Not every food you eat, or even every meal, needs to meet the recommended percentage of calories from fat. You can decide how and when to spend your fat grams.

This allows you some flexibility in choosing foods for personal satisfac-tion, an important mainstay of any eating plan. So go ahead and dip into the guacamole bowl once in a while (with fat-free tortilla chips, of course). Or nibble on some nuts. Both avocados and certain nuts, such as pecans, almonds, peanuts, and cashews, contain primarily heart-healthy monounsaturated fat in addi-tion to many other nutrients.

In planning meals, you can supple-ment your favorite main course with a

---

A Few Words about My Nutrient Analyses

All of the recipes in this book were analyzed for total fat, saturated fat, calories, cholesterol, sodium, protein, carbohydrates, and dietary fiber based on the latest U.S. Department of Agriculture figures and more than 1,000 additional scientific sources. Some additional nutrient data came from food manufacturers. Remember that, as with any nutrient analyses, these numbers are guidelines only. They may vary slightly from those in other nutritional programs, and they may vary from the actual foods you consume.

fabulous fat-free appetizer or soup, a side dish, and a grain dish to bring the total fat for the meal way down.

Adding and Subtracting

Subtracting fat, particularly saturated fat, is important for healthy eating. Adding fruits, vegetables, and grains is just as essential to maintain good health.

The diets of most Americans need improvement. That's the conclusion drawn by the USDA's Healthy Eating Index survey. On this nutritional report card released in 1995, only 12 percent of Americans had scores of 80 or above on a scale of 100. People were most likely to underconsume foods in the fruit, vegetable, and grain groups.

The USDA's Dietary Guidelines recommend 3 to 5 servings of vegetables, 2 to 4 servings of fruits, and 6 to 11 servings of grains (including bread, cereal, rice, and pasta) each day.

If you base your eating plan on these super-nutritious foods, prepared without added fat, your fat consumption will plummet automatically. You won't even need to compute fat grams because these foods are so low in fat. When you choose fat-free dairy products and only small amounts of red meat and poultry, your saturated fat intake will be reduced as well.

Because my fat-free dishes are all based on nutrient-dense vegetables and whole grains, you can confidently incorporate any of them into even the strictest dietary plan.

Cooking at home gives you control over what goes into your food and into your body. Now that you understand the importance of slashing fat—without sacrificing one iota of flavor—you can turn to "Free of Fat, Full of Flavor" (see page 7) to find out just how easy it is to cook the fabulous fat-free way, right in your own kitchen.

Chances are that you have most of what you need in your kitchen to get started right now. My recipes use common ingredients—the kind found in any supermarket. And my easy fat-free cooking techniques are designed to get the most natural flavor out of each ingredient. I'll show you how you can make your meals sizzle without added fat.

Free of Fat, Full of Flavor

Like three on a date or five wheels on a car, fat

added to food can really ruin a good thing. For food

that tastes naturally wonderful, kick the fat out of

your kitchen. You simply don't need it.

My recipes let the flavors of fresh foods shine.

Taste for yourself the crisp-tender crunch of fresh

vegetables in Sweet-and-Sour Turkey and the succu-

lence of Herb-Breaded Orange Roughy. Savor the

gooey goodness of Pineapple Caramel Cake and the

creamy tartness of Key Lime Cheese-cake.

When you allow fresh foods to sing for themselves, you'll never hit an off-note in fat-free cooking.

My shopping list and my pantry look quite different today than they did 5 years ago and very different from 25 years ago as I've gained more knowledge.

In this chapter, I share my experience in shopping for fat-free in-gredients, stocking a fat-free pantry, picking the perfect seasonings, and choosing the best cookware for fat-free cooking. I share the cooking tech-niques that extract maximum flavor from foods without adding fat.

Fat-Free Shopping

With the wide range of ever-improving fat-free and low-fat products in supermarkets today, it's easier than ever to cook absolutely scrump-tious meals with a minimum of fat.

Just remember that, even with fat-free products, calories do still count. So enjoy these items in sensible por-tions, and you'll be well-served.

The first step in buying healthy foods is to read the food labels, so it's important to understand what the terms mean. That way, you can shop confidently, secure in the knowledge

that you can select the most nutritious low-fat or fat-free foods on the market. These are the terms that you need to know.

Fat-free. Less than 0.5 gram of fat per serving.

Low-fat. No more than 3 grams of fat per serving.

Lean. Less than 10 grams of fat, 4 grams of saturated fat, and 95 milligrams of cholesterol per serving.

Light (lite). One-third fewer calories (or no more than half the fat) of the higher-calorie, higher-fat version. Can also mean no more than half the sodium of the higher-sodium version.

Cholesterol-free. Less than 2 milligrams of cho-lesterol and no more than 2 grams of saturated fat per serving.

Get into the habit of comparing fat grams on similar products. You'll be surprised at the savings you can reap on seemingly identical foods. For example, depending on the brand, a ½-cup portion of jarred tomato sauce for pasta can contain anywhere from no fat on up to 6 grams. It obviously pays to read the Nutrition Facts panel on product food labels before you make your selection.

The Fat-Free Kitchen

Life is hard. Grocery shopping should be easy.

Cooking fat-free recipes is

practically effortless when you have the right ingredients at your fingertips. Below I've listed the essentials that you need for pantry, refrigerator, and freezer—with some selection and storage tips.

All the old pantry standbys that have served you well in regular cooking—such as fresh fruits and vegetables, canned tomatoes, all-purpose flour, and even granulated sugar—will continue to perform in your fat-free kitchen.

In the Pantry

Applesauce. Use it to replace or reduce fat in baked goods. It works especially well in muffins, quick breads, and snack cakes.

Broth. Canned fat-free low-sodium chicken or vegetable broth on the shelf means practically effortless soups, stews, sauces, and grain dishes. If you can't find a fat-free chicken broth, refrigerate the can for several hours, then lift off and discard the chilled fat after opening.

Cocoa powder. Here's deep chocolate flavor with nearly all the cocoa butter removed.

Condiments. Piquant seasonings are the life of the fat-free flavor party. Stock items such as dried chipotle peppers, candied ginger, liquid smoke, and low-sodium soy sauce in addition to herbs, spices, and prepared mustard.

Cookies. Fat-free cinnamon and honey cookies, low-fat gingersnaps, low-fat graham crackers, and low-fat vanilla wafers make tasty pie crusts with a fraction of the fat of traditional pastry crusts.

Dried fruit. Apricots, cherries, cranberries, dates, and raisins add sweetness and fiber—but no fat—to baked goods and savory dishes alike.

Dry pasta. Most dry pasta contains only 1 gram of fat per 2-ounce serving, but lower-fat brands that contain 0.5 gram of fat per 2-ounce portion are also available, and I've used them in my recipes. Stock a variety of shapes.

Evaporated skim milk. This mimics the consistency of heavy cream in sauces and soups.

Garlic. Whether you mince it with a knife or squeeze it through a press, this powerful bulb is essential in the fat-free kitchen. Store in a cool, dry place but not in plastic and not in the refrigerator.

Jams, jellies, and preserves. Just a spoonful can brighten both sweet and savory dishes. And they're fat-free musts for topping English muffins, bagels, crumpets, pancakes, and waffles.

Juices. Tomato juice, carrot juice, and vegetable juice cocktail are handy to have on hand for soup or stew bases or just for a nutritious snack.

Oils and sprays. I've called for scant amounts

(continued on page 13)

 9 Free of Fat, Full of Flavor

Herbs and spices are indispensable seasonings in the fat-free kitchen, where they enhance everything from appetizers to desserts.

Herbs are the green leaves or seeds of plants grown in temperate regions. They're used both fresh and dried. To preserve flavor and color, cook fresh herbs only briefly or add them to the dish just before serving. Dried herbs need cooking to rehydrate them and release their flavors. If substituting dried herbs for fresh, add about half the amount.

Spices are the dried bark, flowers, roots, seeds, or stems of tropical plants. They are sold whole or ground. You can crush or grind spices in your kitchen using a small electric grinder, a blender, or a mortar and pestle. Lightly toasting spices and herb seeds in a dry skillet just before using heightens their flavor. Spices benefit from cooking to release their flavors.

Store fresh herbs in loosely closed plastic bags in the vegetable crisper of the refrigerator. Store spices and dried herbs in jars or tightly sealed plastic bags a cool, dark cupboard.

Allspice. The flavor is like a blend of cinnamon, nutmeg, and cloves. Use ground allspice with pumpkin, winter squash, baked apple dishes, carrot cake, or dried-fruit muffins.

Basil. The flavor is like mint and cloves. Use fresh leaves with raw tomatoes, seafood dishes, pasta, or creamy dips. Use dried leaves with Italian tomato sauces, minestrone, fish, and poultry.

Bay leaf. The flavor is woodsy with a hint of cloves. Use dried leaves in a bouquet garni (an herb bundle that includes parsley stems and thyme) or to flavor stocks, soups, stews, chowders, and bean dishes.

Celery seeds. The flavor is like celery but slightly more pungent. Use whole or crushed seeds in salads, poultry, stuffings, soups, stews, vegetables, dips, yeast breads, and relishes.

Chili peppers. The flavor is a combination of ground hot chili peppers and warm spices. Use in chili, chili sauce, guacamole, barbecue sauce, tomato soup, bean dishes, potato salads, salad dressings, stews, egg dishes, and Tex-Mex sauces.

Chives. The flavor is like mild onions. Use sliced fresh chives in salads, egg and vegetable dishes, dips, and soups.

Cilantro. The flavor of these fresh coriander leaves is like citrusy parsley. Use fresh leaves in salsas, seafood dishes, guacamole, and soups, as well as Asian, Hispanic, and North African dishes.

Cinnamon. The flavor is warm and sweet. Use ground cinnamon in fruit pies, fruit sauces, quick breads, coffee cakes, pancakes, French toast, and cookies.

Cloves. The flavor is pungent and sharp. Use ground cloves in relishes, fruit sauces, winter squash or pumpkin dishes, gingerbread, cookies, ham dishes, or meat or poultry stews.

Coriander. The flavor is citrusy with a hint of nuts. Use crushed or ground seeds in couscous, curries, bean dishes, beef, poultry, pork, fruit compotes, or Middle Eastern dishes.

Cumin. The flavor is caraway-like with a hint of heat. Use crushed or ground seeds in chili, fajitas and other Tex-Mex dishes, couscous, bean dishes, poultry and pork preparations, and creamy dips.

Curry powder. The flavor is a blend of various spices, which could include turmeric, ground red pepper, coriander, black pepper, cumin, fenugreek, mustard seeds, cinnamon, and cloves. Use in sauces for seafood or poultry, in egg dishes, with cauliflower or winter squash, or in rice, couscous, or other grain dishes.

Dill. The flavor is refreshing and faintly anise-like. Use fresh or dried leaves with beets, cucumbers, seafood, poultry, cream dips, salad dressings, zucchini, potatoes, and other mild vegetables. Use whole or crushed seeds to make pickles, borscht, or creamy dips and salad dressings.

Fennel seeds. The flavor is sweet and mildly aniselike. Use crushed or ground seeds with seafood, poultry, or pork, and in yeast breads and tomato sauces.

Ginger. The flavor is hot and sweet. Use ground ginger in gingerbread, cookies, curries, marinades, sweet-and-sour dishes, chutneys, stews, or braised meat and poultry dishes. Grated fresh ginger can be used in the same types of dishes.

Ground red pepper. The flavor is of ground dried hot red peppers. Use in chili, stews, marinades, barbecue sauce, tomato sauce, or other dishes that need a hint of heat.

Mint. The flavor is sweet and cool. Use fresh leaves with seafood, poultry, mild vegetables such as cucumbers, in creamy salad dressings, fruit salads, desserts, mint tea, sorbet, jelly, and in Middle Eastern foods. Use dried

(continued)

leaves in tea or cooked fruit or other dessert sauces (strain and discard the leaves before serving).

Nutmeg. The flavor is warm but sharper and less sweet than cinnamon. Use in cheese sauces, spinach dishes, cookies, quick breads, or egg dishes, and with winter squash.

Oregano. The flavor is pungent, sweet, and minty. Use with pizza, pork, seafood, poultry, mushrooms and other vegetables, salads, salad dressing, tomato sauces, and Italian or Mexican dishes.

Paprika. The flavor is of dried ground sweet or hot red peppers. Use in meat and poultry stews, chowders, Hungarian foods, tomato-based sauces, or as a garnish for seafood or light-colored vegetables.

Parsley. The flavor is clean, refreshing, and grassy. Use fresh leaves just before serving in dips, soups, stews, and with seafood, eggs, pasta, and veg-etables. Use fresh stems tied in a bundle with bay leaf and thyme to make a bouquet garni.

Poppy seeds. The flavor is pleasantly bittersweet and nutlike. Use with noodles, eggs, potato salad, coleslaw, creamy salad dressings, or in grain and rice dishes, coffee cakes, and yeast breads.

Rosemary. The flavor is piney. Use fresh or dried leaves with roasted pork and poultry, mushrooms, beans, pizza, focaccia, yeast breads, potatoes, stuffing, and other starchy dishes.

Saffron. The flavor is rich and warm. Use crushed threads in bouillabaisse, paella, tomato soup, poultry dishes, or rice dishes. Saffron needs long cooking to bring out the flavor.

Sage. The flavor is pungent and slightly cam-phorlike. Use fresh or dried leaves in poultry stuffing and stew or with pork or poultry.

Sesame seeds. The flavor is sweet and nutlike. Use in yeast breads, dips, Middle Eastern or Asian dishes, and with pasta or other grains.

Tarragon. The flavor is mildly aniselike. Use with poultry, seafood, cheese, vegetable dishes, or salad dressings.

Thyme. The flavor is peppery with overtones of mint and lemon. Use in stocks, soups, stews, seafood dishes, egg or cheese dishes, or in combination with bay leaf and parsley stems in a bouquet garni.

of oil in only a handful of recipes. Dark sesame oil (often sold in the ethnic section of supermarkets) is used as a seasoning for its intense flavor. Canola oil is used in my Raisin and Spice Oatmeal Cookies (the only dessert with added fat) to enhance the texture.

No-stick spray (either aerosol or pump) is used for lubricating pans. Remember, only a fine mist of the spray is needed.

Fat-free butter-flavored pump spray makes an acceptable substitute for butter on items such as breads, bagels, English muffins, or steamed vegetables.

Prune puree. This product traps moisture in baked goods in much the same way that fat does, and it is especially good in recipes containing cocoa powder. You can use convenient baby-food prunes. Or you can make your own puree by processing 4 ounces pitted prunes with 3 tablespoons hot water in a blender or food processor until smooth.

Sweetened condensed milk. The fat-free version of this classic sweet, thick milk provides a rich consistency in some desserts, such as my Key Lime Cheesecake.

Syrups. Corn syrup can be used in some desserts—such as Citrus-Glazed Carrot Cake—as a fat replacer. You can also stock fat-free caramel topping and chocolate syrup as well as honey, maple syrup, and molasses for drizzling on desserts, pancakes, or French toast.

Tapioca. Cooked with fat-free creamer or skim milk, quick-cooking tapioca makes a wonderfully rich pudding. The dry tapioca granules are also a great thickener for fruit pies.

Vinegar. Vinegar contains absolutely no fat and really brings out the flavor in foods. Try sweet-tart balsamic, cider, red-wine, or white-wine vinegar.

In the Refrigerator

Citrus fruits. You'll want to keep lemons, limes, and oranges on hand always. Store them in a loosely closed plastic bag in the vegetable crisper of your refrigerator for up to two weeks. Use the grated rind (scrub the fruit well and rinse before grating) and the juice to add zest to everything from appetizers to desserts.

Condiments. For perking up stews, sauces, salads, or main dishes, try capers, pickles (dill and sweet). roasted red peppers or pimentos (jarred), salsa, relishes, ketchup, low-sodium Worcestershire sauce, Dijon mustard, fresh ginger, hoisin sauce, horseradish, and hot-pepper sauce.

Dairy whipped topping. Skim milk–based fat-free aerosol whipped topping is a fine substitute for whipped cream on pumpkin pudding, fat-free sundaes, and other desserts.

Eggs. Egg whites are both fat-free and cholesterol-free. They're indispensable for lightening and tenderizing cakes, soufflés, and some cookies.

Liquid creamers. These fat-free nondairy and dairy creamers, found in the dairy case, mimic the consistency of heavy cream in soups and sauces. Choose plain (not flavored) for cooking. Be sure to check the labels—some creamers contain more sweeteners than others.

Liquid egg substitute. This convenient, pasteurized, fat-free product, which is primarily made from egg whites, is great for omelets, frittatas, mayonnaise, pancakes, waffles, French toast, and baked goods. You can substitute ¼ cup egg substitute for each large egg in a recipe.

Mayonnaise. When fat-free mayonnaise is well-seasoned in a sauce or dressing, you won't know it's not the real McCoy.

Milk. Fat-free buttermilk and skim milk are good for baking and sauces.

Parmesan topping. Look for fat-free brands that contain some real Parmesan or Romano cheese in the ingredient list.

Polenta in a tube. This ready-to-serve polenta is not only super-convenient but also fat-free. It comes in several flavors, including plain, mushroom, and sun-dried tomato.

Poultry and meat. Always select "zero trim" meats with no visible fat or marbling. Best beef choices are top round and sirloin. Tenderloin is the leanest pork. Lean ham and Canadian bacon are also good choices.

Canadian bacon is a handy staple for seasoning a variety of dishes. One ounce of this cured, smoked pork tenderloin contains only 2.4 grams of fat, compared with 13.9 grams in regular bacon.

Boneless, skinless turkey breast, trimmed of all visible fat, is as close to fat-free as poultry can be. And some producers are marketing boneless, skinless chicken breasts with only 0.5 gram of fat in a 3-ounce cooked portion. So read labels carefully to always choose the lowest-fat cut possible and always trim off all visible fat.

Fat-free lunchmeat, such as chicken breast, ham, or turkey breast, is convenient for sandwiches and salads.

Semifirm cheeses. Look for fat-free Cheddar, mozzarella, and Swiss. A few years ago, fat-free cheese was a synonym for rubber, but now there are major brands that melt well. I particularly like individually wrapped slices for melting.

Remember that unless you are on a severely fat-restricted diet, you can enjoy low-fat cheeses blended with fat-free cheeses. Each ounce of low-fat cheese (such as Swiss or mozzarella) adds about 3.5 grams of fat to the total recipe.

Soft cheeses. Select fat-free cottage cheese, cream cheese, mozzarella, and ricotta to add a creamy dairy flavor and consistency to a variety of dishes.

Sour cream. Choose fat-free sour cream, which has the added bonus of not separating when heated, as full-fat sour cream does.

Tortillas. Fat-free flour tortillas keep well in the refrigerator for up to a week (and much longer in the freezer). Use for fajitas or tacos, or serve with scrambled egg substitute or bean dishes.

Yogurt. Fat-free plain yogurt is essential for sauces and for making creamy, tangy Yogurt Cheese (see page 304). Flavored and fruit fat-free yogurts are good in sauces and baked goods or eaten as snacks.

In the Freezer

Breads. Keep bagels, bread (40 calories per slice), and pita bread on hand for sandwiches and recipes. Stock English muffins and fat-free crumpets for breakfast.

Homemade vegetable or chicken stock. Make a batch (see pages 93 and 94) and freeze it as a handy base for soups, stews, sauces, and stir-fries.

Nondairy fat-free whipped topping. This is convenient for impromptu desserts.

Phyllo, or filo, dough. These paper-thin sheets of fat-free pastry make wonderful pie crusts or appetizer wrappers for fat-free fillings. Thaw according to package directions. Lightly coat each sheet of phyllo with no-stick spray so the sheets will stay separate and crisp.

Poultry, seafood, and beef. It's convenient to have a variety on hand in recipe-ready portions.

Equipment for Fat-Free Cooking

No-stick cookware is essential for fat-free cooking. And because it's such a breeze to clean up, you may find yourself cooking much more often.

With just a whisper of no-stick spray in a no-stick skillet, you can turn onions and other vegetables into flavor gold as the base for great-tasting dishes. You can also brown turkey cutlets, chicken pieces, stewing beef, and fish fillets with no added fat.

Fat-free surfaces are tremendously improved from the original coatings that chipped and flaked soon after they were put into use. In general, the heavier the pan, the better the heat is conducted for more even cooking. Aluminum, cast iron, and stainless steel (with a bottom pad of aluminum or copper) are all good choices. Check the following list for the pots and pans that you need in your kitchen and then shop for the best pans that you can afford.

No-stick bakeware is nice to have but not essential. All the dessert recipes in this book work beautifully with regular bakeware and no-stick spray. Or you can line baking dishes and sheets with parchment paper, wax paper, or the reusable no-stick sheets that can be cut to fit the dimensions of any pan.

Sharp, good-quality knives are essential for fat-free cooking. They let you trim all fat from meats, as well as skin and fat from fish and poultry. And they make peeling and cutting vegetables and fruits a joy.

High-carbon stainless-steel forged knives are durable, hold an edge well, and won't rust as old-fashioned carbon-steel knives did. Good sizes include a 10" *chef's knife*, a 10" serrated knife, a 4" serrated knife and three 3" or 4" paring knives (I always misplace mine) for peeling fruits and vegetables. A knife sharpener is also a good investment.

I prefer dishwasher-safe knives with molded polyurethane handles, which I always place on the top shelf of the dishwasher away from the drying coils. You may prefer to hand wash and dry your knives to protect them from unwanted bumps that may dull the blades.

Kitchen scissors are great, too, for trimming fat as well as snipping fresh herbs—even for cutting pizza without scratching the pan.

Glass or plastic defatting pitchers are a must for removing fat from stocks, soups, and meat drippings. I prefer large glass ones because they handle more liquid and remain transparent, unlike some of the plastic cups, which can turn cloudy and crack with heavy use. As a safety precaution, don't pour boiling liquid into a glass pitcher.

No-Stick Cookware

✳ Small saucepan (1 quart)

✳ Medium saucepan (2 quarts)

✳ Large saucepan (3 or 4 quarts)

✳ Dutch oven or large pot (6 quarts)

✳ Small skillet (6" or 8")

✳ Large skillet (10" or 12")

✳ Lids (assorted, to fit pans)

Bakeware

✳ Baking dishes (13" x 9"; 12" x 8"; 8" x 8")

✳ Baking sheets

✳ Bundt pan (12 cups)

✳ Cake pans (9")

✳ Loaf pan (8" x 4")

✳ Pie plates (9" regular, 10" deep-dish)

✳ Soufflé dish (1½ quarts)

✳ Springform pan (9")

✳ Tube pan (10")

Kitchen Tools

✳ Blender, food processor, or hand blender

✳ Defatting pitcher

✳ Electric mixer

✳ Kitchen scissors

✳ Knives

✳ Whisks

Fat-Free Preparation and Cooking Methods

Trim it and *skim it.* That's all you need to know to rid excess fat from your food before and after cooking.

Before cooking, trim all visible skin and fat from seafood, poultry, and meat. Don't trust your supermarket meat cutter with this important job. Your motivation to do a thorough job is the desire for improved health.

After cooking stocks, soups, stews, chili, a roast with pan drippings, or any other dish that contains melted fat, skim as much fat from the surface as you can before serving. Melted fat is clear and rises to the top, where it's easy to capture and discard. You can do this in three ways.

Spoon it. Skim off the melted fat with a large spoon.

Pitch it. For clear preparations, such as stock, use a large defatting pitcher. Pour the liquid into the pitcher, which has a spout that starts at the bottom. Wait a few seconds until the clear melted fat rises to the top. Slowly pour out the stock (which comes from the bottom of the pitcher), stopping just before the fat reaches the base of the spout. I usually do two passes with the defatting pitcher to get rid of every drop of fat.

(continued on page 20)

101 Fabulous Fat-Free Foods

The best foods in life are free—from fat. You can feast on any of these 101 satisfying selections, all with less than 1 gram of fat. When you base your eating plan on low-fat, nutrient-rich foods, you get more bang for your fat-gram bucks. When naturally low-fat foods are cooked with unneeded fat, the cost is high. For example, a measly 10 potato chips—hardly a satisfying amount of food—will cost you 6.9 grams of fat. You'd have to eat 34 large baked potatoes to spend the same amount of fat grams.

Amount	Food	Fat (g.)
Fruits and Fruit Juices		
1	apple	0.5
1 cup	apple juice	0.3
6	apricot halves, dried	0.1
1	banana	0.6
1 cup	blueberries	0.6
1 cup	cantaloupe cubes	0.5
⅔ cup	cherries, sweet	0.9
½	grapefruit, pink or red	0.1
1 cup	grapes, Thompson seedless	0.9
1 cup	honeydew cubes	0.2
1	kiwifruit	0.3
1 cup	mango slices	0.5
1	nectarine	0.6
1	orange	0.2
1 cup	orange juice	0.7
1	peach	0.1
1	pear, Bartlett	0.7
1 cup	pineapple chunks	0.7
1	plum	0.4
½ cup	raisins	0.3
1 cup	raspberries, red	0.7
1 cup	cut strawberries	0.5
1	tangerine	0.2
1 cup	watermelon cubes	0.7

Amount	Food	Fat (g.)
Vegetables and Vegetable Juices		
10	asparagus spears, cooked	0.5
½ cup	beans, canned baked vegetarian	0.6
1 cup	beans, green (cooked)	0.4
1 cup	beans, red kidney (cooked)	0.9
1 cup	beans, lima (cooked)	0.5
1 cup	broccoli (chopped), cooked	0.6
1 cup	cabbage (shredded)	0.2
1	carrot	0.1
1 cup	carrots (sliced), cooked	0.3
1 cup	cauliflower (chopped), cooked	0.6
1 cup	corn, frozen (cooked)	0.1
1 cup	lentils (cooked)	0.8
1 cup	lettuce, iceberg (chopped)	0.1
1 cup	lettuce, romaine (chopped)	0.1
1 cup	mushroom pieces (cooked)	0.7
1 cup	peas, frozen (cooked)	0.4
½ cup	peppers, green (chopped)	0.1
1	potato, large with skin (baked)	0.2
1 cup	spinach (cooked)	0.5
1 cup	spinach (chopped)	0.2
1 cup	squash, acorn (cubes), baked	0.3
1	sweet potato, medium (baked)	0.1

Amount	Food	Fat (g.)
1	tomato	0.4
1 cup	tomatoes, canned stewed	0.4
1 cup	tomato juice	0.2
1 cup	zucchini (sliced), cooked	0.1

Grains, Breads, and Cereals

Amount	Food	Fat (g.)
½	bagel, plain	0.5
½ slice	bread, cracked wheat	0.7
½ slice	bread, white sliced sandwich	0.6
1 cup	bulgur (cooked)	0.4
1 cup	cereal, bran flakes	0.7
1 cup	cereal, corn flakes	0.1
1 cup	cereal, frosted bite-size shredded wheat	0.6
1 cup	cereal, bite-size shredded wheat	0.9
1 cup	cereal, wheat flakes	0.5
3	cookies, animal crackers	0.9
2	cookies, fortune	0.4
1 cup	couscous (cooked)	0.3
2	crackers, saltine	0.7
10	crackers, wheat crispbread	0.6
½	English muffin, plain	0.5
1	graham cracker	0.7
1 cup	macaroni (cooked)	0.9
½ cup	oatmeal (cooked)	0.8
1	pita bread, white	0.7
2 cups	popcorn (air-popped)	0.7
½ oz.	pretzels, thin-twist	0.5
1 cup	rice, long-grain white (cooked)	0.6
½ cup	rice, long-grain brown (cooked)	0.9
2	rice cakes, multigrain brown	0.6
1 cup	spaghetti (cooked)	0.9
1	tortilla, corn	0.8

Amount	Food	Fat (g.)
Dairy Foods		
1 cup	cottage cheese, fat-free	0.0
⅓ cup	cottage cheese, 1% low-fat	0.8
2 Tbsp	milk, instant fat-free dry	0.1
1 cup	milk, canned evaporated skim	0.5
¼ cup	milk, 1% low-fat	0.7
1 cup	milk, fat-free skim	0.4
1 cup	yogurt, fat-free with fruit	0.4
1 cup	yogurt, lemon fat-free	0.4
1 cup	yogurt, plain fat-free	0.4

Seafood and Turkey

Amount	Food	Fat (g.)
3 oz.	cod, Atlantic (baked or broiled)	0.7
⅓ cup	crab, blue (steamed)	0.7
2 oz.	flounder (baked or broiled)	0.9
2 oz.	grouper (baked or broiled)	0.7
3 oz.	haddock (baked or broiled)	0.8
1 oz.	halibut (baked or broiled)	0.8
3 oz.	mahimahi (baked or broiled)	0.8
3 oz.	orange roughy (baked or broiled)	0.8
2 oz.	perch (baked or broiled)	0.7
2 oz.	pollack, walleye (baked or broiled)	0.6
1 oz.	scallops (steamed)	0.9
3 oz.	shrimp, large (steamed)	0.9
2 oz.	snapper (baked or broiled)	0.9
2 oz.	sole (baked or broiled)	0.9
2½ oz.	turkey breast, skinless (roasted)	0.8
½ cup	tuna, light, drained, canned in water	0.6

Lift it. Let time do the work for you. This method works especially well for stews and other dishes with lots of chunky ingredients. Refrigerate the finished dish for several hours or overnight, until the fat hardens on the top. Pick off and discard the layer of fat. You'll feel victorious as you toss that fat into the garbage pail.

Fat-Free Cooking Techniques

You might be surprised to learn that you already know a lot of fat-free cooking techniques. You use them in your kitchen every day. The difference is that now you'll be doing them with no-stick cookware and no added fat. Here's the rundown.

Braising. Braising cooks foods in a small amount of liquid in a tightly covered pan or baking dish on the stove top or in the oven. Seafood, poultry, and meat can be browned before braising using the dry-frying technique below. This will boost the flavor of the finished dish. The liquid is often reduced after cooking as the base for an accompanying sauce.

Dry-frying. Dry-frying sears foods to seal in moisture. Lightly coat the food—such as turkey cutlets or fish fillets—with no-stick spray, then sear in a hot skillet. Cast iron or aluminum no-stick skillets work best, because they can be heated to higher temperatures.

Grilling and broiling. These direct-heat methods cook vegetables and small cuts of meat, poultry, and seafood quickly, sealing in juices and browning the surface without added fat.

Brush the grill or broiler pan with a few drops of oil or lightly coat the food with no-stick spray before cooking. To add flavor to low-fat cuts, marinate the food or baste during cooking with de-fatted stock seasoned with herbs or spices.

To grill small pieces of seafood or vegetables, place them on a special cooking rack, perforated with small holes, that sits right on top of the grill rack. Or create your own perforated surface by punching holes in a double thickness of heavy-duty foil.

Microwaving. A microwave is especially useful for moist-heat recipes such as braises, soups, and stews.

Poaching. This method cooks seafood, poultry, and vegetables submerged in simmering seasoned water, juice, wine, or other liquids. Always poach at a gentle simmer, never a boil.

Roasting. This method of oven-cooking food in an uncovered pan is ideal for vegetables and tender cuts of poultry, meat, and seafood. Enhance flavor with dry seasoning rubs or marinades.

Steaming. This method cooks seafood, poultry, or vegetables on a collapsible metal steamer with legs set over boiling liquid in a tightly covered pan.

The steamer unit must sit comfortably inside the pan with some room to spare around the sides, so that the steam rises around the food. Fill the pot with about one inch of water. Place the steamer rack in the pan and put the food to be steamed on the rack. Cover and bring the water to a boil. Reduce the heat slightly and cook for the amount of time specified in the recipe.

Many foods can also be steamed on a grill or in the oven, tightly wrapped in foil packets or in an oven bag, with some seasoned liquid and chopped vegetables added for flavor.

Stewing. Stewing is a method of cooking several foods in a seasoned liquid such as stock or wine. The liquid base, often thickened, is served as part of the dish.

Stir-frying. Cutting seafood, poultry, meat, and vegetables into small pieces is the secret to successful stir-frying with just a coating of no-stick spray in a very hot skillet or wok. For best results, always stir-fry in small batches. If the pan is too crowded, the ingredients will steam instead of brown.

Appetizers, Finger Foods, Dips, and Spreads

Appetizers and predinner nibbles don't have to contain fat to be welcoming and delicious. With fat-free recipes, you can show your family and guests real hospitality—food that tastes good, looks good, and is good for them.

I'll show you how to make delicious party fare that proves you care about the well-being of your guests. You won't spend a fortune or countless hours in the kitchen.

The best parties are celebrations of good health.

I love serving fat-free appetizers because I know that I'm not contributing to anyone's health or weight problems. These satisfying morsels won't make you feel guilty. When you can enjoy tasty appetizers that are free of fat, why not indulge?

Serving such festive, delicious appetizers is possible with the wonderful new fat-free dairy products on the market. Forget the unhealthy full-fat sour cream, cream cheese, and mayonnaise hors d'oeuvres of yesterday.

Something for Every Appetite

Because so many people with lighter appetites can make a meal of appetizers, I have included a section of first courses, several of which could be served together. My seafood appetizers are simple to make and fit this role nicely. Try Broiled Flounder with Fennel, Baked Red Snapper with Clams, Seafood Medley, or Parsleyed Bay Scallops.

Some of my vegetable appetizers, such as Roast Parmesan Asparagus and Summer Zucchini, are celebrations of seasonal bounty and deserve to be showcased as a course of their own. You can also serve them as delicious side dishes at a more casual meal.

Less Work—More Fun

For your casual parties, always put out plenty of fat-free foods to make the offerings look really lavish. Guests will never feel deprived with heaping bowls of fat-free potato chips, fat-free corn chips, pretzels, air-popped popcorn, and fat-free crackers. I always include a huge vegetable platter filled with every vegetable possible.

To go with the chips, crackers, and vegetables, make-ahead dips and spreads are always popular and never go out of style. Try my Pinto Bean Dip, Crunchy Onion Dip, or Dill Dip.

Don't forget luscious fresh fruit for parties. With their vivid colors, fresh fruits dress up any table. And if you're serving perfectly ripe fruit, you really don't have to do anything to it. Make a large paper cone or use a basket cornucopia spilling out with bananas, bunches of grapes, papayas, plums, or whatever fruit is in season. In the summer, cut a melon basket and fill it with bite-size fruit pieces.

For no-cook appetizers, try 100 percent fat-free ham, chicken, and turkey products or fat-free cheese slices. Wrap them around chunks of melon, mangoes, pears, sweet pickles, or dill pickles. Spear with toothpicks.

Tomates à la Marseillaise

quick and easy

My terrific former assistant, Marty Cavendish, loved this tomato dish when she lived in France. She has found that its sunny flavors travel beautifully to this country. The tomatoes have to be garden fresh and very ripe. I like them seasoned with a lot of freshly ground black pepper.

1   clove garlic, cut in half
2   ripe medium tomatoes, at room temperature, cut in half
1   teaspoon dried basil
1   teaspoon dried oregano
1   teaspoon dried thyme
    Ground black pepper
    Salt (optional)
4   medium romaine lettuce leaves (optional)

1   Coat a large no-stick skillet with no-stick spray. Warm the skillet over medium heat. Rub the cut side of the garlic halves around the pan, then discard the cloves.

2   Place the tomatoes, cut side up, in the skillet. Mist with no-stick spray. Sprinkle with the basil, oregano, and thyme. Press the herbs down lightly with the palm of your hand. Season to taste with the pepper and salt (if using). Cover and cook for 4 minutes.

3   Turn the tomatoes. Cover and cook for 4 to 5 minutes, or until the tomatoes are hot. Serve, cut side up, on the lettuce (if using).

Makes **4** servings.

Lynn's Fat-Free Flavor

Garlic doesn't have to be a major part of a recipe to impart great flavor. You can rub the cut side of a split clove around a salad bowl or an olive oil–coated skillet for a subtle, aromatic addition.

nutrition at a glance
per serving

0.3 g.	total fat
0 g.	saturated fat
17	calories
0 mg.	cholesterol
6 mg.	sodium
1 g.	protein
4 g.	carbohydrates
1 g.	dietary fiber

Roast Parmesan Asparagus

quick and easy

So simple, yet it tastes like Italy. My special taster and friend Beth Mendelson calls this the best asparagus ever. Thick spears work better than thin for baking.

1 pound asparagus
½ cup water
2 tablespoons freshly squeezed lemon juice
Ground black pepper
Salt (optional)
½ cup fat-free Parmesan topping

1 Preheat the oven to 375°F. Coat a 12" x 8" baking dish with no-stick spray.

2 Arrange the asparagus in the dish in rows. Add the water and lemon juice. Season to taste with the pepper and salt (if using). Sprinkle with the Parmesan.

3 Cover loosely with foil. Bake for 20 minutes, or until the asparagus is tender.

Makes **4** servings.

nutrition at a glance

per serving

0.2 g.	total fat
0 g.	saturated fat
60	calories
0 mg.	cholesterol
201 mg.	sodium
8 g.	protein
9 g.	carbohydrates
1 g.	dietary fiber

Summer Zucchini

quick and **easy**

The flecks of fresh tomatoes, sun-dried tomatoes, and yellow peppers add color and perk up the flavor of this mild summer squash.

½   cup boiling water
¼   cup dry-pack sun-dried tomato halves
1   pound zucchini, thinly sliced
1   onion, thinly sliced
1   small yellow pepper, diced
2   cloves garlic, minced
¼   cup chopped tomatoes
1   tablespoon thinly sliced fresh basil
2   teaspoons balsamic vinegar
    Ground black pepper
    Salt (optional)

1   Place the water and sun-dried tomatoes in a small bowl. Let stand for 10 minutes. Drain and finely chop. Set aside.

2   Coat a large no-stick skillet with no-stick spray. Add the zucchini, onions, yellow peppers, and garlic. Cover and cook over medium-high heat, stirring occasionally, for 4 to 5 minutes, or until the vegetables soften and start to brown. If necessary, add 1 or 2 teaspoons water to prevent sticking.

3   Add the chopped tomatoes and sun-dried tomatoes. Uncover and cook over medium-high heat, stirring occasionally, for 5 minutes, or until the vegetables are tender. Stir in the basil and vinegar. Season to taste with the black pepper and salt (if using).

Makes **6** servings.

nutrition at a glance
per serving

0.2 g.	total fat
0 g.	saturated fat
36	calories
0 mg.	cholesterol
76 mg.	sodium
2 g.	protein
8 g.	carbohydrates
2 g.	dietary fiber

Tabbouleh with Cucumbers

Tabbouleh—a nutrient-rich Middle Eastern bulgur salad—makes a refreshing appetizer for a summer gathering. Thinly sliced tender young zucchini make a nice alternative to the cucumber. I prefer finely ground bulgur rather than the more coarse types of bulgur.

1   cup water
½   cup bulgur
      Pinch of salt (optional)
1   small tomato, diced
½   cup chopped fresh parsley
¼   cup finely chopped onions or scallions
2   tablespoons shredded carrots
2   tablespoons freshly squeezed lemon juice
1   tablespoon chopped fresh mint
1   tablespoon dried currants or chopped raisins
½   teaspoon ground cumin
      Pinch of ground allspice
      Coarsely ground black pepper
1   medium English cucumber, thinly sliced

1   Bring the water to a boil in a medium no-stick saucepan. Add the bulgur and salt (if using). Reduce the heat to low, cover, and cook for 8 to 10 minutes, or until the bulgur is tender and the liquid is absorbed. Remove from the heat. Fluff with a fork, then set aside to cool. Refrigerate for several hours to chill thoroughly.

2   In a medium bowl, combine the tomatoes, parsley, onions or scallions, carrots, lemon juice, mint, currants or raisins, cumin, and allspice. Toss to mix well. Season to taste with the pepper.

3   Add the bulgur and toss well. Chill if desired.

4   Arrange the cucumbers in a spiral pattern on a platter. Spoon the tabbouleh in the center.

Makes **6** servings.

nutrition at a glance
per serving

0.4 g.	total fat
0.1 g.	saturated fat
63	calories
0 mg.	cholesterol
11 mg.	sodium
2 g.	protein
14 g.	carbohydrates
3 g.	dietary fiber

Broiled Flounder with Fennel

Many fish can take the place of the mild-tasting flounder. Try sole, halibut, orange roughy, whitefish, monkfish, catfish, or turbot. Save the leafy fronds from the fennel to use as a garnish.

1   tablespoon grated lemon rind
2   teaspoons fennel seeds, crushed
1   teaspoon dried thyme
     Pinch of salt (optional)
4   flounder fillets (2½ ounces each)
1½   cups sliced fennel
     Ground black pepper
2   tablespoons freshly squeezed lemon juice (optional)
2   tablespoons freshly squeezed orange juice (optional)

1   In a small bowl, combine the lemon rind, fennel seeds, thyme, and salt (if using); mix well.

2   Rinse the fish and pat dry with paper towels. Coat both sides of the fish with no-stick spray. Place in a single layer on a platter. Sprinkle with the seasoning mix and pat it firmly in place. Cover and refrigerate for 1 to 2 hours.

3   About 15 minutes before cooking the fish, bring 1" of water to a boil in a large no-stick saucepan. Add the sliced fennel and cook for 6 to 7 minutes, or until tender when pierced with a sharp knife. Drain; return to the pan and mist with no-stick spray. Sprinkle with the pepper. Cover and keep warm.

4   Cover a baking sheet with foil. Place the fish on the sheet in a single layer. Broil 4" from the heat for 4 minutes, or until the fish is opaque in the center. (Check by inserting the tip of a sharp knife in the center of 1 fillet.)

5   Serve the fish with the fennel. Sprinkle with the lemon juice (if using) and orange juice (if using).

Makes **4** servings.

nutrition at a glance
per serving
0.9 g. total fat
0.2 g. saturated fat
76 calories
33 mg. cholesterol
70 mg. sodium
12.5 g. protein
4 g. carbohydrates
2 g. dietary fiber

Baked Red Snapper with Clams

quick and easy

This impressive appetizer was inspired by the Baked Mackerel with Clams in *Jane Brody's Good Seafood Book*. I've substituted lean red snapper, which makes a really pretty presentation, but striped bass, croaker, or mullet works well, too.

4   red snapper fillets (2½ ounces each), skin on
1   teaspoon dried rosemary, crumbled
1   teaspoon dried oregano
    Pinch of salt (optional)
8   littleneck clams, scrubbed
¼   cup freshly squeezed lemon juice
¼   cup defatted chicken stock (page 94)
3   cloves garlic, minced
¼   cup chopped fresh parsley
    Ground black pepper

1   Preheat the oven to 450°F.

2   Rinse the fish and pat dry with paper towels. Score the skin side with four or five diagonal slashes. Sprinkle on both sides with the rosemary, oregano, and salt (if using).

3   Coat a 13" x 9" baking dish with no-stick spray. Place the fish in the dish, skin side up, in a single layer.

4   Add the clams to the dish. Sprinkle with the lemon juice, stock, and garlic.

5   Bake for 15 to 20 minutes, or until the fish is cooked (check by inserting the tip of a sharp knife in the center of 1 fillet) and the clams are opened and hot. Discard any unopened clams. Sprinkle with the parsley and season to taste with pepper.

6   Serve the fish and clams with the pan juices spooned over top.

Makes **4** servings.

Photograph on page 51

nutrition at a glance
per serving
0.9 g.   total fat
0.2 g.   saturated fat
72   calories
24 mg.   cholesterol
35 mg.   sodium
13 g.   protein
3.4 g.   carbohydrates
0.5 g.   dietary fiber

Seafood Medley

quick and easy

This skillet dish of shrimp and scallops is a colorful, tasty, and quick appetizer. For a special presentation, serve it in scallop shells (available in cookware shops) or shallow individual baking dishes. Sprinkle with fat-free Parmesan topping and broil for 1 to 2 minutes, or until golden.

5	ounces shelled shrimp
4	ounces sea or bay scallops
1	medium tomato, chopped
4	scallions, sliced diagonally
½	cup clam juice
¼	cup thinly sliced fresh basil
¼	cup white wine or nonalcoholic white wine
1	clove garlic, minced
¼	teaspoon ground black pepper
	Pinch of salt (optional)
1	tablespoon cornstarch
4	teaspoons fat-free Parmesan topping

1 In a large no-stick skillet, combine the shrimp, scallops, tomatoes, scallions, ¼ cup of the clam juice, the basil, wine, garlic, pepper, and salt (if using). Cover and cook over medium-low heat for 7 minutes, or until the scallops are nearly opaque.

2 Place the cornstarch in a cup. Add the remaining ¼ cup clam juice and stir to dissolve the cornstarch. Add to the skillet. Stir for 1 minute, or until the sauce thickens. Sprinkle with the Parmesan.

Makes **4** servings.

nutrition at a glance

per serving

0.9 g.	total fat
0.2 g.	saturated fat
96	calories
74 mg.	cholesterol
456 mg.	sodium
11 g.	protein
6 g.	carbohydrates
0.6 g.	dietary fiber

Parsleyed Bay Scallops

quick and easy

**These succulent bay scallops are bursting with sweet flavor.
Serve them with a crisscross of thinly sliced sweet red peppers.
For a light main course, try them over linguine, white rice, brown
rice, or wild rice. (Omit the cornstarch and toss the linguine or
rice gently with the scallop mixture just before serving.)**

Lynn's
Fun Food
Fact

**Although there are
hundreds of scallop
varieties in the
world, only three
kinds are available
commercially in this
country. Sea scal-
lops are the
largest, sometimes
as big as the palm
of your hand. Bay
scallops are
smaller, about the
size of marbles.
The even more
diminutive calicoes
are a rarer find.**

3	cloves garlic, minced
1	tablespoon water
8	ounces bay scallops
2	tablespoons chopped fresh parsley
¼	teaspoon crushed red-pepper flakes
1	cup white wine or nonalcoholic white wine
2	teaspoons cornstarch
	Ground black pepper
	Salt (optional)

1   Coat a large no-stick skillet
with no-stick spray. Warm the skillet over medium heat.
Add the garlic and water. Cook, stirring, for 2 minutes,
or until the garlic is softened.

2   Reduce the heat to low. Add
the scallops, parsley, red-pepper flakes, and ¾ cup of
the wine. Simmer, stirring occasionally, for 5 minutes,
or until the scallops are opaque.

3   Place the cornstarch in a
cup. Add the remaining ¼ cup wine and stir to dissolve
the cornstarch. Add to the skillet and stir constantly
until the sauce thickens. Season to taste with the
black pepper and salt (if using).

Makes **4** servings.

nutrition at a glance

per serving
0.9 g.	total fat
0.2 g.	saturated fat
52	calories
9 mg.	cholesterol
119 mg.	sodium
5 g.	protein
1 g.	carbohydrates
0.1 g.	dietary fiber

Southwestern Polenta

quick and easy

The crisp texture of skillet-grilled polenta and the richness of black beans and salsa make this meal opener a tight winner.

1	tube (16 ounces) prepared fat-free polenta
½	teaspoon ground cumin
½	teaspoon dried oregano
1	cup salsa
1	cup cooked black beans
4	scallions, finely sliced
¼	cup fat-free sour cream
1	tablespoon chopped fresh cilantro

1 Cut the polenta into 8 slices. Sprinkle evenly on both sides with the cumin and oregano; press gently to adhere.

2 Coat a large no-stick skillet with no-stick spray. Warm over medium-high heat. Place the polenta in the skillet in a single layer. Reduce the heat to medium-low and cook for 5 minutes on each side, or until golden and heated through. Remove the polenta to a platter; cover loosely with foil to keep warm.

3 Add the salsa, beans, and scallions to the skillet. Simmer for 2 to 3 minutes, or until hot.

4 Spoon the salsa mixture over the polenta. Top with the sour cream and sprinkle with the cilantro.

Makes **4** servings.

Photograph on page 155

nutrition at a glance

per serving

0.4 g.	total fat
0.1 g.	saturated fat
189	calories
0 mg.	cholesterol
687 mg.	sodium
8 g.	protein
37 g.	carbohydrates
8 g.	dietary fiber

Bruschetta with Tomatoes

quick and easy

My guests have never guessed that these salad-topped garlic toasts—so evocative of the Mediterranean—contain no fat. Bruschetta is so versatile that it can be served hot, warm, at room temperature, or chilled. You can prepare the topping and the garlic toasts ahead, but don't spoon on the topping until serving time, or the toasts will get soggy.

16 rounds (about ¼" thick x 1½" wide) Italian or French bread
3 cloves garlic
1 medium onion, coarsely chopped
2 large plum tomatoes, diced
¼ cup thinly sliced fresh basil
2 teaspoons balsamic vinegar
Ground black pepper
Salt (optional)

1 Preheat the oven to 325°F. Cover a baking sheet with foil.

2 Place the bread on the sheet in a single layer. Coat both sides with no-stick spray. Bake for 20 minutes, or until golden.

3 Cut 1 clove of the garlic in half. Rub the cut sides over the tops of the toast; discard the garlic halves.

4 Meanwhile, coat a large no-stick skillet with no-stick spray. Add the onions. Mist with no-stick spray. Cover and cook over medium-high heat, stirring occasionally, for 3 to 4 minutes, or until the onions start to release liquid. Reduce the heat to medium. Uncover and cook, stirring occasionally, for 3 to 4 minutes, or until golden. If necessary, add 1 to 2 teaspoons water to prevent sticking.

5 Add the tomatoes. Mince the remaining 2 cloves garlic and add to the skillet. Cook, stirring occasionally, for 2 to 3 minutes, or until the tomatoes soften slightly. Remove from the heat.

Stir in the basil and vinegar. Season to taste with the pepper and salt (if using).

6 Place a spoonful of the topping on each garlic toast.

Makes **16** servings.

Photograph on page 47

nutrition at a glance

per serving

0.2 g. total fat
0 g. saturated fat
20 calories
0 mg. cholesterol
34 mg. sodium
1 g. protein
4 g. carbohydrates
0 g. dietary fiber

Gingery Stuffed Tomatoes

Very Asian and very simple, this refreshing summer appetizer is slightly hot from the fresh ginger.

¼	cup rice vinegar or cider vinegar
2	tablespoons sugar
1½	teaspoons minced fresh ginger
1	teaspoon low-sodium soy sauce
½	teaspoon dark sesame oil
1	cucumber, peeled, seeded, and shredded
20	cherry tomatoes
2	teaspoons toasted sesame seeds (optional)

Lynn's Fun Food Fact
Fresh ginger is often referred to as ginger root, but it is actually an underground stem, or rhizome.

1 In a medium bowl, combine the vinegar, sugar, ginger, soy sauce, and oil. Add the cucumbers and mix well. The mixture will be watery. Lightly smash with a potato masher or the bottom of a heavy glass. Let stand for 20 to 30 minutes.

2 Slice ⅛" from the stem end of each tomato. Cut a thin slice from the tomato bottoms, if necessary, so the tomatoes can stand without wobbling. With a small metal spoon or small melon baller, remove the flesh from inside the tomatoes; discard.

3 Drain the cucumbers. With your fingers or a small spoon, stuff the cucumber mixture into the tomatoes. Sprinkle with the sesame seeds (if using).

Makes **20** tomatoes.

nutrition at a glance

per 2 tomatoes

0.4 g. total fat
0.1 g. saturated fat
24 calories
0 mg. cholesterol
24 mg. sodium
1 g. protein
5 g. carbohydrates
1 g. dietary fiber

Japanese Pork Dumplings

These savory morsels will win raves at your next party. Using purchased wonton skins, they really aren't difficult to make. And you can assemble them several hours before serving. Place the sealed dumplings in a single layer on a damp tray, cover loosely with plastic wrap, and refrigerate.

<table>
<tr><td colspan="2">Lynn's Kitchen Tip</td></tr>
</table>

Lynn's Kitchen Tip

Wontons also make convenient wrappers for home-made ravioli stuffed with fat-free cheeses or mush-rooms. These square or round dough wrappers can be found nestled in the produce department, or occasionally in the frozen food case, in most large supermarkets.

Soy Dipping Sauce

5	tablespoons low-sodium soy sauce
2	teaspoons rice vinegar
2	teaspoons minced garlic
1	teaspoon grated fresh ginger
1	teaspoon sugar
	Hot-pepper sauce

Pork Dumplings

8	ounces thinly sliced baby bok choy or napa cabbage
5	ounces lean ground pork tenderloin, all visible fat removed before grinding
½	cup diced or shredded carrots
3	cloves garlic, minced
1	tablespoon low-sodium soy sauce
2	teaspoons dry sherry or ½ teaspoon sherry extract (optional)
1	teaspoon packed brown sugar
½	teaspoon dark sesame oil
32	square or round wonton wrappers

1 *To make the soy dipping sauce:* In a small bowl, combine the soy sauce, vinegar, garlic, ginger, and sugar; mix well. Season to taste with the hot-pepper sauce. Set aside.

2 *To make the pork dumplings:* In a large microwaveable bowl, combine the cabbage, pork, carrots, and garlic. Cover and microwave on high power for a total of 4 minutes, or until the pork is no longer pink; stop and stir every 60 seconds during this time. Pour off and discard any liquid.

3 Stir in the soy sauce, sherry or sherry extract (if using), brown sugar, and sesame oil. Transfer to a blender or food processor. Process until finely chopped. (The mixture can also be chopped in the bowl with a hand blender.)

4   Place 4 wonton wrappers at a time on a work surface. Have a small bowl of water at hand. Dip your index finger in the water and wet the border of each wonton. Place a marble-size ball of the pork mixture in the center of each wonton. Fold the wonton in half diagonally to make a triangle or crescent. Fold the seam edges slightly back on themselves. Press to seal tightly.

5   Repeat to use all the remaining wontons and filling.

6   Bring about 1" of water to a boil in a large pot.

7   Arrange half of the wontons on a steamer rack. Place the rack in the pot, cover, and cook for 3 to 4 minutes, or until the stuffing is cooked (test a wonton with the tip of a sharp knife). Transfer the dumplings to a warm platter; keep warm.

8   Repeat with the remaining wontons. Serve with the soy dipping sauce.

Makes **32** dumplings.

nutrition at a glance	
per 2 dumplings	
0.7 g.	total fat
0.2 g.	saturated fat
69	calories
7 mg.	cholesterol
326 mg.	sodium
4 g.	protein
11 g.	carbohydrates
0 g.	dietary fiber

Mediterranean Shrimp

You can purchase your shrimp already steamed and chilled, which cuts the effort. You can also replace the peppers with snow peas.

16	medium shrimp, shelled with tails left on
16	thin green pepper slices
⅓	cup freshly squeezed orange juice
2	tablespoons white-wine vinegar
4	cloves garlic, minced
1	teaspoon crushed fennel seeds
1	bay leaf
½	teaspoon ground cumin
½	teaspoon dried tarragon
4	large lettuce leaves (optional)

Lynn's Fat-Free Flavor

Wine vinegar costs a bit more than distilled vinegar, but it's worth it. The flavor is more mellow, an important consideration when cooking with no added oil or other fats.

1   Fill a large bowl with ice water. Set aside.

2   Bring about 1" of water to a boil in a large no-stick saucepan. Add the shrimp and peppers. Cover and cook, stirring once, for 3 minutes, or until the shrimp just begin to turn pink. Drain and transfer to the ice water. Let stand for 2 minutes. Drain and pat dry with paper towels.

3   In a resealable plastic bag, combine the orange juice, vinegar, garlic, fennel seeds, bay leaf, cumin, and tarragon. Seal the bag and squeeze the package to mix. Open the bag and add the shrimp and peppers. Seal the bag and refrigerate for up to 2 hours.

4   Drain before serving; discard the marinade and bay leaf. Serve on the lettuce (if using).

Makes **8** servings.

Photograph on page 50

nutrition at a glance	
per serving	
0.6 g.	total fat
0 g.	saturated fat
54	calories
80 mg.	cholesterol
94 mg.	sodium
10 g.	protein
4 g.	carbohydrates
0 g.	dietary fiber

Pesto Pita Wedges

quick and easy

These pita wedges are exceptionally tasty and can be served as a snack by themselves or with my **Pinto Bean Dip (page 43)** or **Crunchy Onion Dip (page 44)**. Be sure to purchase the flattest pitas that you can find; they crisp nicely in the oven. I prefer my pepper coarsely ground for this appetizer.

½   cup finely chopped fresh basil
1   tablespoon fat-free Parmesan topping
¾   teaspoon ground black pepper
4   fat-free white or whole-wheat pita breads (8" diameter)

1   Preheat the oven to 400°F.

2   In a small bowl, combine the basil, Parmesan, and pepper. Coat the tops of the pitas with no-stick spray. Spread the basil mixture evenly over the tops of the pitas. Coat with the spray.

3   Cut each pita into 8 wedges. Transfer to a baking sheet and bake for 5 to 8 minutes, or until golden and crisp.

Makes **32** wedges.

Photograph on page 49

Lynn's Kitchen Tip
When you find a good source for Middle Eastern pita breads, be sure to buy several packages. Pita breads freeze beautifully and are handy for snacks and sandwiches.

nutrition at a glance
per 2 wedges
0 g.   total fat
0 g.   saturated fat
21   calories
0 mg.   cholesterol
32 mg.   sodium
1 g.   protein
4 g.   carbohydrates
0 g.   dietary fiber

Herbed Stuffed Mushrooms

Hot and savory stuffed mushrooms don't have to be swimming in butter to taste rich. You can make these elegant appetizers ahead, refrigerate them, and then bake just before serving.

16   medium button mushrooms
2   ounces Canadian bacon, trimmed of all visible fat and finely chopped
2   cremini mushrooms, finely chopped
1   small onion, finely chopped
1   tablespoon Madeira wine or Worcestershire sauce
3   tablespoons herbed bread crumbs
2   teaspoons balsamic vinegar
2   tablespoons chopped fresh parsley
     Ground black pepper
     Salt (optional)
2   tablespoons fat-free Parmesan topping

1   Preheat the oven to 375°F.

2   Remove the stems from the button mushrooms and chop; set aside. Set the caps aside.

3   Coat a large no-stick skillet with no-stick spray. Add the bacon, cremini mushrooms, onions, and reserved mushroom stems. Mist with no-stick spray. Cook over medium-high heat, stirring often, for 5 minutes.

4   Add the wine or Worcestershire sauce. Cook, stirring, for 1 minute. Add the bread crumbs, vinegar, and 1 tablespoon of the parsley. Stir to combine. Season to taste with the pepper and salt (if using).

5   Spoon the stuffing into the reserved mushroom caps. Place in a single layer in a large baking dish. Sprinkle with the Parmesan. Cover with foil and bake for 25 minutes, or until the mushrooms are hot. Sprinkle with the remaining 1 tablespoon parsley.

Makes **16** mushrooms.

nutrition at a glance

per 2 mushrooms
0.8 g. total fat
0.2 g. saturated fat
42 calories
4 mg. cholesterol
201 mg. sodium
4 g. protein
6 g. carbohydrates
0.9 g. dietary fiber

Baked Potato Skins

This popular contemporary appetizer is a cinch to make free of fat. To cut down on the baking time, you can microwave the scrubbed potatoes for 7 minutes, turning them 4 times for even cooking. Wet the potatoes and bake at 350°F for 30 minutes, or until tender. After you've scooped out the potato flesh, save it for another use, such as mashed potatoes or potato pancakes.

4 medium russet potatoes
8 slices fat-free cheese, cut in half
¼ cup fat-free sour cream
3 tablespoons finely chopped fat-free ham
½ green pepper, finely chopped
½ sweet red pepper, finely chopped
½ cup diced tomatoes
4 scallions, sliced
  Ground black pepper

Lynn's Kitchen Tip Wrapping potatoes in foil before baking actually steams them and softens the skin. So scrap the foil. Instead, scrub the potatoes and then place them (still wet) directly on the oven baking rack. This technique crisps the skin beautifully.

1 Preheat the oven to 350°F.

2 Wash and gently scrub the potatoes, but don't dry. Poke each potato several times with a fork. Place at least 4" apart on the oven rack and bake for 1 hour, or until tender. Remove from the oven. Cut each potato in half lengthwise. Set aside for 10 minutes, or until cool enough to handle.

3 With a large spoon, scoop out the potato flesh, leaving a sturdy shell; reserve the flesh for another use. Using kitchen scissors, cut each skin in half lengthwise. Place the potato skins on a baking sheet.

4 Coat both sides of each skin with no-stick spray. Top each skin with a half slice of cheese. Broil 4" from the heat for 4 minutes, or until the cheese partially melts.

5 Remove from the oven. Transfer the skins to a platter. Top with the sour cream and sprinkle with the ham, green peppers, red peppers, tomatoes, and scallions. Season to taste with the black pepper.

Makes **16** skins.

nutrition at a glance
per 4 skins
0.2 g. total fat
0 g. saturated fat
210 calories
8 mg. cholesterol
723 mg. sodium
13.4 g. protein
38.5 g. carbohydrates
3.1 g. dietary fiber

Baba Ghannouj

Serve this lush Middle Eastern puree as a dip with crackers or pita bread. Or use it as a stuffing for celery or halved hard-cooked egg whites. Top with a sprig of parsley or a slice of pimento.

1	eggplant (1½–2 pounds)
2	tablespoons freshly squeezed lemon juice
2	tablespoons balsamic vinegar
3	cloves garlic, minced
2	teaspoons grated fresh ginger
½	cup finely chopped onions
⅓	cup shredded carrots
	Ground black pepper
	Salt (optional)
2	tablespoons capers, rinsed and drained

1   Pierce the eggplant in several spots with a sharp knife. Microwave on high power for a total of 9 minutes, or until soft; turn the eggplant after 4 minutes. Set aside until cool enough to handle.

2   Cut the eggplant in half, scoop out the pulp, and transfer the pulp to a food processor. Discard the eggplant skin. Add the lemon juice, vinegar, garlic, and ginger; process until almost smooth but not pureed. Add the onions and carrots; pulse once or twice to combine. Season to taste with the pepper and salt (if using).

3   Chill for several hours. Sprinkle with the capers just before serving.

Makes **6** servings.

Lynn's Kitchen Tip

Here's an alternate way to prepare the eggplant, which is a member of the nightshade family and related to the potato and tomato. Pierce the eggplant in several spots with a sharp knife. Place in a shallow baking dish and bake at 375°F for 1¼ hours, or until soft, slightly charred, and collapsed.

nutrition at a glance
per serving

0.3 g.	total fat
0 g.	saturated fat
45	calories
0 mg.	cholesterol
113 mg.	sodium
1 g.	protein
11 g.	carbohydrates
3 g.	dietary fiber

Pinto Bean Dip

quick and easy

You can give this bean dip an even more pronounced Tex-Mex flair by adding ½ teaspoon chili powder. Serve with fat-free tortilla chips, plain toasted pita wedges, or small leafy celery stalks as dippers.

1	can (15 ounces) pinto beans, rinsed and drained
½	sweet red pepper, finely chopped
1	stalk celery, finely chopped
1	small onion, finely chopped
2	cloves garlic, minced
2	tablespoons cider vinegar
2	teaspoons freshly squeezed lemon juice
1	teaspoon dried oregano
½	teaspoon ground cumin
	Ground black pepper
	Salt (optional)

1   Place the beans in a blender or food processor. Process to a chunky puree. Add the red peppers, celery, onions, garlic, vinegar, lemon juice, oregano, and cumin. Pulse once or twice to combine. Season to taste with the black pepper and salt (if using).

Makes about **2½** cups.

nutrition at a glance

per ¼ cup

0.2 g.	total fat
0 g.	saturated fat
46	calories
0 mg.	cholesterol
73 mg.	sodium
3 g.	protein
9 g.	carbohydrates
3 g.	dietary fiber

Crunchy Onion Dip

quick and easy

A confetti of chopped fresh vegetables makes this dip come alive. For a tasty variation, add ½ cup tiny steamed shrimp, more lemon juice, and hot-pepper sauce to taste.

2	cups fat-free sour cream
½	cup finely chopped onions
½	cup finely chopped scallions
⅓	cup finely chopped sweet red peppers
¼	cup finely chopped fresh chives
¼	cup finely chopped carrots
1	tablespoon cider vinegar
1	teaspoon freshly squeezed lemon juice
1	teaspoon chopped fresh parsley
1	clove garlic, minced
½	teaspoon garlic salt
½	teaspoon hot-pepper sauce
¼	teaspoon finely chopped jalapeño peppers (wear plastic gloves when handling)

1 In a medium bowl, combine the sour cream, onions, scallions, red peppers, chives, carrots, vinegar, lemon juice, parsley, garlic, garlic salt, hot-pepper sauce, and jalapeño peppers. Stir well.

Makes about **3** cups.

Photograph on page 48

Photograph on page 48

Lynn's Lore

The term *dip* has evolved with time, according to John Mariani writing in *The Dictionary of American Food and Drink*. From a pork-fat sauce for fish in the mid-1800s to a dessert sauce in the early 1900s, dip now refers to a creamy condiment for crackers, chips, or raw vegetables.

---

nutrition at a glance

per ¼ cup

0 g.	total fat
0 g.	saturated fat
58	calories
0 mg.	cholesterol
128 mg.	sodium
3 g.	protein
10 g.	carbohydrates
0 g.	dietary fiber

Dill Dip

quick and easy

Dill is one of those refreshing, delightful herbs that's pleasing to almost everyone. This appetizer gets a double dill kick with the addition of dill pickles.

1	cup fat-free cottage cheese
1	tablespoon skim milk (optional)
1	cup fat-free plain yogurt cheese (page 304)
¼	cup chopped onions
¼	cup chopped fresh dill
4	teaspoons chopped low-sodium dill pickles
½	teaspoon sugar
½	teaspoon ground black pepper

1 In a blender or food processor, process the cottage cheese for at least 2 minutes. Add the milk, if necessary, to facilitate blending. Add the yogurt cheese; process to combine.

2 Add the onions, dill, pickles, sugar, and pepper. Pulse just to combine.

Makes about **2** cups.

nutrition at a glance

per ¼ cup

0.1 g.	total fat
0 g.	saturated fat
55	calories
3 mg.	cholesterol
127 mg.	sodium
7 g.	protein
6 g.	carbohydrates
0 g.	dietary fiber

Cream Cheese and Chutney

quick and **easy**

The old standby of sweet and spicy, this updated simple 1950s appetizer is a tasty spread on melba toast rounds or any fat-free cracker. Our testers loved it in celery stalks and snow peas.

2 cups mild or hot chutney
2 nectarines, peeled and cut into quarters
¼ cup fat-free liquid creamer
8 scallions, chopped
1 package (8 ounces) fat-free cream cheese, at room temperature

1 In a blender or food processor, combine the chutney, nectarines, and creamer. Process to break up any large chunks of fruit and make a coarse puree. Add all but 2 tablespoons of the scallions; pulse once or twice to combine.

2 Place the cream cheese on a serving dish. Pour the chutney sauce over the cream cheese, letting it drip down the sides. Sprinkle with the remaining 2 tablespoons scallions.

Makes **8** servings.

nutrition at a glance

per serving

0.7 g.	total fat
0.2 g.	saturated fat
154	calories
2 mg.	cholesterol
295 mg.	sodium
6 g.	protein
34 g.	carbohydrates
3 g.	dietary fiber

Bruschetta with Tomatoes (page 34)

Crunchy Onion Dip (page 44)

Pesto Pita Wedges (page 39)

Mediterranean Shrimp (page 37)

Baked Red Snapper with Clams (page 30)

Springtime Asparagus Soup (page 65)

Corn Chowder (page 89)

Fresh Tomato Soup (page 67)

New Orleans Spicy Bean Soup (page 80)

Gazpacho with Shrimp and Avocado (page 66)

Tossed Antipasto Salad (page 97)

Caesar Salad with Turkey (page 99)

Tomato, Basil, and Mozzarella Salad (page 106)

Spinach-Orange Salad (page 109)

Turkey Salad with Orange Dressing (page 100)

Cran-Blackberry Gelatin Salad (page 110)

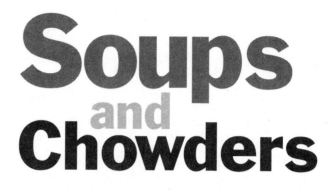

Soups and Chowders

Soups are so easy to love because soups are so

easy to make. Even a novice can create fine soups.

Most require only one pot and little attention as they

simmer. In my kitchen, soups are among the most

gratifying dishes to prepare free of unwanted fat. It's

easy to start your soup with fat-free homemade

stock or canned broth, if you follow my easy recipes

on pages 93 and 94.

Big-batch soups are a powerful arsenal in the

war against fat. With my larger recipes, you can serve a delicious meal and have extra portions to refrigerate or freeze for brown-bag lunches or fast weeknight meals. Most soups keep beautifully, actually improving in flavor. (Cook no-yolk noodles, potatoes, or other starches just before serving.)

Bowling for Health

For ladling out good nutrition, you can't make a better choice than a big bowlful of low-fat home-cooked soup. Made primarily from vegetables, legumes, and grains, a serving or two of soup each day can deliciously help you meet the healthful eating guidelines of the U.S. Department of Agriculture Food Guide Pyramid.

The vegetables in soup are complex carbohydrates that provide a density of nutrients—vitamins A, C, and sometimes B, plus various minerals. They also fortify your body with fiber and powerful substances called antioxidants, which may destroy the free radicals that can lead to cancer and heart disease.

The grains, rice, and pasta in soup provide complex carbohydrates, an important source of energy. They also contain fiber, vitamins, and minerals. The Food Guide Pyramid suggests 6 to 11 servings of these foods each day.

The dry beans, lentils, and peas in soup are excellent sources of fiber, vitamins, minerals, and lean protein. Cook them from scratch (page 259) or use rinsed and drained canned beans.

Ready to Serve

How much soup is a serving? One cup or less is an appropriate appetizer size. Chicken stock with tiny pasta or a refreshing gazpacho is the type of lighter soup that makes a perfect meal opener. Eating a nutritious soup can actually curb your appetite to prevent overeating later in the meal.

For a soup-and-sandwich lunch, I recommend 1½ cups of soup per serving. Cream of Broccoli Soup and my other cream soups are great companions for savory sandwiches made with fat-free cheeses, roasted vegetables, or bean spreads.

Sometimes you'll want to make a meal of soup, accompanied by whole-grain bread. Try my robust Gumbo z'Herbes, U.S. Senate Bean Soup, or Winter Potato and Fish Chowder. For those occasions, 1½ to 2 cups is a reasonable serving.

I've given recipe yields in cups. The nutrient analyses are calculated per 1-cup serving. You can adjust your nutritional totals depending upon the amount that you actually eat.

Springtime Asparagus Soup

quick and easy

This thick soup is an edible celebration of springtime's finest vegetable. Garnish it with a squeeze of lemon or a dollop of fat-free plain yogurt. For a cream soup variation, substitute 2 cups fat-free liquid creamer or buttermilk for the final 2 cups water. Stir in 2 teaspoons fat-free Parmesan topping just before serving.

1   pound asparagus
1   chicken bouillon cube
1   medium leek, white and some green stem, chopped
1   small onion, coarsely chopped
1   small potato, coarsely chopped
1   large stalk celery, cut into ½" pieces
3   cups water
    Ground black pepper
    Salt (optional)
2   tablespoons all-purpose flour
    Pinch of ground nutmeg

1   Remove the tough ends from the asparagus. Chop the tips finely and set aside. Cut the stalks into ½" pieces.

2   Place the stalks in a medium no-stick saucepan. Add the bouillon cube, leeks, onions, potatoes, celery, and 1 cup of the water. Cover and simmer over medium-low heat for 15 minutes, or until the asparagus is very tender.

3   Season to taste with the pepper and salt (if using). Whisk in the flour.

4   Pour the soup into a blender or food processor. Process for 3 to 4 minutes, or until very smooth. Return the soup to the saucepan. (The soup can also be pureed in the saucepan with a hand blender.)

5   Whisk in the remaining 2 cups water. Add the nutmeg and reserved asparagus tips. Cover and simmer, stirring occasionally, for 4 minutes, or until the tips are tender and bright green.

Makes about **4** cups.

Photograph on page 52

Photograph on page 52

Lynn's Kitchen Tip

Keep asparagus chilled and cook it as soon as possible. If refrigerated longer than a few days, asparagus spears wilt, dry out, and toughen. If you can't use asparagus soon after purchase, freeze it. Boil or steam the spears for 2 to 3 minutes, then plunge them into a large bowl of ice water. Drain and pat dry. Place in a heavy-duty resealable plastic bag and freeze.

---

nutrition at a glance

per 1 cup

0.4 g.	total fat
0.1 g.	saturated fat
68	calories
0 mg.	cholesterol
314 mg.	sodium
3 g.	protein
14 g.	carbohydrates
2.4 g.	dietary fiber

Gazpacho with Shrimp and Avocado

quick and easy

If your ingredients are cold from the refrigerator, you won't have to chill the gazpacho before serving. Pass additional hot-pepper sauce and some lemon wedges at the table so that people can make the soup as spicy or tart as they like. For extra crunch and fiber, I like to reserve the pepper seeds and stir them into the chunky soup.

½	large cucumber (peeled if waxed), cut in half crosswise
1	large very ripe tomato, cut into quarters
½	green pepper, cut into quarters
½	sweet red pepper, cut into quarters
½	large yellow or Spanish onion, cut into quarters
3	tablespoons chopped fresh cilantro
2	sprigs fresh parsley
1	small clove garlic, minced
2	tablespoons cider vinegar
5	tablespoons freshly squeezed lemon juice or lime juice
	Hot-pepper sauce
2	cups tomato juice
1	cup cold water
	Salt (optional)
¼	cup finely diced avocado
3	cooked medium shrimp, chilled and cut in half lengthwise
6	sprigs fresh cilantro

1 In a food processor, combine half of the cucumber, half of the tomatoes, half of the green peppers, half of the red peppers, and half of the onions. Add the chopped cilantro, parsley, garlic, vinegar, and 4 tablespoons of the lemon juice or lime juice. Process until nearly pureed. Season to taste with the hot-pepper sauce.

2 Add the remaining cucumber, tomatoes, green peppers, red peppers, and onions. Pulse 2 or 3 times, so that the mixture remains chunky. Stir in the tomato juice and water. Season to taste with the salt (if using).

Lynn's Nutrition Note

Avocados are high in fat, but most of it is heart-healthy monounsaturated fat. They also contain folate, potassium, and vitamin C. The Fuerte avocado, a smooth-skinned variety usually grown in Florida, has one-third less fat than the alligator-skinned Haas, usually grown in California. With very little saturated fat, avocados (especially the Fuertes) can and should be enjoyed in moderation in a low-fat diet.

3 In a small bowl, toss the avocado with the remaining 1 tablespoon lemon juice or lime juice. Serve the soup garnished with the avocado, shrimp, and cilantro sprigs.

Makes about **6** cups.

Photograph on page 56

Fresh Tomato Soup

quick and easy

You'll want to pick the ripest red tomatoes from your garden or farmers market for this summery soup. This version is chunky, but you can puree it if you like. Garnishing ideas: fat-free sour cream, fat-free plain yogurt, lemon or lime wedges, chopped jalapeño peppers, or fat-free croutons. For extra spice, add a dash of hot-pepper sauce.

¼ cup all-purpose flour
2 cups vegetable stock (page 93) or water
5 large ripe tomatoes, coarsely chopped
1 medium onion, coarsely chopped
1 stalk celery with leafy top, coarsely chopped
2 cloves garlic, minced
2 teaspoons dried oregano
1 teaspoon packed brown sugar
   Juice of ½ lemon
   Salt (optional)
8 large fresh basil leaves, thinly sliced

Lynn's Nutrition Note

We Americans eat 18 pounds of tomatoes each year, in quantities second only to the potato. That's smart eating. A single tomato can provide nearly half the vitamin C that you need each day. Tomatoes also contain lycopene, an awesome antioxidant that may aid in cancer prevention.

1 Place the flour in a large no-stick pot. Gradually whisk in the stock or water until smooth. Add the tomatoes, onions, celery, garlic, oregano, and brown sugar.

2 Cook over medium-high heat, stirring constantly, until the soup almost comes to a boil. Reduce the heat to medium-low, cover, and simmer, stirring occasionally, for 15 minutes, or until the vegetables are soft. Stir in the lemon juice and season to taste with the salt (if using). Sprinkle with the basil just before serving.

Makes about **6** cups.

Photograph on page 54

Cavendish Green-Pepper Soup

My former assistant, Marty Cavendish, shared her mother's unique recipe for green-pepper soup for those of us who never get enough green peppers. I love all that vitamin C! I scatter the sweet, crunchy pepper seeds over the soup before serving.

1	medium onion, chopped
2	cloves garlic, minced
4	medium green peppers, coarsely chopped
½	teaspoon dried thyme
1	teaspoon dried marjoram
2	cans (14 ounces each) low-sodium chicken broth, defatted
⅓–½	cup instant potato flakes
1	tablespoon Worcestershire sauce
2	tablespoons chopped fresh parsley
¼	teaspoon hot-pepper sauce
2	cups fat-free liquid creamer or evaporated skim milk
	Freshly ground black pepper
	Salt (optional)

1 Coat a large no-stick pot with no-stick spray. Add the onions and garlic. Sauté over medium heat for 4 minutes, or until translucent. (Add 1 to 2 tablespoons water to the pot if the onions start to stick.) Add the green peppers, thyme, marjoram, and 1 cup of the broth. Simmer for 12 to 15 minutes, or until the peppers are tender.

2 In a blender or food processor, puree 2 cups of the soup mixture. Return to the pot. Pour the remaining broth into the pot. Cover and simmer over medium heat for 10 minutes.

3 Add ⅓ cup of the potato flakes and cook, whisking, for 4 minutes, or until thickened. (Add 1 to 2 tablespoons more flakes, if needed, to thicken.) Stir in the Worcestershire sauce, parsley, and hot-pepper sauce. Add the creamer or milk. Season to taste with the black pepper and salt (if using). Cook for 3 minutes, or until the soup is hot.

Makes about **10** cups.

nutrition at a glance

per 1 cup

0.2 g.	total fat
0.1 g.	saturated fat
68	calories
2 mg.	cholesterol
133 mg.	sodium
6.7 g.	protein
9.9 g.	carbohydrates
1 g.	dietary fiber

Cabbage and Potato Soup with Ham

To make this soup even quicker, start with shredded cabbage, which can be purchased at most large markets in convenient cellophane bags.

1   cup chopped onions
8   cups water
5   cups shredded green cabbage
2   large potatoes, diced
6   tablespoons diced lean ham or Canadian bacon
2   vegetable bouillon cubes
1   teaspoon crushed dill seed
2   tablespoons cider vinegar
    Ground black pepper
    Salt (optional)
2   tablespoons chopped fresh parsley

1   Coat a large no-stick pot with no-stick spray. Add the onions. Cover and cook over medium heat, stirring occasionally, for 5 to 6 minutes, or until the onions start to color. Uncover and cook for 3 to 4 minutes, or until golden. If necessary, add 1 or 2 teaspoons water to prevent sticking.

2   Add the water, cabbage, potatoes, ham or bacon, bouillon cubes, and dill seed. Cover and bring almost to a boil.

3   Reduce the heat to low and simmer for 15 to 20 minutes, or until the potatoes are very tender. If a slightly thicker soup is desired, mash some of the potatoes against the side of the pot with the back of a large spoon. Stir in the vinegar. Season to taste with the pepper and salt (if using). Sprinkle with the parsley.

Makes about **10** cups.

nutrition at a glance

per 1 cup
0.5 g. total fat
0.1 g. saturated fat
65   calories
2 mg. cholesterol
139 mg. sodium
3 g. protein
13 g. carbohydrates
2 g. dietary fiber

Carrot and Almond Soup

I like this vitamin-rich puree served with a dollop of fat-free yogurt cheese on top. I take a sip of soup and then a bite of cheese. You can also serve it with a spoonful of fat-free plain yogurt, which blends more easily with the soup when you stir it in at the table.

6	medium carrots, cut into 2" pieces
1	medium potato, cut into eighths
½	stalk celery, sliced
1	small onion, cut in half
2	shallots, cut in half
6	unblanched almonds
½	teaspoon sugar
½	teaspoon salt (optional)
¼	teaspoon ground nutmeg
	Pinch of ground allspice
	Pinch of ground ginger
2–3	cups vegetable stock (page 93) or water
4	whole cloves
2	cloves garlic, unpeeled
	Ground black pepper
1	cup fat-free plain yogurt cheese (page 304) or fat-free plain yogurt
1	tablespoon snipped chives or scallion stems

1 In a large no-stick saucepan, combine the carrots, potatoes, celery, onions, shallots, almonds, sugar, salt (if using), nutmeg, allspice, ginger, and 2 cups of the stock or water. Place the cloves and garlic in a mesh tea ball or wrap in a small piece of cheesecloth and tie with kitchen string. Place in the saucepan.

2 Cover and bring almost to a boil over medium-high heat. Reduce the heat to low and simmer for 35 minutes, or until the carrots and potatoes are tender. Remove the tea ball or cheesecloth bundle; discard the cloves. Squeeze the garlic from its skin and add the soft paste to the soup.

3 Working in batches if necessary, pour the soup into a blender or food processor. Process for several minutes, or until pureed. (The soup can also be pureed in the saucepan with a hand blender.) Return the soup to the pan. If the soup is too thick, thin with the remaining 1 cup stock or water. Season to taste with the pepper. Serve topped with the yogurt cheese or yogurt and chives or scallions.

Makes about **6** cups.

Salt Substitutes

Nearly everyone wants a little salt in soup, and frankly, most soups taste better with it. Salt intensifies flavors. Of course, you should follow your physician's advice about sodium consumption. If you have to watch the saltshaker, here are some seasonings that will heighten flavors without contributing sodium.

Try a tablespoon or two of vinegar or a few squeezes of lemon juice or lime juice. Worcestershire sauce and soy sauce, which contain some salt, also do the trick. Just remember that regular Worcestershire sauce (a low-sodium brand is also available) contains a third less sodium than even low-sodium soy sauce. Crushed red-pepper flakes, fresh or pickled chili peppers, and commercial salt-potassium seasoning blends are also good flavor boosters.

On occasions when you want real salt, remember that, by weight, sea salt and kosher salt have more sodium chloride than table salt, which contains anticlumping agents and starches. (Valid comparisons are difficult to make by volume measurement, because the density of these salts differs.)

Better-Than-French Onion Soup

quick and easy

This simple soup with a secret ingredient (coffee!) has all the flavor of the finest onion soup you ever tasted. It requires some attention while cooking, but the results are well worth it. A small piece of toast and 2 tablespoons finely shredded fat-free mozzarella will add close to 1 gram of fat per serving. Ladle the soup into 6 ovenproof bowls, then top with the toast piece and cheese. Bake in a preheated 450°F oven for 10 minutes, or until the cheese melts.

2   large onions, sliced
3   tablespoons unflavored brewed coffee
1   beef bouillon cube
4   cups water
¼   cup port wine (optional)

1   Coat a large no-stick saucepan with no-stick spray. Warm the saucepan over medium-high heat. Add the onions and coffee. Cook, stirring constantly, to coat the onions well with the coffee. Cook for 3 minutes, or until the coffee is nearly evaporated.

2   Add the bouillon cube and ½ cup of the water. As the cube melts, mash it with the back of a large spoon and stir into the water. Cook, stirring, until the water is nearly evaporated.

3   Add ¼ cup of the remaining water and cook, stirring occasionally, for 7 minutes, or until the water evaporates. Add ¼ cup of the remaining water and cook for another 7 minutes, or until the onions are soft.

4   Add the wine (if using) and the remaining 3 cups water. Cook over medium-high heat until the soup comes to a light boil.

Makes about **6** cups.

nutrition at a glance

per 1 cup
0.1 g.	total fat
0 g.	saturated fat
18	calories
0 mg.	cholesterol
149 mg.	sodium
0.6 g.	protein
3.9 g.	carbohydrates
0.5 g.	dietary fiber

Lemongrass Egg-Drop Soup

This aromatic Asian broth studded with vegetables is sure to be a welcome addition to your soup repertoire. You can add 1½ ounces shrimp, 2 ounces turkey breast, or 2 ounces no-yolk noodles to the recipe and still keep it fat-free. If you don't have a fresh hot red pepper, use ¼ teaspoon crushed red-pepper flakes.

2 tablespoons dried flaked lemongrass or 1 stalk fresh
4 cups defatted chicken stock (page 94)
1 medium tomato, chopped
1 small hot red pepper, chopped (wear plastic gloves when handling)
2 tablespoons chopped scallions
1 tablespoon freshly squeezed lemon juice
2 teaspoons sugar
1 teaspoon grated fresh ginger
2 tablespoons chopped fresh cilantro
   Salt (optional)
1 egg white
½ teaspoon dark sesame oil

1 If using dried lemongrass, place it in a mesh tea ball. Place the ball in a medium no-stick saucepan. Add 1 cup of the stock. Warm over medium-low heat; turn off the heat and let soak for 1 hour. Add the remaining 3 cups stock.

2 (If using fresh lemongrass, peel the root end of the stalk to expose the pinkish-white center. Thinly slice and place in a medium no-stick saucepan. Add all the stock; do not soak.)

3 Add the tomatoes, peppers, scallions, lemon juice, sugar, ginger, and 1 tablespoon of the cilantro. Bring to a boil over medium-high heat; reduce the heat to medium. Cover and simmer for 5 minutes. Season to taste with the salt (if using).

4 In a small bowl, lightly beat the egg white with a fork. While stirring the soup, add the egg white in a thin stream and cook for 1 minute. Remove from the heat. Stir in the sesame oil and the remaining 1 tablespoon cilantro. If using dried lemongrass, remove the tea ball and discard the lemongrass.

Makes about **4** cups.

nutrition at a glance

per 1 cup

0.9 g.	total fat
0.1 g.	saturated fat
52	calories
5 mg.	cholesterol
41 mg.	sodium
5 g.	protein
7 g.	carbohydrates
0.8 g.	dietary fiber

Cream of Broccoli Soup

quick and easy

The little bit of sharp Cheddar really enlivens the taste of this simple soup. (I like to use New York Cheddar.) You can make this soup into a meal by serving it over 1 cup no-yolk noodles, rice, or mashed potatoes. The starch will raise the fat content by about 1 gram.

2	pounds broccoli
2	cups vegetable stock (page 93) or defatted chicken stock (page 94)
1	medium onion, finely chopped
¼	cup shredded carrots
1	small clove garlic, minced
1	cup skim milk
1	cup fat-free liquid creamer
3	tablespoons all-purpose flour
	Juice of 1 lemon
	Ground black pepper
	Salt (optional)
6	tablespoons shredded fat-free sharp Cheddar cheese
1	tablespoon shredded sharp Cheddar cheese

1   Take one bunch of the broccoli and cut the florets away from the stalks; cut the florets into slivers lengthwise and set them aside.

2   Finely chop the stalks and the remaining broccoli; place in a medium no-stick saucepan.

3   Add the stock, onions, carrots, and garlic. Cover and cook over medium heat, stirring often, for 6 to 7 minutes.

4   Add the reserved broccoli florets. Cook, stirring, for 2 to 3 minutes, or until the florets are bright green.

5   Whisk in the milk and creamer. Bring almost to a boil over medium heat.

6 Hold a large, fine sieve over the saucepan; add the flour to the sieve and shake into the soup, whisking to incorporate. Cook over low heat, stirring, for 3 to 4 minutes, or until the soup is thick. Stir in the lemon juice. Season to taste with the pepper and salt (if using).

7 Serve sprinkled with the fat-free Cheddar and sharp Cheddar.

Makes about **8** cups.

Barley Soup with Beef

Beef and barley soup is a thick, aromatic soup traditional among Middle European Jewish families. The soup should be hearty. You can make it thick or thin it with water or broth. I love it both ways.

1	beef knuckle or marrow bone with meat attached
3	quarts vegetable stock (page 93) or water
2	bay leaves
2	beef bouillon cubes (optional)
1	cup extra-large dry lima beans
2	medium onions, chopped
2	stalks celery, chopped
2	carrots, chopped
½	cup chopped fresh parsley
½	cup barley
4	cloves garlic, minced
	Ground black pepper
	Salt (optional)
2	tablespoons chopped fresh parsley

Lynn's Lore

Barley has nourished humans for thousands of years. It was grown 10,000 years ago in Jericho, 5,000 years ago in Japan, and 3,000 years ago in Babylonia for both food and beer. In the Dark Ages, bread was made primarily of barley.

1 In a large no-stick pot, combine the beef knuckle or marrow bone, stock or water, bay leaves, and bouillon cubes (if using). Simmer for 1¼ hours over low heat.

2 Strain the liquid into a large bowl and defat it (see page 17).

3 Wash the pot with soapy water and rinse.

(continued)

4 Discard the bay leaves. Cut the lean meat from the bone; discard the fat. Dice the meat and set aside 6 tablespoons; reserve any remainder for another use.

5 Return the liquid and the meat to the pot. Add the beans, onions, celery, carrots, parsley, barley, and garlic. Cover and cook over low heat for 2½ hours, or until the beans are tender. (If the soup becomes too thick, add some water. If the soup is too watery, remove the lid for the last 30 minutes of cooking.)

6 Season to taste with the pepper and salt (if using). Sprinkle with the parsley.

Makes about **12** cups.

nutrition at a glance	
per 1 cup	
0.5 g.	total fat
0.1 g.	saturated fat
115	calories
4 mg.	cholesterol
37 mg.	sodium
6.4 g.	protein
22.2 g.	carbohydrates
5.6 g.	dietary fiber

Mushroom and Wild Rice Soup

Garnish this chunky soup with lemon slices and paprika. To make a creamy variation, stir 1½ cups fat-free liquid creamer into the soup just before serving. Heat through but do not boil.

½	cup wild rice
8	cups defatted chicken stock (page 94) or vegetable stock (page 93)
1½	pounds large button mushrooms, thickly sliced
1	large onion, chopped
1	carrot, chopped
1	stalk celery, chopped
3	shallots, chopped
3	cloves garlic, minced
1	teaspoon dried basil
¼	teaspoon ground nutmeg
4	tablespoons dry sherry or 2 teaspoons sherry extract (optional)
3	tablespoons all-purpose flour
½	cup chopped fresh parsley

1 Cook the rice according to the package directions. Set aside and keep warm.

2 Meanwhile, in a large no-stick pot, combine the stock, mushrooms, onions, carrots, celery, shallots, and garlic. Bring to a boil over medium-high heat. Add the basil, nutmeg, and 2 tablespoons of the sherry or 1 teaspoon of the sherry extract (if using). Reduce the heat to medium, cover, and simmer for 30 minutes.

3 Hold a large, fine sieve over the saucepan; add the flour and shake over the soup, whisking to incorporate. Cook over medium-high heat, stirring, for 3 to 4 minutes, or until thick. Add the parsley and the remaining 2 tablespoons sherry or 1 teaspoon sherry extract (if using). Mix well. Cook for 1 minute but do not boil. Serve the soup over the wild rice.

Makes about **12** cups.

nutrition at a glance

per 1 cup

0.4 g.	total fat
0.1 g.	saturated fat
68	calories
0 mg.	cholesterol
23 mg.	sodium
3 g.	protein
14.3 g.	carbohydrates
2 g.	dietary fiber

Wheat Berry Soup

If you've never tasted wheat berries—hulled whole grains of wheat—you'll be delighted by their nutty flavor and chewy texture. If wheat berries are unavailable, you can use bulgur, which will cook in only 40 minutes. Serve the soup garnished with a little shredded fat-free mozzarella and some pimento-stuffed olive slices. If you don't have Cajun spice blend, substitute ¼ teaspoon ground red pepper and ¼ teaspoon sugar.

1	cup wheat berries
4	cups water or defatted chicken stock (page 94)
1	pound button mushrooms, sliced
3	ripe plum tomatoes, diced
1	medium onion, finely diced
6	cloves garlic, minced
1	teaspoon dried thyme
1	teaspoon dried rosemary, crumbled
½	teaspoon Cajun spice blend
	Salt (optional)

1   Place the wheat berries in a large bowl. Cover with at least 6 cups cold water. Set aside to soak for at least 4 hours. Drain and place in a large no-stick saucepan.

2   Add the water or stock. Cover and bring to a boil over medium-high heat. Reduce the heat to medium and simmer for 1 hour. Add the mushrooms, tomatoes, onions, garlic, thyme, rosemary, and Cajun spice blend.

3   Cover and simmer, stirring occasionally, for 30 to 45 minutes, or until the wheat berries are tender. Season to taste with the salt (if using).

Makes about **9** cups.

Lynn's Fun Food Fact

Wheat berries are whole, unprocessed kernels of ripe wheat that are high in fiber and other nutrients. Look for them in natural food stores, specialty flour catalogs, or large supermarkets. Soak wheat berries for several hours in cold water before cooking and cook them in a generous amount of water for 1½ hours, or until tender. You can cook a large amount of wheat berries, drain them, and freeze them in recipe-ready portions. They're a nutritious addition to soups, casseroles, and mixed-grain pilafs.

nutrition at a glance

per 1 cup

0.5 g.	total fat
0.1 g.	saturated fat
50	calories
0 mg.	cholesterol
21 mg.	sodium
2.6 g.	protein
11.1 g.	carbohydrates
2.2 g.	dietary fiber

If a soup is properly thickened to a luscious consistency, you'll never notice that it has no fat.

For clear or translucent soups, such as Asian broths or chicken soup, use cornstarch, arrowroot, rice flour, or tapioca flour.

For opaque soups that don't already contain starchy ingredients, use all-purpose flour, bread crumbs, mashed potatoes, pureed cooked rice, red lentils (which disintegrate quickly), or mashed potatoes.

Of course, the simplest and purest way to thicken a soup made with vegetables or legumes is to pour a small portion of the soup into a blender or food processor, puree it, and stir it into the soup.

All-purpose flour. For each quart of liquid, whisk 2 tablespoons flour into ½ cup cool water. Whisk into the hot soup over medium heat for at least 3 minutes, or until the soup thickens and the flour loses its raw taste. Flour-thickened soups can usually be reheated without losing their consistency.

Cooked rice. For each quart of liquid, process ½ to 1 cup cooked rice with ¼ cup water until pureed. Whisk into the soup over medium heat for 4 minutes, or until thickened.

Cornstarch. For each quart of liquid, whisk 2 tablespoons cornstarch into ½ cup cold water. Whisk into the hot soup over medium heat for 30 seconds, or until thickened. Any refrigerated leftover soup may need to be rethickened after reheating.

Mashed potatoes. For each quart of liquid, whisk 1 cup mashed potatoes into the soup over medium heat for 4 minutes or until thickened.

Potato flour or mashed potato powder. For each quart of liquid, whisk 2 tablespoons potato flour or mashed potato powder into ½ cup cool water. Whisk into the soup over medium heat for 4 minutes, or until thickened.

Rice flour. For each quart of liquid, whisk 2 tablespoons rice flour into ¼ cup cool water. Whisk into the soup over medium heat for 2 minutes, or until thickened.

Tapioca flour. For each quart of liquid, whisk 2 tablespoons tapioca flour into ¼ cup cool water. Whisk into the soup over medium heat for 30 seconds, or until thickened.

New Orleans Spicy Bean Soup

I like Zatarain's Creole seasoning, which can be bought in most markets nationwide, for this Crescent City specialty. Creole seasoning is spicy hot, so you may want to start with the minimum amount and add more later if the soup needs it.

3	quarts water
1	smoked ham hock with meat attached
1	bay leaf
1	pound dry navy or kidney beans
2	large onions, chopped
2	stalks celery with leafy tops, chopped
1	carrot, shredded or chopped
½	sweet red pepper, chopped
1	cup chopped fresh parsley
1	tablespoon chopped fresh cilantro
2	teaspoons ground cumin
1	teaspoon dried oregano
1–2	teaspoons Creole seasoning
4	cloves garlic, minced
	Hot-pepper sauce

1 In a large no-stick pot, combine the water, ham hock, and bay leaf. Bring to a boil over medium-high heat. Reduce the heat to medium-low, cover, and simmer for 1 hour. Uncover and simmer for 30 minutes.

2 Strain into a large bowl. Discard the bay leaf. Remove the meat from the bone. Trim off all visible fat and cut the meat into small dice. Set aside about ¾ cup of the meat; reserve any remainder for another use. Defat the stock (see page 17).

3 Wash the pot with soapy water and rinse. Return the stock to the pot.

Lynn's Kitchen Tip

When using several cloves of garlic in a long-cooked dish, don't bother to peel and dice them. Place the cloves in a mesh tea ball, clip it shut, and put it right in the pot to cook with the soup. After cooking, remove the ball, rinse the cloves to cool them, and squeeze out the sweet, cooked garlic. Whisk the garlic paste into the soup for a mellow flavor accent.

4   Add the beans, onions, celery, carrots, red peppers, parsley, cilantro, cumin, oregano, Creole seasoning, and garlic. Set over medium-high heat and bring almost to a boil. Reduce the heat to low, cover, and simmer for 2½ to 3 hours, or until the beans are tender.

5   Transfer 4 cups of the soup to a blender or food processor. Puree, then stir back into the soup. If the soup is not thick enough, continue pureeing in 1-cup batches until the soup is the desired consistency. (The soup can also be partially pureed in the pot using a hand blender.) Stir in the reserved ham. Season to taste with the hot-pepper sauce.

Makes about **14** cups.

Photograph on page 55

U.S. Senate Bean Soup

This thick soup has a rich history and great depth of flavor. Scatter some chopped parsley, chives, scallion greens, or slivered sweet red peppers over the top for color. A few dashes of hot-pepper sauce will add some spunk.

3   quarts water
1   smoked ham hock with meat attached
1   pound dry navy or Great Northern beans
3   medium onions, chopped
3   stalks celery, chopped
1   large russet potato, chopped
¼   cup chopped fresh parsley
3   cloves garlic, minced
    Ground black pepper

1   In a large no-stick pot, combine the water and ham hock. Bring to a boil over medium-high heat. Reduce the heat to medium-low, cover, and simmer for 1 hour. Uncover and simmer for 30 minutes.

2   Strain into a large bowl. Remove the meat from the bone. Trim off all visible fat and cut the meat into small dice. Set aside about

Lynn's Lore

The original recipe for this bean soup has been made for decades in the dining room of the United States Senate. Some of the more senior stewards tell me that the recipe came from the family of the late Henry Cabot Lodge and features foods from many parts of the country, such as celery and garlic from Florida or Washington State, potatoes from Maine, onions from California, ham from Virginia, and beans from Michigan. Like a seasoned politician, this all-American potage adapts beautifully to the (low-fat) times.

(continued)

¾ cup of the meat; reserve any remainder for another use. Defat the stock (see page 17).

3   Wash the pot with soapy water and rinse. Return the stock to the pot.

4   Add the beans, onions, celery, potatoes, parsley, and garlic. Set over medium-high heat and bring almost to a boil. Reduce the heat to low, cover, and simmer for 2½ to 3 hours, or until the beans are tender.

5   Working in batches, transfer half of the soup to a blender or food processor. Puree, then stir back into the soup. (The soup can also be partially pureed in the pot with a hand blender.)

6   Stir in the reserved ham. Season to taste with the pepper.

Makes about **18** cups.

nutrition at a glance	
per 1 cup	
0.8 g.	total fat
0.3 g.	saturated fat
114	calories
2 mg.	cholesterol
32 mg.	sodium
7.7 g.	protein
19.4 g.	carbohydrates
5.7 g.	dietary fiber

Chili Soup

quick and easy

Garnish with chopped scallions or fresh cilantro.

6 ounces lean ground top round, all visible fat removed before grinding
1 large onion, coarsely chopped
1 green pepper, cut into 1" pieces
1 sweet red pepper, cut into 1" pieces
3 cloves garlic, minced
4 cups water
1 can (28 ounces) crushed tomatoes (with juice)
1 can (15 ounces) dark red kidney beans, rinsed and drained
1 can (8 ounces) tomato sauce
2 teaspoons chili powder
1 teaspoon ground cumin
1 teaspoon dried oregano
1 teaspoon hot-pepper sauce
½ teaspoon cocoa powder
   Salt (optional)

1 Coat a no-stick Dutch oven with no-stick spray. Warm over medium heat. Add the meat and cook, stirring occasionally, for 4 to 5 minutes, or until no longer pink. Place the meat in a colander to drain and then rinse under hot tap water to remove any residual fat. Set aside.

2 Wipe the Dutch oven with paper towels. Add the onions, green peppers, red peppers, and garlic. Mist with no-stick spray. Cover and cook over medium-high heat, stirring occasionally, for 4 minutes, or until the onions start to release liquid. Remove the cover and reduce the heat to medium. Cook, stirring, for 2 to 3 minutes, or until golden.

3 Add the water, tomatoes (with juice), beans, tomato sauce, chili powder, cumin, oregano, hot-pepper sauce, cocoa powder, and the reserved meat. Bring to a boil. Reduce the heat to medium, cover, and simmer for 8 minutes. Remove the cover and simmer, stirring occasionally, for 10 minutes. Season to taste with the salt (if using).

Makes about **12** cups.

Lynn's Lore

Chili—both the dried spice blend and the spicy stew—is a product of the New World chili pepper. Texans say that chili (the stew) originated in the Lone Star state. But it is really just a modern name given to the stews and soups that have been served for centuries in South America, Central America, Mexico, lower California, New Mexico, and Texas.

nutrition at a glance

per 1 cup

0.9 g.	total fat
0.2 g.	saturated fat
74	calories
9 mg.	cholesterol
188 mg.	sodium
6.6 g.	protein
10.9 g.	carbohydrates
3.3 g.	dietary fiber

Double Lentil Soup

Oh, you lucky lentil lovers! This soup has lots of invaluable nutrients and fiber. You can add ½ ounce crumbled regular feta cheese (or 1 ounce low-fat feta) per serving and still come in under 1 gram of fat. Or try ¼ cup diced tomatoes mixed with 1 tablespoon sliced scallions as a fresh topper.

2	tablespoons water
1½	cups diced or shredded carrots
1	cup diced celery stalks with leafy tops
1	large yellow onion, chopped
3	cloves garlic, minced
5	cups vegetable stock (page 93) or defatted chicken stock (page 94)
1	cup brown or green lentils
½	cup red lentils, rinsed
2	teaspoons Worcestershire sauce
½	teaspoon dried thyme
⅛	teaspoon ground allspice
1	bay leaf
	Ground black pepper
	Salt (optional)

1 Coat a large no-stick pot with no-stick spray. Add the water. Warm over medium-high heat. Add the carrots, celery, onions, and garlic. Cook, stirring frequently, for 6 minutes, or until the carrots are tender. If necessary, add 1 or 2 teaspoons more water to prevent sticking.

2 Add the stock, brown or green lentils, red lentils, Worcestershire sauce, thyme, allspice, and bay leaf. Bring to a boil. Reduce the heat and simmer for 35 to 40 minutes, or until the red lentils disintegrate.

3 Remove and discard the bay leaf. Season to taste with the pepper and salt (if using).

Makes about **8** cups.

Lynn's Kitchen Tip

Lentils keep for months stored in a cool, dry spot. There are a great many varieties, which are used in soups, salads, stews, and especially in the spicy Indian dish called dal. Red lentils break down quickly in cooking, making them a nutritious thickener for soups and stews. Unlike beans, lentils don't have to be soaked. They cook in just 20 to 35 minutes, depending upon the variety.

nutrition at a glance

per 1 cup

0.5 g.	total fat
0.1 g.	saturated fat
152	calories
0 mg.	cholesterol
47 mg.	sodium
11 g.	protein
27.4 g.	carbohydrates
6.3 g.	dietary fiber

Split Pea Soup

Split pea soup is always welcome at my house. It's a cinch to make fat-free, even with all the savory ham flavor. Serve with low-fat crackers.

10	cups water
1	smoked ham hock with meat attached
1	bay leaf
2	carrots, chopped
2	stalks celery with leafy tops, chopped
1	large onion, chopped
1	large potato, coarsely chopped
8	ounces dry green split peas
½	cup beer or nonalcoholic beer (optional)
½	teaspoon dried thyme
	Ground black pepper

1 In a large no-stick pot, combine the water, ham hock, and bay leaf. Bring to a boil over medium-high heat. Reduce the heat to medium-low, cover, and simmer for 1 hour. Uncover and simmer for 30 minutes.

2 Strain into a large bowl. Discard the bay leaf. Remove the meat from the bone. Trim off all visible fat and cut the meat into small dice. Set aside about 6 tablespoons of the meat; reserve any remainder for another use. Defat the stock (see page 17).

3 Wash the pot with soapy water and rinse. Add the stock to the pot.

4 Add the carrots, celery, onions, potatoes, split peas, beer (if using), and thyme. Cover and simmer for 45 minutes, or until the split peas are soft.

5 Working in batches, transfer the soup to a blender or food processor. Puree and return to the pot. (The soup can also be pureed in the pot with a hand blender.) Season to taste with the pepper. Serve sprinkled with the reserved ham.

Makes about **12** cups.

nutrition at a glance

per 1 cup

0.9 g.	total fat
0.3 g.	saturated fat
107	calories
3 mg.	cholesterol
50 mg.	sodium
8.4 g.	protein
16.7 g.	carbohydrates
2.3 g.	dietary fiber

Gumbo z'Herbes

This New Orleans gumbo is traditionally made with seven different greens, but the results are just as delicious using only two or three. Choose from spinach, collard greens, kale, beet greens, dandelion, mustard greens, lettuce, young radish tops, cilantro, or celery leaves.

9   cups water
1   smoked ham hock with meat attached
¾   cup quick-cooking brown rice (ready in 30 minutes)
1   onion, chopped
1   cup chopped spinach leaves
1   cup chopped fresh collard greens or kale
½   cup chopped fresh parsley
½   cup chopped cabbage
½   cup chopped watercress
1   bay leaf
     Pinch of dried thyme
     Pinch of dried tarragon
½   cup all-purpose flour
1   pound okra, sliced into rounds
     Pinch of salt
     Pinch of ground black pepper
     Hot-pepper sauce
     Wine vinegar or lemon wedges

1   In a large no-stick pot, combine the water and ham hock. Bring to a boil over medium-high heat. Reduce the heat to medium-low, cover, and simmer for 1 hour. Uncover and simmer for 30 minutes.

2   Strain into a large bowl. Remove the meat from the bone. Trim off all visible fat and cut the meat into small dice. Set aside about ¾ cup of the meat; reserve any remainder for another use. Defat the stock (see page 17).

3   Wash the pot with soapy water and rinse. Return the stock to the pot.

4   Add the rice. Cover and cook over very low heat for 25 minutes, or until the rice is nearly tender.

5   Add the onions, spinach, collard greens or kale, parsley, cabbage, watercress, bay leaf, thyme, and tarragon. Simmer for 20 minutes, or until the rice is tender.

6   Meanwhile, place the flour in a large no-stick skillet. Cook over medium-high heat, stirring frequently, for 3 to 4 minutes, or until golden. Set aside to cool slightly.

7   Transfer the flour to a large plastic bag. Add the okra, salt, and pepper. Holding the bag closed with one hand, shake to coat the okra with flour.

8   Coat the same skillet with no-stick spray. Remove the okra from the bag, shaking lightly to remove excess flour. Discard the remaining flour. Place the okra in the skillet. Coat lightly with no-stick spray. Cook over medium heat, tossing occasionally, for 10 minutes, or until cooked.

9   When the rice is cooked, remove and discard the bay leaf. Stir the okra and reserved ham into the gumbo. If the gumbo is too thick, stir in a little extra water to thin it slightly. Serve with the hot-pepper sauce and vinegar or lemon wedges for seasoning.

Makes about **16** cups.

nutrition at a glance	
per 1 cup	
0.8 g.	total fat
0.2 g.	saturated fat
56	calories
2 mg.	cholesterol
34 mg.	sodium
3.7 g.	protein
8.8 g.	carbohydrates
1.1 g.	dietary fiber

Cream of Celery Soup

quick and easy

This simply wonderful creamed soup—which is also delicious chilled—can serve as a blueprint for many tasty variations. Just substitute broccoli, cauliflower, asparagus, or fennel for the celery. A dash of ground nutmeg is always welcome in any cream soup.

2   cups chopped celery stalks with leafy tops
½   cup water
¼   cup chopped onions
2   tablespoons all-purpose flour
1   cup skim milk
½   cup fat-free liquid creamer
     Ground black pepper
     Salt (optional)
4   small leafy celery sprigs

1   In a medium no-stick saucepan, combine the chopped celery, water, and onions. Bring almost to a boil over medium-high heat. Reduce the heat to medium-low. Cover and cook for 12 to 15 minutes, or until the celery is tender.

2   Meanwhile, place the flour in a small bowl. Gradually whisk in the milk until blended. Whisk the milk mixture into the saucepan. Whisk in the creamer.

3   Pour the soup into a blender or food processor. Process for several minutes, or until pureed. (The soup can also be pureed in the saucepan with a hand blender.) Return the soup to the saucepan.

4   Cook over medium heat, stirring constantly, for 4 minutes, or until the soup thickens. Season to taste with the pepper and salt (if using). Serve garnished with the celery sprigs.

Makes about **4** cups.

nutrition at a glance

per 1 cup

0.2 g.	total fat
0.1 g.	saturated fat
69	calories
1 mg.	cholesterol
84 mg.	sodium
3.1 g.	protein
13 g.	carbohydrates
1.2 g.	dietary fiber

Corn Chowder

quick and easy

This soup reminds me of the many summer trips I took with my mother to her childhood Iowa, where sweet, heavenly corn filled the fields along the narrow roads near Brighton. If you like more vegetables, add ½ cup chopped carrots. Plenty of chopped parsley makes a pretty and nutritious garnish.

1   cup water
2   cups fresh whole-kernel corn
2   medium onions, chopped
1   medium potato, diced
1   medium leek, white and some green stem, chopped
¾   cup finely diced sweet red peppers
¼   cup finely diced green peppers
½   teaspoon sugar
½   teaspoon ground cumin
¼   teaspoon dried thyme
½   teaspoon curry powder
    Salt (optional)

1   In a blender or food processor, combine the water, 1 cup of the corn, half of the onions, and half of the potatoes. Process to a coarse puree.

2   Pour into a large no-stick saucepan. Bring almost to a boil over medium-high heat. Reduce the heat to low and simmer, stirring occasionally, for 10 minutes.

3   Add the leeks, red peppers, green peppers, sugar, cumin, thyme, and curry powder. Add the remaining corn, onions, and potatoes. Cover the pan and cook for 10 to 12 minutes, or until the potatoes are tender. Add more water if a thinner consistency is desired. Season to taste with the salt (if using).

Makes about **8** cups.

Photograph on page 53

Photograph on page 53

Lynn's Kitchen Tip

To cut corn kernels from the cob, use a sharp, heavy 8" or 10" chef's knife. First, trim the wider end of the ear so that it will stand steadily on a cutting board when held upright. Holding the ear upright with one hand, carefully but firmly slice the kernels in rows, from top to bottom, as close to the cob as possible. Rotate the ear to repeat slicing the kernels in rows. Then, with the blunt side of the knife, scrape the cob to remove all the sweet, milky juice.

nutrition at a glance

per 1 cup

0.7 g.	total fat
0.1 g.	saturated fat
82	calories
0 mg.	cholesterol
14 mg.	sodium
2.4 g.	protein
18.9 g.	carbohydrates
2.6 g.	dietary fiber

Winter Potato and Fish Chowder

If you like fish chowder and you like creamy potato soup, this savory merger will suit you just fine. I like to use red snapper or tilapia, both of which hold their shape well. (You could also substitute catfish, pike, pollack, kingfish, or monkfish.) You adventurous eaters may want to substitute smoked chub or the milder smoked sablefish for half the amount of fish in the recipe.

1	medium onion, coarsely chopped
2	stalks celery, sliced
½	teaspoon fennel seeds, crushed
2	tablespoons water
3	cups skim milk
1	large yellow or white potato, cut into ½" cubes
2	cups fat-free liquid creamer
6	ounces red snapper or tilapia fillets, cut into 1" cubes
1	cup fresh or frozen whole-kernel corn
	Ground black pepper
	Salt (optional)

1   Coat a medium no-stick saucepan with no-stick spray. Add the onions, celery, and fennel seeds. Mist lightly with no-stick spray. Add the water. Cook over medium heat, stirring, for 10 minutes, or until the onions are translucent.

2   Add the milk and potatoes. Simmer over medium-low heat, stirring occasionally, for 15 minutes, or until the potatoes are soft.

3   Pour the soup into a blender or food processor. Pulse about 5 times, or until the soup is partially pureed but still chunky. (The soup can also be partially pureed in the saucepan with a hand blender.)

4   Return the soup to the saucepan. Add the creamer, fish, and corn. Cook over medium-low heat for 5 minutes, or just until the fish is cooked. Season to taste with the pepper and salt (if using).

Makes about **6** cups.

nutrition at a glance

per 1 cup
- 0.9 g.   total fat
- 0.3 g.   saturated fat
- 169   calories
- 9 mg.   cholesterol
- 89 mg.   sodium
- 9.7 g.   protein
- 28.9 g.   carbohydrates
- 1.6 g.   dietary fiber

Manhattan Clam Chowder

Try to find salt pork that has a wide streak of lean meat in it. Slab bacon can also be used.

5 ounces lean salt pork
2 cups water
3 medium potatoes, diced
1 medium onion, finely chopped
2½ stalks celery, finely chopped
1 can (14 ounces) diced tomatoes (with juice)
1 medium tomato, diced
⅓ cup diced green peppers
½ cup white wine or nonalcoholic white wine
½ teaspoon dried thyme
1 can (10 ounces) baby clams (with juice)
2 cups tomato juice
½ cup chopped fresh parsley
  Ground black pepper

1 In a large no-stick saucepan over medium-high heat, fry the salt pork, turning often, for 4 minutes, or until some of the fat is rendered. Add the water and bring to a boil.

2 Reduce the heat to medium, cover, and simmer for 20 minutes. Strain into a bowl and defat (see page 17). Remove the salt pork to a work surface. Cut the lean meat from the fat; discard the fat. Dice the meat and set aside 3 tablespoons; reserve any remainder for another use.

3 Wash the saucepan with soapy water and rinse. Return the broth and meat to the saucepan. Add the potatoes, onions, celery, canned tomatoes (with juice), diced tomatoes, green peppers, wine, and thyme. Drain the juice from the clams into the saucepan; set the clams aside.

4 Cover and cook over low heat for 15 minutes, or until the potatoes are soft. Stir in the tomato juice, parsley, and the reserved clams. Cover and bring to a boil over medium-high heat. Reduce the heat to medium-low and cook for 4 minutes. Season to taste with the black pepper.

Makes about **8** cups.

nutrition at a glance

per 1 cup

0.9 g.	total fat
0.2 g.	saturated fat
111	calories
14 mg.	cholesterol
426 mg.	sodium
7.8 g.	protein
17 g.	carbohydrates
2 g.	dietary fiber

I like to create visual excitement with a contrasting garnish color, such as finely chopped scallion greens sprinkled over an ivory potato soup or a dollop of fat-free sour cream on black bean soup.

Here are some garnishes that complement various types of soups.

Clear Soups

* Fresh herb sprigs—cilantro, parsley, basil, watercress, dill, or mint
* Thinly sliced scallions
* Cooked pasta stars, alphabets, or other tiny shapes

Cream Soups or Vegetable Purees

* Grated fresh ginger
* Chiffonade-cut lettuce or spinach leaves
* Ground nutmeg or paprika
* Chopped apples
* Fat-free plain or herb croutons
* Poppy seeds or toasted sesame seeds
* Air-popped popcorn

Bean and Legume Soups

* Raw vegetables such as diced tomatoes, cucumber slices, celery-leaf sprigs, sliced scallions, or sweet red or yellow pepper strips
* Banana slices
* Fat-free plain or herb croutons
* Diced hard-cooked egg whites
* Hot-pepper sauce or chopped fresh jalapeño peppers or serrano peppers
* Fat-free sour cream or plain yogurt

Chunky Vegetable Soups

* Bean sprouts or alfalfa sprouts
* Toasted squash seeds or toasted pumpkin seeds
* Fat-free Parmesan topping

Seafood Chowders

* Cooked mussels, clams, or oysters, in or out of the shell
* Cooked small crab claws or crayfish in the shell
* Cooked scallops or shrimp
* Lemon, lime, or orange slices

Vegetable Stock

Vegetable stock is easy to make as a tasty, nutrient-rich base for many soups. It's so satisfying to know exactly what ingredients are in your soup base. If you like, double the recipe and freeze in recipe-ready amounts.

4   quarts water
8   ounces butternut squash, peeled, seeded, and cut into 2" chunks
3   stalks celery, coarsely chopped
2   large tomatoes, diced
2   large onions, coarsely chopped
2   carrots, coarsely chopped
½   cup chopped fresh parsley
3   shallots, coarsely chopped
4   cloves garlic, minced
1   teaspoon dried basil
1   large bay leaf
¼   teaspoon dried thyme
¼   teaspoon dried rosemary

1   In a large no-stick pot, combine the water, squash, celery, tomatoes, onions, carrots, parsley, shallots, and garlic.

2   Place the basil, bay leaf, thyme, and rosemary in a mesh tea ball or wrap in a small piece of cheesecloth and tie with kitchen string. Add to the pot. Bring to a boil over medium-high heat. Reduce the heat to medium-low, cover, and simmer for 1 hour.

3   Strain the stock through a colander into a large bowl. Discard the vegetables and herbs. Refrigerate or freeze for use in recipes.

Makes about **12** cups.

nutrition at a glance	
per 1 cup	
0.1 g.	total fat
0 g.	saturated fat
11	calories
0 mg.	cholesterol
14 mg.	sodium
0.5 g.	protein
2.1 g.	carbohydrates
0 g.	dietary fiber

Chicken Stock

Here's a flavorful fat-free stock that can be the basis of many recipes. To turn it into chicken and vegetable soup, add 1 tablespoon chopped cooked chicken and ⅓ cup cooked vegetables to each cup of stock. For another variation, add ⅓ cup cooked no-yolk noodles, low-fat pasta, white rice, wheat berries, or bulgur plus 1 tablespoon chopped chicken to each cup of stock.

4	quarts water
1	broiler-fryer chicken
2	carrots, cut into large chunks
1	medium onion, cut into quarters
1	large stalk celery with leafy tops, cut into large chunks
1	large leek, white and some green stem, cut into large chunks
¼	cup chopped fresh parsley
3	cloves garlic
	Pinch of dried thyme
	Pinch of dried rosemary
	Pinch of dried tarragon

1 In a large no-stick pot, combine the water, chicken, carrots, onions, celery, leeks, parsley, garlic, thyme, rosemary, and tarragon.

2 Bring almost to a boil over medium-high heat. Reduce the heat to low, cover, and cook for 1¼ to 1½ hours.

3 With a large slotted spoon, remove the chicken and vegetables. Discard the vegetables. Remove the skin, bones, and fat from the chicken and discard. Reserve the cooked chicken for another use.

4 Defat the stock (see page 17). Refrigerate or freeze for use in recipes.

Makes about **14** cups.

nutrition at a glance

per 1 cup

0.1 g.	total fat
0 g.	saturated fat
14	calories
0 mg.	cholesterol
20 mg.	sodium
0.4 g.	protein
3.3 g.	carbohydrates
0 g.	dietary fiber

Salads and Dressings

Salads are natural fat fighters. Composed primarily

of fresh vegetables and fruits, salads can easily

help us fulfill the U.S. Department of Agriculture

Food Guide Pyramid recommendations of three to

five servings of vegetables and two to four servings

of fruit a day.

Vegetable and fruit salads are bundles of color,

texture, and flavor that are loaded with fiber,

vitamins, and minerals. Try my Spinach-Orange

Salad, Asian Coleslaw, and Fruit Salad with Cantaloupe Dressing to taste just how delicious good nutrition can be.

Add a small amount of protein-rich cooked beans, lean poultry, fat-free cheese, or seafood to a simple vegetable salad, and it turns into a fat-free feast. My Turkey Salad with Orange Dressing, and Mexicali Pasta Salad, make great light meals.

Dressed for Success

Salads are indeed fat-free wonders, but salad dressing is the serpent lurking in this Garden of Eden.

Just 1 tablespoon of vegetable oil—less than many people unthinkingly pour on a serving of salad—contains 13.5 grams of fat. You can see that by liberally pouring on the oil-based dressing, you can quickly send the fat content of a salad into the double digits.

Fortunately, great-tasting fat-free dressings are a cinch to make, as my Creamy Italian Dressing, Thai Peanut Dressing, and others attest. There are many alternatives that perform the same role as oil: namely, to buffer the sharpness of the vinegar.

Choose from fat-free sour cream, fat-free buttermilk, fat-free plain yogurt, fat-free mayonnaise, defatted chicken stock, vegetable stock, fruit juices, or vegetable juices as a base for your homemade dressings.

If you still think that you simply must have some oil, mist it lightly on your salad from a plastic spray bottle. And be sure to choose an oil that offers plenty of flavor—such as extra-virgin olive oil or dark sesame oil—in exchange for the fat calories that you'll be spending.

Sharpen Flavors

I often dress my salads with only vinegar, but I suspect that most people don't care for salads quite that sharp. Vinegar or citrus juices should heighten natural flavors without overpowering them. Unlike most other vinegars, balsamic vinegar has a natural sweetness that makes it mellow enough to drizzle alone on a salad.

Other options include red- or white-wine vinegar, malt vinegar, cider vinegar, Asian rice vinegar, lemon juice, lime juice, and orange juice.

After combining the fat-free base and vinegar or citrus juice, season the dressing with ketchup, mustard, Worcestershire sauce, hot-pepper sauce, fresh or dried herbs, ground spices, crushed herb seeds, ground black pepper, minced garlic, grated fresh ginger, chopped fresh hot peppers, chopped pickles, or capers.

Tossed Antipasto Salad

quick and easy

This satisfying main-dish salad is a colorful blend of chick-peas, roasted peppers, and fresh vegetables. The parsley takes the place of traditional greens. Serve with a crusty country bread and soup for a delightful meal.

1	sweet red pepper
1	yellow pepper
½	cup coarsely chopped fresh parsley
½	cup diced celery
⅓	cup canned chick-peas, rinsed and drained
1	medium onion, chopped
6	cherry tomatoes, cut in half
3	tablespoons water
2	tablespoons balsamic vinegar
2	teaspoons dried basil
½	teaspoon dried oregano
1	large clove garlic, minced
	Ground black pepper

1   Cut the red and yellow peppers in half lengthwise. Discard the stems, membranes and seeds. Line a baking sheet with foil and place the peppers, cut side down, on the sheet. Broil 4" from the heat for 10 minutes, or until the skins are blackened. Wrap the foil around the peppers, sealing the edges securely, and set aside for 10 minutes, or until the peppers are cool enough to handle.

2   In a medium bowl, combine the parsley, celery, chick-peas, onions, tomatoes, water, vinegar, basil, oregano, and garlic. Toss to blend.

3   Remove the peppers from the foil. With a sharp paring knife, remove and discard the blackened skin. Cut the peppers into thin strips. Add to the bowl. Season to taste with the black pepper. Toss to combine.

Makes **4** servings.

Photograph on page 57

nutrition at a glance	
per serving	
0.8 g.	total fat
0.1 g.	saturated fat
71	calories
0 mg.	cholesterol
57 mg.	sodium
2.9 g.	protein
14.9 g.	carbohydrates
3.7 g.	dietary fiber

Mexicali Pasta Salad

If you want more heat, add ½ teaspoon finely diced jalapeño peppers. Garnish with a few tablespoons shredded fat-free cheese. Make the salad a few hours ahead of time for the flavors to blend. If desired, replace the macaroni with other small pasta shapes.

4   ounces low-fat macaroni (0.5 g. fat per 2-ounce serving)
1   ear corn
½   cup defatted chicken stock (page 94)
¼   cup chopped fresh cilantro
2   cloves garlic, minced
1   tablespoon Dijon mustard
1   teaspoon chili powder
1   cup canned pinto beans, rinsed and drained
1   cup finely diced celery
1   cup finely diced onions
1   yellow pepper, diced
1   can (4½ ounces) diced mild green chili peppers
4   cups chopped or shredded romaine lettuce

1   Bring a large pot of water to a boil over high heat. Add the macaroni and cook for 5 minutes. Add the corn and cook for 4 minutes, or until the pasta is just tender.

2   Remove the corn with tongs and place in a large bowl of ice water for several seconds to cool.

3   Drain the pasta and let stand in the colander.

4   Remove the corn from the ice water. With a sharp knife, cut the corn kernels from the cob. Set aside.

5   In a large bowl, combine the stock, cilantro, garlic, mustard, and chili powder. Whisk to combine. Add the pasta, corn, beans, celery, onions, yellow peppers, and chili peppers; toss gently to mix. Cover and refrigerate for at least 1 hour. Just before serving, add the lettuce. Toss to mix.

Makes **8** servings.

Photograph on page 145

Photograph on page 145

Lynn's Kitchen Tip

Pinto beans are often used to make the Mexican specialty refried beans. For an easy fat-free version, rinse and drain 1 can pinto beans. Mash well and season to taste with chili powder and garlic powder. Add 1 to 2 tablespoons water or chicken stock if the beans are dry. Shape into patties. Coat with no-stick spray and cook in a no-stick skillet for 2 to 3 minutes per side, or until the patties are hot in the center.

nutrition at a glance
per serving
0.8 g. total fat
0.1 g. saturated fat
123 calories
0 mg. cholesterol
155 mg. sodium
5.2 g. protein
24.6 g. carbohydrates
4.5 g. dietary fiber

Caesar Salad with Turkey

quick and easy

This classic salad has become positively trendy in fashionable restaurants. It's so easy to make at home as a luncheon main dish. Fat-free egg substitute replaces the raw egg used in traditional recipes.

½	large head romaine lettuce
1½	cups cubed cooked boneless, skinless turkey breast
½	cup freshly squeezed lemon juice
¼	cup fat-free egg substitute
2	large cloves garlic, minced
1	teaspoon Worcestershire sauce
¼	teaspoon anchovy paste (optional)
	Ground black pepper
¼	cup fat-free Parmesan topping
	Garlic croutons (optional)

1 Tear the lettuce into large pieces and place in a large bowl. Add the turkey.

2 In a small bowl, combine the lemon juice, egg substitute, garlic, Worcestershire sauce, and anchovy paste (if using). Whisk to combine. Season to taste with the pepper. Pour over the lettuce and turkey. Toss to combine.

3 Sprinkle with the Parmesan and croutons (if using). Toss to combine.

Makes **4** servings.

Photograph on page 58

nutrition at a glance
per serving
- 0.9 g. total fat
- 0.2 g. saturated fat
- 129 calories
- 45 mg. cholesterol
- 247 mg. sodium
- 22 g. protein
- 8.8 g. carbohydrates
- 1.2 g. dietary fiber

Turkey Salad with Orange Dressing

This turkey salad is so special that I served it at a friend's wedding. I can guarantee that none of the wedding guests missed the fat. As a cool main-dish summer salad, it's beautiful served with a rainbow of fresh fruit: grapes, strawberries, cantaloupe, honeydew, watermelon, or fresh pineapple.

Orange Dressing

½	cup orange juice
½	cup fat-free plain yogurt
2	cloves garlic, minced
2	teaspoons freshly squeezed lime juice
2	teaspoons low-sodium soy sauce
1	teaspoon Dijon mustard
1	teaspoon dried tarragon

Turkey Salad

8	ounces boneless, skinless turkey breast, trimmed of all visible fat and cut into ½" cubes
1	teaspoon lemon-pepper seasoning
1	cup coarsely chopped celery
1	cup seedless red or green grapes, cut in half
1	cup coarsely chopped fresh pineapple
¾	cup canned sliced water chestnuts, cut into matchsticks
⅔	cup thinly sliced scallions
6	hard-cooked egg whites, sliced into wedges
1	head Bibb lettuce
¼	cup chopped pimentos
1½	cups garlic sourdough croutons (optional)

1 *To make the orange dressing:* In a small bowl, combine the orange juice, yogurt, garlic, lime juice, soy sauce, mustard, and tarragon. Cover and refrigerate.

2 *To make the turkey salad:* Season the turkey with the lemon-pepper seasoning. Place in an ovenproof plastic cooking bag. Microwave on high power for 4 minutes, or until the turkey is no longer pink in the center when tested with the point of a sharp knife. Transfer to a large bowl and refrigerate for 30 minutes, or until chilled.

3 Add the celery, grapes, pineapple, water chestnuts, scallions, and egg whites.

nutrition at a glance

per serving

0.9 g.	total fat
0.2 g.	saturated fat
139	calories
26 mg.	cholesterol
314 mg.	sodium
15.3 g.	protein
18.7 g.	carbohydrates
2.8 g.	dietary fiber

4   Remove 6 lettuce leaves and place on a platter. Chop the remaining lettuce and add to the turkey mixture. Pour the dressing over the salad. Toss gently to coat. Spoon over the lettuce. Sprinkle with the pimentos and croutons (if using).

Makes **6** servings.

Photograph on page 61

Shrimp Salad

quick and easy

You can also make this special seafood salad with lobster, crab, scallops, imitation crab, or a combination of seafoods. It makes a wonderful appetizer or sandwich filling. Serve with chilled fresh melon slices and grapes for a refreshing summer luncheon salad.

¼   cup fat-free mayonnaise
¼   cup fat-free sour cream
2   tablespoons freshly squeezed lemon juice
2   tablespoons water
¼   teaspoon hot-pepper sauce
½   cup diced cucumbers
2   large stalks celery, diced
1   medium onion, diced
2   tablespoons diced dill pickles
1   tablespoon capers, rinsed and drained
1   teaspoon chopped fresh dill
8   ounces cooked and chilled shelled shrimp, cut into bite-size pieces
     Ground black pepper
     Paprika

1   In a small bowl, combine the mayonnaise, sour cream, lemon juice, water, and hot-pepper sauce. Whisk until smooth.

2   In a medium bowl, combine the cucumbers, celery, onions, pickles, capers, and dill. Toss lightly to mix. Add the dressing and shrimp; toss gently to combine. Season to taste with the pepper and paprika.

Makes **4** servings.

---

nutrition at a glance

per serving

0.8 g.	total fat
0.2 g.	saturated fat
102	calories
111 mg.	cholesterol
473 mg.	sodium
14 g.	protein
10 g.	carbohydrates
1 g.	dietary fiber

Barley-Lentil Salad

quick and easy

Make this hearty main-dish grain salad when you have leftover cooked barley and lentils on hand.

8	cremini mushrooms, sliced
2	cloves garlic, minced
½	cup defatted chicken stock (page 94)
3	tablespoons balsamic vinegar
2	teaspoons Dijon mustard
1	teaspoon freshly squeezed lemon juice
1	cup cooked barley
1	cup cooked lentils
1	cup cooked peas or thawed frozen peas
½	cup sliced scallions
8	baby carrots, sliced
1	medium tomato, diced
	Ground black pepper
	Salt (optional)
6	curly lettuce leaves (optional)
1	tablespoon chopped fresh parsley

1 Coat a large no-stick skillet with no-stick spray. Add the mushrooms and garlic and mist with no-stick spray. Cover and cook over medium heat for 3 to 4 minutes, or until the mushrooms start to lose their moisture. Uncover and cook, stirring, for 1 to 2 minutes, or until the mushrooms are tender.

2 In a large bowl, combine the stock, vinegar, mustard, and lemon juice; whisk until smooth. Add the barley, lentils, peas, scallions, carrots, tomatoes, and mushroom mixture. Toss gently to coat the salad with dressing. Season to taste with the pepper and salt (if using).

3 Line a platter with the lettuce leaves (if using). Top with the salad. Sprinkle with the parsley.

Makes **6** servings.

nutrition at a glance

per serving

0.7 g.	total fat
0.1 g.	saturated fat
123	calories
0 mg.	cholesterol
57 mg.	sodium
6.2 g.	protein
24.5 g.	carbohydrates
5.6 g.	dietary fiber

Artichoke Salad

quick and easy

If frozen artichoke hearts aren't available, you may use canned ones, but they'll be higher in sodium. Garnish with capers and paprika, if you like, for extra piquancy and color.

2   packages (9 ounces each) frozen artichoke hearts, thawed
1   cup shredded carrots
1   sweet red pepper, cut into matchsticks
1   small onion, thinly sliced
3   ounces fat-free mozzarella cheese, diced
1   teaspoon dried thyme
3   tablespoons balsamic vinegar
3   tablespoons freshly squeezed lemon juice
2   tablespoons water
    Ground black pepper
1   head iceberg lettuce
3   tablespoons chopped fresh parsley

1   Place the artichokes on several layers of paper towels. Let them drain for 5 minutes, then pat dry. Cut the artichokes in half lengthwise. Place in a large bowl.

2   Add the carrots, red peppers, onions, mozzarella, thyme, vinegar, lemon juice, and water. Toss to combine. Season to taste with the black pepper.

3   Remove the outer leaves of lettuce and arrange on a platter.

4   Coarsely chop the remaining lettuce. Add to the bowl; toss to combine. Spoon the salad over the lettuce on the platter. Sprinkle with the parsley.

Makes **4** servings.

nutrition at a glance

per serving
0.9 g.   total fat
0.2 g.   saturated fat
136   calories
3 mg.   cholesterol
230 mg.   sodium
12 g.   protein
23.4 g.   carbohydrates
7.9 g.   dietary fiber

Greek Salad

quick and easy

Garnish each salad with ½ teaspoon diced kalamata olives, and you'll increase the fat to only 1 gram per serving.

¼ cup defatted chicken stock (page 94)
2 tablespoons red-wine vinegar
2 teaspoons freshly squeezed lemon juice
1 teaspoon sugar
1 teaspoon thinly sliced fresh basil or ½ teaspoon dried
½ teaspoon dried oregano
2 cups torn romaine lettuce
12 thin slices cucumber
1 cup chilled cooked green beans cut into 1" pieces
¼ cup finely chopped red onions
2 tablespoons finely chopped fresh parsley
1 tablespoon crumbled low-fat feta cheese
1 large tomato, cut into 8 wedges
4 peperoncini
Ground black pepper

1 In a large bowl, combine the stock, vinegar, lemon juice, sugar, basil, and oregano. Whisk until smooth. Add the lettuce, cucumbers, beans, onions, and parsley. Toss to combine the salad with the dressing.

2 Serve topped with the feta, tomatoes, and peperoncini. Season to taste with the pepper.

Makes **4** servings.

Photograph on page 143

Photograph on page 143

Lynn's Fat-Free Flavor

Peperoncini are imported pickled peppers that are moderately hot. They're seldom mentioned in recipes but are a constant in Greek restaurant salads and salad bars. You can find them in any large supermarket.

---

nutrition at a glance

per serving

0.9 g.	total fat
0.4 g.	saturated fat
46	calories
1 mg.	cholesterol
222 mg.	sodium
2.4 g.	protein
8.5 g.	carbohydrates
2.2 g.	dietary fiber

Cuke and Zuke Raita

quick and easy

This raita—an Indian salad with yogurt dressing—is a refreshing blend of cucumbers, zucchini, and mint. It beautifully balances any spicy main dish.

¾ cup fat-free plain yogurt
¼ cup fat-free sour cream
¼ cup chopped fresh chives
3 tablespoons chopped fresh mint
2 cloves garlic, minced
1 cucumber, diced
1 cup diced zucchini

1 Line a fine sieve with cheesecloth or a coffee filter. Add the yogurt. Set over a bowl to drain for 5 minutes. Discard the whey that drains into the bowl.

2 Transfer the yogurt to a medium bowl. Add the sour cream, chives, mint, and garlic. Stir to mix well. Add the cucumbers and zucchini. Toss to coat with the dressing. Let stand for 10 to 15 minutes to blend the flavors. Pour off any excess water that accumulates.

Makes **4** servings.

nutrition at a glance
per serving
0.3 g. total fat
0.1 g. saturated fat
69 calories
1 mg. cholesterol
60 mg. sodium
5 g. protein
11 g. carbohydrates
2 g. dietary fiber

Tomato, Basil, and Mozzarella Salad

quick and easy

Make this superb Italian salad in the summer, when garden tomatoes, zucchini, and yellow squash are abundant. If yellow tomatoes aren't available, simply use all red ones. You'll need only a few drops of balsamic vinegar to enhance the sweetness of the tomatoes.

30	large fresh basil leaves
½	cup small spinach leaves
4	small yellow tomatoes, thinly sliced
1	zucchini, thinly sliced
4	ounces fat-free mozzarella cheese, thinly sliced
4	small red tomatoes, thinly sliced
1	yellow squash, thinly sliced
	Balsamic vinegar
4	pitted black or green olives, sliced (optional)
	Ground black pepper

1 Stack 6 of the basil leaves on top of each other. Roll lengthwise into a tight bundle and then cut into thin slices. Unfurl the slices into shreds and set aside.

2 Line the outer edge of a round platter with the spinach leaves. Alternate the remaining basil leaves, yellow tomatoes, zucchini, mozzarella, red tomatoes, and yellow squash, slightly overlapping, in circles going around the plate.

3 Sprinkle lightly with the vinegar. Sprinkle with the reserved basil and olives (if using). Season to taste with the pepper.

Makes **4** servings.

Photograph on page 59

Lynn's Kitchen Tip

Chiffonade is a French term meaning "made of rags," according to *The New Food Lover's Companion* by Sharon Tyler Herbst. Strips of green herbs, such as basil, make a pretty garnish in a soup or salad. To cut any herb leaves, lettuce, or other greens into chiffonade, stack the leaves, then roll them into a tight bundle. Cut crosswise into thin slices.

nutrition at a glance
per serving

0.9 g.	total fat
0.1 g.	saturated fat
117	calories
4 mg.	cholesterol
218 mg.	sodium
12 g.	protein
18 g.	carbohydrates
4 g.	dietary fiber

Asian Coleslaw

quick and easy

Roasting brings out the flavor of seeds and nuts. Use a bit of dark sesame oil or dark roasted peanut oil, and you'll experience the distinctive flavor note that just a few drops of roasted nut oils add to foods.

3	tablespoons white-wine vinegar or cider vinegar
1	teaspoon sugar
1	teaspoon low-sodium soy sauce
½	teaspoon minced fresh ginger
¼	teaspoon five-spice seasoning
1	clove garlic, minced
1	teaspoon sesame seeds (optional)
¼	teaspoon crushed red-pepper flakes (optional)
1	medium cucumber, diced
1	cup shredded bok choy or cabbage
½	cup shredded carrots
½	sweet red pepper, finely diced
1	can (6 ounces) sliced water chestnuts, drained and cut in half
1	tablespoon chopped fresh cilantro
	Dark sesame oil in a spray bottle

1   In a large bowl, combine the vinegar, sugar, soy sauce, ginger, five-spice seasoning, and garlic. Add the sesame seeds (if using) and red-pepper flakes (if using). Whisk to combine.

2   Add the cucumbers, bok choy or cabbage, carrots, red peppers, water chestnuts, and cilantro. Spray lightly with the oil; toss to combine.

Makes **4** servings.

Photograph on page 144

Lynn's Kitchen Tip

Storing flavorful oils, such as extra-virgin olive oil or dark sesame oil, in a plastic spray bottle is a convenient way to flavor salads with a scant amount. To make sure that you're spritzing the amount that you want, do a test. Spray oil into a ½ teaspoon measuring spoon, counting the number of spritzes. Make a note of the number and you'll always know exactly how much oil you're spraying. Remember that each ½ teaspoon oil contains 2.3 grams of fat.

nutrition at a glance
per serving

0.8 g.	total fat
0.1 g.	saturated fat
54	calories
0 mg.	cholesterol
71 mg.	sodium
2 g.	protein
11 g.	carbohydrates
2 g.	dietary fiber

Potato Salad with Caramelized Onions

quick and easy

On the day of testing, several guests arrived just at the moment this potato salad was finished. Some testers barely got a taste of the salad because it disappeared so fast. Garnish with extra finely chopped parsley, if you like, to perk up the color.

1½ pounds small red potatoes
1 large onion, chopped
2 tablespoons white-wine vinegar
2 tablespoons finely chopped fresh parsley
1 clove garlic, minced
¼ cup fat-free mayonnaise
¼ cup fat-free sour cream
2 tablespoons freshly squeezed lemon juice
½ teaspoon sugar
1 sweet red pepper, diced
   Ground black pepper
   Salt (optional)

1 Place the potatoes in a medium no-stick saucepan. Add enough water to cover. Bring to a boil over medium-high heat. Reduce the heat to medium. Cook for 15 minutes, or until the potatoes are tender when pierced with a fork.

2 Meanwhile, coat a large no-stick skillet with no-stick spray. Add the onions and coat with no-stick spray. Cover and cook over medium-high heat, stirring occasionally, for 5 minutes, or until the onions start to give off moisture. Uncover and cook over medium heat, stirring occasionally, for 6 to 8 minutes, or until golden. If necessary, add 1 to 2 teaspoons water to prevent sticking.

3 Drain the potatoes, then cut into large bite-size pieces. Place in a large bowl. Sprinkle with 1 tablespoon of the vinegar; toss. Sprinkle on the parsley, garlic, and onions; toss and set aside.

4 To serve the salad cold, cover the potatoes and refrigerate for several hours.

5 In a small bowl, combine the mayonnaise, sour cream, lemon juice, sugar, and the remaining 1 tablespoon vinegar. Whisk to combine.

6 Pour over the potatoes. Add the red peppers. Season to taste with the black pepper and salt (if using). Toss gently to combine.

Makes **4** servings.

<table>
<tr><td colspan="2">nutrition at a glance</td></tr>
<tr><td colspan="2">per serving</td></tr>
<tr><td>0.3 g.</td><td>total fat</td></tr>
<tr><td>0.1 g.</td><td>saturated fat</td></tr>
<tr><td>228</td><td>calories</td></tr>
<tr><td>0 mg.</td><td>cholesterol</td></tr>
<tr><td>121 mg.</td><td>sodium</td></tr>
<tr><td>6 g.</td><td>protein</td></tr>
<tr><td>51 g.</td><td>carbohydrates</td></tr>
<tr><td>5 g.</td><td>dietary fiber</td></tr>
</table>

Spinach-Orange Salad

quick and **easy**

This salad is a bright addition to the winter table when fresh tomatoes are out of season.

½ cup fat-free buttermilk
2 teaspoons Dijon mustard
1 clove garlic, finely chopped
4 cups torn spinach leaves
2 navel oranges, peeled and separated into segments
1 small red onion, sliced
¼ cup finely chopped scallions
  Ground black pepper

Lynn's Fat-Free Flavor

Mustard—such as Dijon, stone-ground, honey, or horseradish—offers a mighty amount of flavor with barely any fat. Use a tea-spoon or two to spark flavor in salad dressings and sauces.

1 In a large bowl, combine the buttermilk, mustard, and garlic; whisk to mix well. Add the spinach, oranges, onions, and scallions. Toss to coat with the dressing. Serve sprinkled with the pepper.

Makes **4** servings.

Photograph on page 60

<table>
<tr><td colspan="2">nutrition at a glance</td></tr>
<tr><td colspan="2">per serving</td></tr>
<tr><td>0.5 g.</td><td>total fat</td></tr>
<tr><td>0.1 g.</td><td>saturated fat</td></tr>
<tr><td>66</td><td>calories</td></tr>
<tr><td>1 mg.</td><td>cholesterol</td></tr>
<tr><td>138 mg.</td><td>sodium</td></tr>
<tr><td>3.8 g.</td><td>protein</td></tr>
<tr><td>13.7 g.</td><td>carbohydrates</td></tr>
<tr><td>3.3 g.</td><td>dietary fiber</td></tr>
</table>

Cran-Blackberry Gelatin Salad

The contrast of tart berries and rich, sweet sour cream is irresistible in this molded gelatin salad. It's ideal for a party. In fact, you can make it several days ahead and store, tightly covered, in the refrigerator.

Sour Cream Layer

¼   cup orange juice
1   teaspoon plain gelatin
1   tablespoon sugar
1   cup fat-free sour cream

Cran-Blackberry Gelatin

2½   cups fresh or frozen cranberries
½   cup sugar
2   tablespoons freshly squeezed lemon juice or lime juice
¼   teaspoon ground cinnamon
2¾   cups orange juice
1¼   cups blackberries
5   teaspoons plain gelatin
   Bibb lettuce leaves or fresh mint leaves (optional)

Lynn's Lore
To speed up the setting of any gelatin mixture, place the bowl with the gelatin in a larger bowl filled partially with ice water. Set aside for 15 minutes, stirring occasionally, or until the mixture gets thick enough to coat a spoon.

1 *To make the sour cream layer:* Place the orange juice in a medium microwaveable bowl. Sprinkle with the gelatin. Let stand for 2 minutes, or until the gelatin softens. Microwave on high power for 45 seconds, or until hot. Stir in the sugar.

2 Whisk in the sour cream until well-combined. Pour into a 6-cup ring mold. Refrigerate while preparing the cran-blackberry gelatin.

3 *To make the cran-blackberry gelatin:* Meanwhile, in a medium no-stick saucepan, combine the cranberries, sugar, lemon juice or lime juice, cinnamon, and 2 cups of the orange juice. Bring to a boil over medium heat. Reduce the heat to low, cover, and simmer for 5 minutes, or until the sugar dissolves.

4 Add the blackberries. Cover and simmer, stirring occasionally, for 10 minutes.

5 Place the remaining ¾ cup orange juice in a small microwaveable bowl. Sprinkle with the gelatin. Let stand for 2 minutes, or until the gelatin softens. Microwave on high power for 1 to 2 minutes, or until hot; stir to dissolve the gelatin.

6 Add to the berry mixture and stir well. Transfer to a large bowl. Refrigerate for 45 minutes, stirring occasionally, until the mixture is thickened enough to mound when dropped from a spoon.

7 Pour the berry mixture into the mold. Refrigerate for at least 4 hours, or until set.

8 To unmold, run a knife around the outer and inner edges of the mold. Dip the bottom of the mold into hot water for a few seconds. Cover with a serving plate and flip the mold over. Allow to stand for a few seconds before gently lifting off the mold.

9 Tuck lettuce leaves or mint leaves (if using) under the edges of the salad.

Makes **8** servings.

Photograph on page 62

nutrition at a glance	
per serving	
0.3 g.	total fat
0.1 g.	saturated fat
161	calories
0 mg.	cholesterol
27 mg.	sodium
4.2 g.	protein
36 g.	carbohydrates
2.2 g.	dietary fiber

Fruit Salad with Cantaloupe Dressing

quick and easy

The creamy cantaloupe dressing is also refreshing for any fruit, poultry, or shrimp salad. The following recipe yields about 1 cup dressing. The cantaloupe can be pureed in a blender for a smoother dressing, if you like.

Cantaloupe Dressing

¼	cup fat-free lemon yogurt
2	teaspoons freshly squeezed lime juice or lemon juice
1	teaspoon Dijon mustard
½	teaspoon honey
¾	cup finely chopped cantaloupe

Fruit Salad

2	bananas
1	tablespoon freshly squeezed lemon juice
2	ruby red grapefruit, peeled and cut into wedges
2	pears, cut into chunks
1	cup blueberries
1	cup thinly sliced celery
2	kiwifruit, cut into wedges
2	plums, cut into wedges
1	tablespoon finely chopped fresh mint

1   *To make the cantaloupe dressing:* In a medium bowl, combine the yogurt, lime juice or lemon juice, mustard, and honey. Whisk to combine. Add the cantaloupe and stir to combine. Set aside.

2   *To make the fruit salad:* Cut the bananas into slices and place in a medium bowl; toss with the lemon juice. Arrange on a large platter. Arrange the grapefruit, pears, blueberries, celery, kiwifruit, plums, and mint in a pretty design.

3   Drizzle with the dressing just before serving.

Makes **6** servings.

Lynn's Nutrition Note

Just 1 cup cubed cantaloupe supplies more than 100 percent of the Daily Value for vitamins A and C.

---

nutrition at a glance

per serving

0.9 g.	total fat
0.1 g.	saturated fat
163	calories
0 mg.	cholesterol
30 mg.	sodium
2.8 g.	protein
40 g.	carbohydrates
6 g.	dietary fiber

Thousand Island Dressing

quick and easy

For those of you who have given up on your old favorite chunky salad dressing because of the outrageous fat content, I've created this fat-free version that tastes zestier than the original.

1   cup fat-free mayonnaise
¼   cup chunky chili sauce
¼   cup finely chopped green peppers
3   tablespoons finely chopped onions
3   tablespoons sweet pickle relish
2   tablespoons chopped fresh parsley
½   teaspoon paprika
¼   cup skim milk or fat-free sour cream (optional)
3   hard-cooked egg whites, finely chopped

1   In a medium bowl, combine the mayonnaise, chili sauce, peppers, onions, relish, parsley, and paprika. Stir to mix well. Add the milk or sour cream (if using) for a thinner dressing. Fold in the egg whites.

Makes about **2** cups.

Lynn's Lore

John Mariani reports in *The Dictionary of American Food and Drink* that Thousand Island dressing most likely was named after the Thousand Islands in the St. Lawrence River, which cuts between New York and Ontario.

nutrition at a glance

per 2 tablespoons

0 g.	total fat
0 g.	saturated fat
22	calories
0 mg.	cholesterol
194 mg.	sodium
0.8 g.	protein
4.2 g.	carbohydrates
0.2 g.	dietary fiber

Green Goddess Dressing

quick and easy

This old-favorite salad dressing can double as a condiment for broiled or grilled beef, fish, or shellfish.

¾ cup fat-free mayonnaise
½ cup fat-free sour cream
2 tablespoons white-wine vinegar
2 teaspoons freshly squeezed lemon juice
1 teaspoon anchovy paste or Worcestershire sauce
½ teaspoon Dijon mustard
3 tablespoons chopped fresh parsley
2 tablespoons chopped fresh chives
1 scallion, finely chopped
1 clove garlic, minced
¼ teaspoon dried tarragon

1 In a medium bowl, combine the mayonnaise, sour cream, vinegar, lemon juice, anchovy paste or Worcestershire sauce, and mustard. Mix with a whisk until blended. Stir in the parsley, chives, scallions, garlic, and tarragon.

Makes about **1¼** cups.

nutrition at a glance

per 2 tablespoons

0 g.	total fat
0 g.	saturated fat
22	calories
0 mg.	cholesterol
194 mg.	sodium
0.8 g.	protein
4.2 g.	carbohydrates
0.2 g.	dietary fiber

Creamy Italian Dressing

quick and easy

If you don't have fresh basil for this dressing, you can substitute 1½ teaspoons dried basil.

⅓ cup fat-free sour cream
¼ cup fat-free buttermilk
2 tablespoons red-wine vinegar
2 tablespoons thinly sliced fresh basil
2 cloves garlic, minced
¾ teaspoon dried oregano
 Ground black pepper
 Salt (optional)

1 In a small bowl, combine the sour cream, buttermilk, vinegar, basil, garlic, and oregano. Whisk to combine. Season to taste with the pepper and salt (if using).

Makes about ⅔ cup.

nutrition at a glance
per 2 tablespoons
0 g. total fat
0 g. saturated fat
23 calories
0 mg. cholesterol
24 mg. sodium
1.5 g. protein
4 g. carbohydrates
0 g. dietary fiber

Thai Peanut Dressing

quick and easy

This distinctive dressing is wonderful over greens, sprouts, snow peas, carrots, sugar snap peas, and many other vegetables. It's also delicious spooned over grilled fish or poultry. Some minced chives or scallions are a nice addition.

1½	teaspoons low-fat peanut butter
6	tablespoons freshly squeezed lime juice or lemon juice
2	tablespoons low-sodium soy sauce
2	tablespoons water
1	teaspoon sugar
¼	teaspoon hot-pepper sauce
3	tablespoons chopped fresh cilantro
2	tablespoons thinly sliced fresh basil
2	teaspoons chopped fresh mint
3	cloves garlic, minced

1 Place the peanut butter in a medium bowl. Gradually add the lime juice or lemon juice, whisking constantly until smooth. Add the soy sauce, water, sugar, and hot-pepper sauce. Whisk to blend. Add the cilantro, basil, mint, and garlic. Stir to combine.

Makes about ¾ cup.

Photograph on page 319

nutrition at a glance

per 2 tablespoons

0.6 g.	total fat
0.1 g.	saturated fat
22	calories
0 mg.	cholesterol
211 mg.	sodium
1 g.	protein
3.9 g.	carbohydrates
0.3 g.	dietary fiber

Poppy Seed Dressing

quick and easy

This tangy dressing is great for coleslaw. Toasting the poppy seeds in a small skillet for a few minutes over medium heat will bring out their flavor.

½ cup cider vinegar
1 tablespoon honey
1 tablespoon freshly squeezed lemon juice
1 teaspoon poppy seeds

1 In a small bowl, combine the vinegar, honey, lemon juice, and poppy seeds. Mix well with a fork.

Makes about ⅔ cup.

nutrition at a glance

per 2 tablespoons

0.1 g.	total fat
0 g.	saturated fat
13	calories
0 mg.	cholesterol
0 mg.	sodium
0 g.	protein
3.3 g.	carbohydrates
0 g.	dietary fiber

Slim Salad Sidekicks

Transform a tossed salad from simple to sensational with any of these fat-free additions.

✳ Matchsticks of fat-free ham, turkey, or chicken

✳ Diced fat-free, Cheddar or Monterey Jack cheese

✳ Fat-free Parmesan topping

✳ Diced or sliced hard-cooked egg whites

✳ Chopped dried dates, figs, apricots, or raisins

✳ Chopped or sliced fresh apples, nectarines, peaches, or grapes

✳ Sliced pickled peppers, such as peperoncini or jalapeños

✳ Sliced pickled vegetables, such as okra, capers, beets, green beans, asparagus, or baby onions

✳ Frozen peas or corn (sprinkle on the salad and they'll thaw in minutes)

✳ Rinsed and drained canned kidney beans, pinto beans, navy beans, or chick-peas

Ranch Dressing

quick and easy

If you don't have dried celery flakes, use chopped celery leaves or finely chopped celery.

1	cup fat-free sour cream
½	cup fat-free buttermilk
2	teaspoons cider vinegar
¼	teaspoon sugar
½	cup shredded carrots
1	tablespoon finely chopped fresh parsley
1	large clove garlic, minced
½	teaspoon celery seeds
½	teaspoon dried celery flakes
½	teaspoon onion powder

1 In a medium bowl, combine the sour cream, buttermilk, vinegar, and sugar. Mix to blend. Add the carrots, parsley, garlic, celery seeds, celery flakes, and onion powder. Mix to combine.

Makes about **2** cups.

nutrition at a glance

per 2 tablespoons

0 g.	total fat
0 g.	saturated fat
21	calories
0 mg.	cholesterol
22 mg.	sodium
0.1 g.	protein
3.7 g.	carbohydrates
0.1 g.	dietary fiber

Fish

Shellfish

Fish and Shellfish

Seafood, an excellent source of lean protein, is like manna from heaven to the fat-free cook. Plenty of fish and shellfish contain less than 1 gram of fat for each 3½-ounce portion (see "The Skinny on Seafood" on page 125), which is about the size of a deck of cards. And that fat is overwhelmingly the better-for-you unsaturated variety.

Seafood is generally lower in total fat—and certainly lower in saturated fat—than pork, beef, lamb, and poultry. Although the cholesterol content from clam to lamb and turkey to jerky is comparable, cholesterol doesn't impact weight control and is a far less important contributing factor to heart disease than saturated fat.

Don't be scared off by fish that has more than 1 gram of fat per serving. The types that have the most fat, like mackerel and herring, are also high in health-enhancing omega-3 fatty acids, which may help reduce the risk of stroke and heart attacks. Other seafood, such as sea bass, catfish, turbot, and oysters, has only a few grams of fat per 3½ ounces and fits nicely into a healthful diet.

Preparing the Catch

Start by shopping at a reliable fishmonger—one with a brisk business to help guarantee a fresh product.

Before cooking, rinse the fish gently in cold water. Scrub the shells of mollusks and crustaceans. (Discard any mollusks that don't close after a light tapping.) Pat the seafood dry.

You can marinate seafood for up to one hour before cooking to add flavor. Zesty fat-free marinades can include vinegar, citrus juice, white or red wine, vegetable juice, low-sodium soy sauce, teriyaki sauce, Worcestershire sauce,

defatted stock or broth, bouillon, clam juice, and fat-free salad dressing. Herbs, spices, and other aromatics can also add intrigue.

Seafood is spectacularly easy to prepare with no added fat. Be sure to cook it just until done so it remains moist. For finfish, check by inserting a sharp knife into the center of a fillet. It should be opaque and no longer translucent. A good rule of thumb is to allow 10 minutes of cooking time for each inch thickness of the fish.

For lobster, shrimp, crab, and scallops, cook until the flesh turns opaque and is set but not overly firm to the touch. Cook mussels and clams until the shells open and the flesh is hot.

Perfect Portions

Remember that my seafood main dishes are designed to be just part of a meal. To boost your nutrients and satisfy your appetite, you'll want to include plenty of fresh vegetables, a low-fat salad, and a whole-grain side dish.

Every serving of my seafood dishes contains less than 1 gram of fat. Of course, the number of servings that you'll eat will vary depending upon your gender, body type, and personal calorie needs. Even if you double the servings, however, your total fat intake will still be extremely low.

Red Snapper with Creamed Dill Sauce

quick and easy

This creamy sauce, pungent with fresh dill, tastes decadent. You can replace the snapper with other low-fat seafood, such as orange roughy, halibut, cod, scrod, catfish, flounder, or scallops.

4	red snapper fillets (3 ounces each), skin on
½	teaspoon crushed black peppercorns
1½	cups fat-free liquid creamer
2½	tablespoons all-purpose flour
2	tablespoons chopped fresh dill or 2 teaspoons dried dillweed
1	tablespoon white wine or white-wine Worcestershire sauce (optional)
	Salt (optional)

1 Rinse the fish and pat dry with paper towels. Score the skin side with several diagonal slashes. Rub ¼ teaspoon of the pepper into the flesh.

2 Coat a large no-stick skillet with no-stick spray. Warm the skillet over medium-high heat. Add the fish and cook for 1 minute on each side, or until golden. Reduce the heat to low.

3 Partially cover the skillet and cook for 10 minutes, or until the fish is cooked. (Check by inserting the tip of a sharp knife in the center of 1 fillet.)

4 Meanwhile, in a small no-stick saucepan, combine the creamer, flour, dill, wine or Worcestershire sauce, and the remaining ¼ teaspoon pepper. Whisk over low heat for 5 minutes, or until thickened. Season to taste with the salt (if using).

5 Put the fish on dinner plates. Pour the sauce across of each fillet.

Makes **4** servings.

nutrition at a glance
per serving

0.8 g.	total fat
0.2 g.	saturated fat
136	calories
21 mg.	cholesterol
26 mg.	sodium
12.3 g.	protein
16 g.	carbohydrates
0.2 g.	dietary fiber

Mahimahi with Shrimp and Tropical Salsa

quick and easy

This dish looks like a tropical sunset and tastes like paradise. For a summer dinner party, it doesn't get any better than this vibrant mélange of seafood and fruity salsa. If you like, you can cook the seafood in a no-stick skillet on the stove top.

Mahimahi and Shrimp

4	mahimahi fillets (2½ ounces each)
2	teaspoons freshly squeezed lime juice or lemon juice
4	ounces shelled shrimp, tails left on

Tropical Salsa

¾	cup fresh pineapple chunks
½	cup diced mangoes or peaches
1	slice (½" thick) honeydew, muskmelon, or cantaloupe, cut into ½" pieces
¼	green pepper, cut into ½" pieces
¼	sweet red pepper, cut into ½" pieces
⅓	cup freshly squeezed lime juice or lemon juice
¼	cup chopped fresh cilantro
4	scallions, sliced
½	teaspoon finely diced jalapeño peppers (wear plastic gloves when handling)

1 *To make the mahimahi and shrimp:* Rinse the fish and pat dry with paper towels. Place in a large shallow baking dish. Drizzle with the lime juice or lemon juice; turn to coat both sides. Coat both sides with no-stick spray.

2 Prepare a charcoal grill. Coat the barbecue grill rack with no-stick spray.

3 Place the fish on the rack. Grill for 3 to 5 minutes, or until opaque on the bottom. Turn the fish. Carefully place the shrimp on the grill. Grill for 3 to 5 minutes, or until the mahimahi and shrimp are opaque in the center. (Check by inserting the tip of a sharp knife in the center of 1 fillet and 1 shrimp).

Lynn's Kitchen Tip

To dice a fresh mango, cut it in half lengthwise, slightly off center, just grazing the flat, oval pit. Score the flesh on the pitless side into ½" cubes with a small, sharp knife, cutting down to, but not through, the skin. Holding the piece with both hands, push the skin side upward to display the fruit cubes. Cut the fruit cubes away from the skin. On the remaining half, use the tip of the knife to cut the pit away from the flesh. Cut the flesh as above.

4 *To make the tropical salsa:*
While the fish is cooking, in a medium bowl, mix the pineapple, mangoes or peaches, melon, green peppers, red peppers, lime juice or lemon juice, cilantro, scallions, and jalapeño peppers. Serve with the fish and shrimp.

Makes **4** servings.

Photograph on front cover

Sole Française

quick and easy

This succulent fat-free version of a timeless French classic is always perfect for a special occasion. Serve with parsleyed potatoes, tender young green beans, Boston lettuce salad, and sorbet with fruit. If sole is not available, use flounder. I like to serve the fish with lemon wedges.

4 Dover sole or gray sole fillets (3 ounces each)
¼ cup white wine or nonalcoholic white wine
¼ cup chopped fresh parsley
1 tablespoon freshly squeezed lemon juice

Lynn's Health Watch

Color is a clue to the fat content of fish. Light-colored flesh usually indicates leaner fish. White-fleshed halibut and sole, for example, are low in fat. Darker mackerel, salmon, and tuna contain more fat.

1 Rinse the fish and pat dry with paper towels. Coat both sides with no-stick spray.

2 Warm a large no-stick skillet over medium-high heat. Add the fish and cook for 2 minutes, or until lightly browned on the bottom.

3 Add the wine, parsley, and lemon juice. Reduce the heat to low, cover, and cook for 4 minutes, or until the fish is opaque. (Check by inserting the tip of a sharp knife in the center of 1 fillet.)

4 Remove the fish to warm plates. Boil the sauce over medium-high heat for 1 minute to reduce slightly. Pour over the fish.

Makes **4** servings.

Cod with Ginger-Orange Sauce

quick and easy

This recipe makes plenty of sprightly ginger-orange sauce. Spoon it over angel hair pasta, cellophane noodles, or spaghettini as a low-fat accompaniment to the cod. A green vegetable, sweet grapes, and a salad will complete the menu. You may replace the temple orange with a 6-ounce can of mandarin oranges, drained and cut into chunks.

4	cod fillets (3¼ ounces each)
1	tablespoon minced fresh ginger
1½	tablespoons freshly squeezed lemon juice
1	teaspoon Dijon mustard
1	teaspoon low-sodium soy sauce
1½	cups freshly squeezed orange juice
2	tablespoons cornstarch
1	cup temple orange pieces
4	scallions, chopped

1 Rinse the fish and pat dry with paper towels. Set aside.

2 Coat a large no-stick skillet with no-stick spray. Add the ginger and cook over medium-high heat, stirring often, for 2 minutes, or until lightly browned. Add the lemon juice, mustard, soy sauce, and 1 cup of the orange juice; stir to combine.

3 Add the fish in a single layer. Cover and cook over low heat for 6 to 8 minutes, or until the fish is opaque. (Check by inserting the tip of a sharp knife in the center of 1 fillet.) Remove the fish to a plate; cover to keep warm.

4 Place the cornstarch in a cup. Add the remaining ½ cup orange juice and stir to dissolve the cornstarch. Add to the skillet. Cook, stirring constantly, for 1 minute, or until the sauce thickens. Stir in the oranges; cover and cook for 1 minute, or until the oranges are hot. Serve the sauce over the fish. Sprinkle with the scallions.

Makes **4** servings.

Photograph on page 149

nutrition at a glance
per serving
0.8 g. total fat
0.1 g. saturated fat
141 calories
26 mg. cholesterol
97 mg. sodium
12.1 g. protein
21.5 g. carbohydrates
0.5 g. dietary fiber

The Skinny on Seafood

Get your hooks into these low-fat seafoods for delicious, nutritious meals. The fat content listed is for 3½ ounces fish (raw weight).

Seafood	Fat (g.)
Alaska king crab leg	0.6
Pacific cod	0.6
Atlantic cod	0.7
Haddock	0.7
Mahimahi	0.7
Orange roughy	0.7
Pumpkinseed sunfish	0.7
Abalone	0.8
Bay scallops	0.8
Walleye pollack	0.8
Northern lobster	0.9
Ocean pout	0.9
Perch	0.9
Atlantic pollack	1.0
Clams (large)	1.0
Dungeness crab	1.0
Grouper	1.0
Octopus	1.0
Blue crab	1.1
Flounder	1.2
Queen crab	1.2
Sole	1.2
Snapper	1.3
Squid	1.4
Spiny lobster	1.5
Atlantic ocean perch	1.6
Large shrimp	1.7
Sea bass	2.0
Atlantic/Pacific halibut	2.2
Blue mussels	2.2
Pacific oysters	2.3
Striped bass	2.3
Tilefish	2.3
Tilapia	2.4
Eastern oysters	2.5
European turbot	2.9
Atlantic croaker	3.1

Pollack with Cajun Sauce

quick and easy

Serve this spunky fish dish over rice, with okra on the side, for an authentic taste of Louisiana. Orange roughy makes a good substitute for the pollack. If you don't have Cajun spice blend, use ground red pepper.

4	pollack fillets (4 ounces each)
2	cups tomato juice
1	small onion, cut into quarters
½	stalk celery, cut in half crosswise
¼	sweet red pepper, sliced (optional)
3	cloves garlic, minced
¼	teaspoon dried basil leaves
¼	teaspoon dried oregano
¼–½	teaspoon Cajun spice blend
	Salt (optional)
¼	cup chopped fresh parsley

1 Rinse the fish and pat dry with paper towels. Set aside.

2 In a blender or food processor, combine the tomato juice, onions, celery, red peppers (if using), garlic, basil, and oregano. Process until pureed. Pour into a large no-stick skillet. Stir in the Cajun spice blend.

3 Bring to a boil over medium-high heat. Reduce the heat to medium-low and cook, stirring occasionally, for 15 minutes, or until the mixture thickens into a sauce.

4 Add the fish. Cover and cook for 7 minutes, or until the fish is opaque. (Check by inserting the tip of a sharp knife in the center of 1 fillet.) Season to taste with the salt (if using).

5 Spoon the sauce onto dinner plates. Top with the fish. Sprinkle with the parsley.

Makes **4** servings.

nutrition at a glance

per serving

0.9 g.	total fat
0.2 g.	saturated fat
116	calories
70 mg.	cholesterol
561 mg.	sodium
18.5 g.	protein
8 g.	carbohydrates
1 g.	dietary fiber

Scrod Baked in Foil Packets

quick and **easy**

Preparing fish in foil packets is quick, easy, and fat-free—a cook's dream. Serve with a green vegetable or two plus new potatoes, baked potatoes, or rice.

4	scrod fillets (4 ounces each)
2	medium carrots, julienned
1	large stalk celery, julienned or chopped
1	onion, thinly sliced
1	tablespoon capers, rinsed and drained
1	teaspoon dried thyme
8	thin slices lime or lemon
¼	cup dry sherry or 2 teaspoons sherry extract
	Ground black pepper
	Salt (optional)

1 Preheat the oven to 400°F. Rinse the fish and pat dry with paper towels.

2 Place four 18" x 12" pieces of heavy-duty foil on a work surface. Tip the edges up slightly. Place 1 fillet in the center of each foil piece. Sprinkle with the carrots, celery, onions, capers, and thyme.

3 Top with the lime slices or lemon slices. Sprinkle with the sherry or sherry extract, pepper, and salt (if using). Fold the edges of the foil tightly to seal, leaving some air space within each packet for steam to rise.

4 Bake for 20 minutes. Remove from the oven. Let stand for 2 to 3 minutes. Open 1 packet carefully, pointing it away from you to vent the hot steam. Check for doneness by inserting the tip of a sharp knife in the center of the fillet.

5 If the fish is still translucent, reclose the opened packet and return all the packets to the oven to bake for 2 to 3 minutes more. Carefully unwrap the packets. Slide the fish and vegetables onto dinner plates to serve.

Makes **4** servings.

nutrition at a glance

per serving

0.6 g.	total fat
0.1 g.	saturated fat
101	calories
30 mg.	cholesterol
146 mg.	sodium
13.1 g.	protein
6.9 g.	carbohydrates
1.9 g.	dietary fiber

Herb-Breaded Orange Roughy

quick and easy

The orange roughy stays exceptionally moist inside a garlicky herb and bread crumb coating. Serve with a green vegetable and wild rice, spaetzle, or oven-fried potatoes. Red snapper is also a good choice for the fish.

4	orange roughy fillets (2¼ ounces each)
⅓	cup fat-free mayonnaise
¼	cup fat-free Parmesan topping
1	teaspoon dried basil
1	teaspoon dried oregano
1	teaspoon freshly squeezed lemon juice
2	cloves garlic, minced
¼	cup fine dry plain bread crumbs
	Gound black pepper
2	teaspoons chopped fresh parsley

1 Preheat the oven to 350°F. Rinse the fish and pat dry with paper towels.

2 In a small bowl, combine the mayonnaise, Parmesan, basil, oregano, lemon juice, and garlic. Stir well to combine. Place the bread crumbs on a dinner plate.

3 Spread both sides of the fish with the mayonnaise mixture, then coat with the bread crumbs. Place in a 13" x 9" baking dish. Season to taste with the pepper. Bake for 20 to 25 minutes, or until the fish is opaque in the center. (Check by inserting the tip of a sharp knife in the center of 1 fillet.) Sprinkle with the parsley.

Makes **4** servings.

Lynn's Kitchen Tip

It is easy to make bread crumbs instantly with a hand blender. You can use stale or fresh bread, bagels, even pretzels. First, break the bread, bagels, or pretzels into chunks. Place in a medium mixing bowl. Lift the hand blender up and down into the bowl. In a few seconds, it will be crumbs. Season with ¼ teaspoon dried oregano, dried basil, dried tarragon, dried thyme or garlic salt.

nutrition at a glance

per serving

0.9 g.	total fat
0.2 g.	saturated fat
126	calories
16 mg.	cholesterol
391 mg.	sodium
15.7 g.	protein
13.2 g.	carbohydrates
0.3 g.	dietary fiber

Crispy Fish with Tartar Sauce

quick and easy

Satisfy cravings for fried fish with this heart-healthy baked version. For a bit more color in the crust, add ¼ teaspoon paprika. To vary the tartar sauce, you can substitute sweet pickles for the dill.

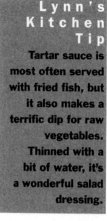

Fish

4	flounder or cod fillets (3 ounces each)
	Salt (optional)
1	egg white
¼	cup grated onions
½	cup dry herbed bread crumbs

Tartar Sauce

1	cup fat-free mayonnaise
2	tablespoons chopped dill pickles
2	tablespoons chopped onions
1	teaspoon freshly squeezed lemon juice
½	teaspoon capers, rinsed, drained and finely chopped (optional)

1 *To make the fish:* Preheat the oven to 400°F. Rinse the fish and pat dry with paper towels.

2 Season the fish lightly with the salt (if using). Place the egg white in a wide shallow bowl and beat lightly with a fork. Add the onions and mix well. Place the bread crumbs on a piece of wax paper or foil. Dip the fish into the egg mixture, then the crumbs, to coat evenly on both sides.

3 Set the fish in an ovenproof grill pan or on a baking sheet topped with a wire rack. Place in the oven and reduce the heat to 375°F. Bake for 10 minutes, or until the fish is opaque in the center. (Check by inserting the tip of a sharp knife in the center of 1 fillet.)

4 *To make the tartar sauce:* While the fish is baking, in a small bowl, mix the mayonnaise, pickles, onions, and lemon juice. Add the capers (if using) to the bowl. Mix well. Serve with the fish.

Makes **4** servings.

---

nutrition at a glance

per serving

0.8 g.	total fat
0.2 g.	saturated fat
144	calories
23 mg.	cholesterol
877 mg.	sodium
12.5 g.	protein
19.3 g.	carbohydrates
0.3 g.	dietary fiber

Hawaiian Mahimahi-Shrimp Kabobs

You can substitute scallops, turbot or monkfish for the mahimahi without changing the fat content of this spicy island entrée. Serve the kabobs over steamed rice, with green beans, sliced bananas, and a green salad containing tiny yellow pear tomatoes. You'll need some long metal or bamboo skewers for this dish.

Lynn's Lore

Mahimahi means "strong strong" in Hawaiian. Although this extremely low fat fish is sometimes called dolphinfish, it is not related to the dolphin, which is a mammal.

1   mahimahi fillet (14 ounces), 1" thick
2   tablespoons freshly squeezed lemon juice
4   cloves garlic, minced
2   teaspoons chili powder
½   teaspoon ground cumin
¼   teaspoon ground red pepper or several drops hot-pepper sauce
¼   teaspoon ground cinnamon
   Pinch of ground cloves
3   ounces shelled medium shrimp
½   pineapple, peeled, cut in half lengthwise, and cut into 24 (1") cubes
1   large green pepper, cut into 24 (1") squares
1   large sweet red pepper, cut into 24 (1") squares
1   large Spanish onion, cut into 24 (1") wedges

1   If using bamboo skewers, submerge 6 long ones in cold water for 30 minutes (to prevent burning during cooking).

2   Meanwhile, rinse the fish and pat dry with paper towels. Cut into 12 (1") cubes.

3   In a resealable plastic bag, combine the lemon juice, garlic, chili powder, cumin, ground red pepper or hot-pepper sauce, cinnamon, and cloves. Seal the bag and knead until blended.

4   Add the fish and shrimp to the bag; seal, then turn gently to coat the fish and shrimp with the marinade. Refrigerate for 30 minutes.

5   Preheat the oven broiler or prepare a charcoal grill. Coat a broiler pan or barbecue grill rack with no-stick spray.

6   Remove the fish and shrimp from the marinade; set the marinade aside. Thread the fish and shrimp alternately on the skewers with the pineapple, green peppers, red peppers, and onions.

7   Broil or grill the kabobs 4" from the heat, basting several times with the reserved marinade, for 7 minutes. Turn and cook, basting several times, for 2 to 3 minutes, or until the fish is opaque. (Check by inserting the tip of a sharp knife in the center of 1 cube.) Discard any remaining marinade. Serve hot, on or off the skewers.

Makes **6** kabobs.

nutrition at a glance	
per kabob	
0.9 g.	total fat
0.2 g.	saturated fat
106	calories
68 mg.	cholesterol
88 mg.	sodium
15.2 g.	protein
9.7 g.	carbohydrates
1.5 g.	dietary fiber

Spicy Shrimp

quick and easy

To use this dish as an appetizer, peel the shrimp and serve with a dip (leave the tip of the tail attached as a handle) or as part of a crudité tray. For a casual meal, serve with other finger foods, such as grilled chunks of corn on the cob, baked zucchini, and carrot sticks.

2	cups water
½	cup white wine or nonalcoholic white wine
2	tablespoons tomato paste
1	teaspoon crushed fennel seeds
1	teaspoon dried basil
½	teaspoon crushed red-pepper flakes
½	teaspoon dried oregano
½	teaspoon dried thyme
¼	teaspoon hot-pepper sauce
¼	teaspoon onion salt
12	ounces shrimp in the shell
2	tablespoons chili powder

Lynn's Fat-Free Flavor

Five-spice powder is a delightfully aromatic Chinese spice mixture usually made up of ground cinnamon, cloves, fennel, star anise, and Szechuan peppercorns. It's sold in Asian food stores and some supermarkets. Try a pinch on carrots, sweet potatoes, or squash for a flavor boost.

1   In a large no-stick saucepan, combine the water, wine, tomato paste, fennel seeds, basil, red-pepper flakes, oregano, thyme, hot-pepper sauce, and onion salt. Whisk to combine.

2   Bring to a boil over medium-high heat. Add the shrimp. Reduce the heat to medium, cover, and cook for 2 minutes. Add the chili powder and stir to combine. Cover and cook for 1 to 1½ minutes, or until all the shrimp are bright pink. Remove from the heat and drain. Serve hot or chilled.

Makes **4** servings.

Photograph on page 146

nutrition at a glance	
per serving	
0.9 g.	total fat
0.2 g.	saturated fat
71	calories
121 mg.	cholesterol
165 mg.	sodium
13.2 g.	protein
1 g.	carbohydrates
0 g.	dietary fiber

Shrimp with Shiitakes in Orange Sauce

quick and easy

This rich-looking dish of earthy mushrooms dotted with tender pink shrimp will please the most discerning palate. Scallops or chunks of flounder, cod, scrod, or halibut can replace the shrimp.

2	tablespoons low-sodium soy sauce
1	teaspoon Worcestershire sauce
2	cloves garlic, minced
¾	cup freshly squeezed orange juice
10	ounces shiitake mushroom caps, thinly sliced
1	large onion, thinly sliced
1	tablespoon cornstarch
12	ounces medium shelled shrimp
2	scallions, sliced into 2" thin shreds

1 In a large no-stick saucepan, combine the soy sauce, Worcestershire sauce, garlic, and ½ cup of the orange juice. Add the mushrooms and onions. Cook over medium heat, stirring often, for 10 to 12 minutes, or until the mushrooms and onions are nearly cooked.

2 Place the cornstarch in a small bowl. Add the remaining ¼ cup orange juice and stir to dissolve the cornstarch. Add to the saucepan. Stir over medium-high heat for 1 minute, or until the mixture thickens.

3 Add the shrimp. Cook, stirring, for 3 minutes, or until the shrimp are bright pink. Serve sprinkled with the scallions.

Makes **4** servings.

nutrition at a glance

per serving

0.9 g.	total fat
0.2 g.	saturated fat
153	calories
121 mg.	cholesterol
458 mg.	sodium
15.4 g.	protein
22.1 g.	carbohydrates
2.2 g.	dietary fiber

Braised Rice with Mushrooms and Shrimp

quick and easy

Sweet shrimp and meaty mushrooms complement each other in this satisfying main-course rice dish. It also makes an excellent appetizer that will serve 8.

1	large onion, chopped
6	ounces portobello mushrooms, sliced
4	shiitake mushroom caps, sliced
1	cup short-grain white rice
1¼–1½	cups defatted chicken stock (page 94) or water
7	ounces shelled shrimp, cut in half lengthwise
	Salt (optional)
2	scallions, chopped
2	tablespoons chopped fresh cilantro

1 Coat a large no-stick skillet with no-stick spray. Add the onions and cook over medium-high heat, stirring, for 3 minutes. Add the portobello mushrooms and shiitake mushrooms. Cook, stirring, for 3 minutes.

2 Add the rice, mixing well. Add ½ cup of the stock or water. Cook, stirring, for 4 minutes, or until the liquid is absorbed. Add an additional ½ cup stock or water. Cook, stirring occasionally, for 4 minutes, or until the liquid is absorbed.

3 Add the shrimp and ¼ cup of the remaining stock or water. Cook, stirring occasionally, for 4 minutes, or until the rice is tender and the liquid is absorbed. (If the rice isn't cooked, add the remaining ¼ cup stock or water and continue cooking until tender.) Season to taste with the salt (if using). Stir in the scallions and cilantro.

Makes **4** servings.

nutrition at a glance
per serving

0.9 g.	total fat
0.2 g.	saturated fat
207	calories
71 mg.	cholesterol
92 mg.	sodium
11.8 g.	protein
38 g.	carbohydrates
2.2 g.	dietary fiber

Scallop Risotto Primavera

Arborio rice, a type of rounded, starchy rice, is essential for an authentic Italian risotto. Risotto takes a little bit of tending to make, but it is not difficult. The key to success is to add the liquid gradually, cooking at a medium simmer, so the rice grains can absorb the liquid. A perfect risotto will have distinct tender grains suspended in a creamy sauce.

8	ounces button mushrooms, sliced
4	ounces baby carrots, cut in half lengthwise
1	onion, chopped
1	clove garlic, minced
⅔	cup Arborio rice
1	chicken or vegetable bouillon cube
2¼–2¾	cups defatted chicken stock (page 94)
4	ounces snow peas or sugar snap peas, cut in half crosswise
½	cup chopped spinach leaves
1	jarred roasted red pepper, thinly sliced
4	ounces bay scallops
½	cup dry white wine or nonalcoholic white wine
	Dash of Cajun spice blend
¼	cup fat-free Parmesan topping
2	tablespoons chopped fresh parsley
3	dry-pack sun-dried tomato halves, finely chopped

1   Coat a large no-stick skillet with no-stick spray. In the skillet, combine the mushrooms, carrots, onions, and garlic. Cover and cook over medium-high heat, stirring occasionally, for 3 to 4 minutes, or until the mushrooms release some liquid. Uncover and cook over medium heat, stirring occasionally, for 2 to 3 minutes, or until the liquid evaporates.

2   Stir in the rice, bouillon cube, and ¼ cup of the stock. Reduce the heat slightly, if necessary; the liquid should be absorbed by the rice, not just evaporate. When the rice has absorbed the liquid, continue adding the stock in ¼- to ½-cup increments.

3   Cook, stirring after each addition, for a total of 20 minutes, or until the rice is tender but firm. Add the snow peas or sugar snap peas, spinach, and peppers.

4 Meanwhile, in a small no-stick skillet, combine the scallops, wine, and Cajun spice blend. Cook over medium-high heat for 3 minutes, or until the scallops barely turn opaque. Drain the liquid into the risotto, stirring lightly to mix. Cook for 2 to 3 minutes.

5 Stir in the scallops, Parmesan, parsley, and tomatoes. Remove from the heat; cover and set aside for 2 minutes to steam.

Makes **8** servings.

Photograph on page 148

<table>
<tr><td colspan="2">nutrition at a glance</td></tr>
<tr><td colspan="2">per serving</td></tr>
<tr><td>0.8 g.</td><td>total fat</td></tr>
<tr><td>0.1 g.</td><td>saturated fat</td></tr>
<tr><td>108</td><td>calories</td></tr>
<tr><td>4 mg.</td><td>cholesterol</td></tr>
<tr><td>191 mg.</td><td>sodium</td></tr>
<tr><td>6.6 g.</td><td>protein</td></tr>
<tr><td>19.3 g.</td><td>carbohydrates</td></tr>
<tr><td>2.2 g.</td><td>dietary fiber</td></tr>
</table>

Malaysian Shrimp Fried Rice

quick and easy

Malaysian fried rice is usually served with a red-pepper sauce and sliced cucumbers with hot chili peppers, according to Indian cooking authority Madhur Jaffrey, whose recipe inspired this dish. For authentic Malaysian flavor, add part of a stalk of fresh or dried lemongrass—which is available in some supermarkets or Asian food stores—to the rice as you cook it. Discard the stalk after cooking.

1	cup finely shredded bok choy
½	sweet red pepper, chopped
¼	cup water
3	cloves garlic, minced
	Pinch of five-spice powder (optional)
1	cup hot cooked long-grain white rice
5	scallions
2	tablespoons low-sodium soy sauce
2	tablespoons chopped fresh cilantro
1	tablespoon chopped fresh parsley
¾	cup fat-free egg substitute
½	cup frozen peas, thawed
4	ounces tiny shrimp or large shrimp, shelled and cut into ¼" slices
½–1	teaspoon Chinese chili paste
¼	teaspoon dark sesame oil

Lynn's Lore

In rice-eating cultures, this ingredient is treated with great care. The Japanese often rinse their rice 10 times or more, placing the rice in the bottom of a pan filled with water and rubbing the kernels together by hand to get rid of all the starchy coating. The rice is rinsed and drained until the water is clear.

1   Coat a large no-stick skillet with no-stick spray. Add the bok choy, peppers, water, garlic, and five-spice powder (if using). Stir to mix. Cover and cook over medium heat for 5 minutes, or until the bok choy wilts. If necessary, add additional water, 1 tablespoon at a time, to keep the bok choy from sticking.

2   Stir in the rice. Cook over medium heat for 4 minutes, or until hot, adding a few tablespoons water to moisten if necessary.

3   Slice 4 of the scallions and add to the skillet. Stir in the soy sauce, cilantro, and parsley. Cook for 1 minute, or until hot, adding 1 table-spoon water if necessary to keep moist.

4   When the mixture is hot, drizzle half of the egg substitute into the skillet in a thin stream, stirring the rice constantly. Make a shallow well in the center of the rice mixture; pour the rest of the egg substitute into the well. Reduce the heat to low and cover the skillet.

5   Cook for 4 minutes, or until the egg substitute in the center is firm. Dice the egg with the tip of a sharp knife. Add the peas, shrimp, chili paste, and oil, stirring gently. Cover and let stand for 3 minutes on very low heat.

6   Chop the remaining scallion and sprinkle over the rice.

Makes **4** servings.

nutrition at a glance	
per serving	
0.8 g.	total fat
0.2 g.	saturated fat
148	calories
46 mg.	cholesterol
460 mg.	sodium
13 g.	protein
21.5 g.	carbohydrates
2.1 g.	dietary fiber

Golden Rice with Shrimp and Shiitakes

Serve with steamed green beans or broccoli. For dessert, serve fresh berries over angel food cake slices and top with fat-free whipped topping or fat-free frozen yogurt.

1	medium onion, coarsely chopped
1	cup sliced shiitake mushroom caps
1¼	cups basmati or long-grain white rice
3	cups water or defatted chicken stock (page 94)
1	package (12 ounces) frozen cooked squash, thawed
⅛	teaspoon ground nutmeg
	Salt (optional)
4	ounces shelled medium shrimp, cut in half lengthwise
1	tablespoon chopped fresh parsley (optional)

1   Coat a no-stick Dutch oven with no-stick spray. Warm the pan over medium heat. Add the onions and mushrooms; mist with no-stick spray. Cook, stirring, for 4 to 5 minutes.

2   Add the rice. Cook, stirring, for 2 minutes. Add the water or stock. Increase the heat to high and bring to a boil. Reduce the heat to medium, cover, and cook for 10 minutes.

3   Add the squash and nutmeg. Season to taste with the salt (if using). Reduce the heat to low, cover, and cook for 5 minutes. Check to make sure that the rice is not sticking.

4   Top with the shrimp; cover and cook for 4 minutes, or until the shrimp turn pink. Set aside a few shrimp for a garnish. Stir to mix the ingredients. Let stand for 3 minutes, or until the mixture thickens somewhat. Garnish with the reserved shrimp. Sprinkle with the parsley (if using).

Makes **4** servings.

nutrition at a glance

per serving

0.9 g.	total fat
0.3 g.	saturated fat
316	calories
40 mg.	cholesterol
57 mg.	sodium
11.1 g.	protein
66.4 g.	carbohydrates
4.5 g.	dietary fiber

Shrimp Creole

This fine old New Orleans dish never tasted so good—or was ever quite so low in fat. Serve with 1 cup cooked rice per portion. It's a great entrée for company because you can double it and make it in advance. (Don't stir in the shrimp until after reheating, however, or they will toughen.) On the side, I like okra or greens.

½ cup defatted chicken stock (page 94)
1 small onion, chopped
½ green pepper, chopped
½ cup chopped celery
2 cloves garlic, minced
1 can (16 ounces) tomatoes, chopped (with juice)
¾ cup tomato sauce
2 teaspoons Worcestershire sauce
2 teaspoons chopped fresh thyme or 1 teaspoon dried
1 teaspoon chopped fresh oregano or ½ teaspoon dried
1 bay leaf
2 teaspoons hot-pepper sauce
1 teaspoon cornstarch
1 tablespoon water
8 ounces shelled medium shrimp, cut in half lengthwise

1 In a large no-stick skillet over medium-high heat, bring the stock to a boil. Reduce the heat to medium. Add the onions, peppers, celery, and garlic. Cook for 3 minutes, or until the onions begin to turn translucent.

2 Add the tomatoes (with juice), tomato sauce, Worcestershire sauce, thyme, oregano, bay leaf, and 1 teaspoon of the hot-pepper sauce. Bring to a boil. Reduce the heat to medium-low and simmer, stirring occasionally, for 20 minutes.

3 Place the cornstarch in a cup. Add the water and stir to dissolve the cornstarch. Add to the skillet. Stir for 1 to 2 minutes, or until the sauce thickens slightly.

4 Add the shrimp; cook for 2 to 3 minutes, or until pink. Taste and add the remaining 1 teaspoon hot-pepper sauce if needed.

Makes **4** servings.

nutrition at a glance
per serving
0.9 g. total fat
0.2 g. saturated fat
101 calories
81 mg. cholesterol
596 mg. sodium
11.3 g. protein
13 g. carbohydrates
2.3 g. dietary fiber

Dungeness Crab Cakes

quick and easy

Sweet Dungeness crab inspired these luscious morsels, but any good-quality lump crabmeat is fine for the recipe. Try them with Rémoulade Sauce (page 300). If you serve them on an English muffin or bun, it will boost the fat content only slightly.

½	cup whole-kernel corn
1¼	cups backfin or lump crabmeat, flaked
1	cup cold cooked rice
2	tablespoons finely chopped scallions
2	tablespoons finely chopped celery
2	tablespoons chopped fresh parsley
2	tablespoons + ½ cup dry plain bread crumbs
½	cup fat-free egg substitute
3	tablespoons fat-free mayonnaise
2	teaspoons freshly squeezed lemon juice
1	teaspoon Worcestershire sauce
½	teaspoon dry mustard
4	dashes hot-pepper sauce
	Pinch of ground black pepper
	Pinch of salt (optional)

1   In a blender or food processor, process the corn until finely chopped. Place in a medium bowl. Add the crab, rice, scallions, celery, parsley, and 2 tablespoons of the bread crumbs.

2   In a small bowl, combine the egg substitute, mayonnaise, lemon juice, Worcestershire sauce, mustard, hot-pepper sauce, black pepper, and salt (if using). Add to the crab mixture and stir to combine. Form the mixture into 8 cakes.

3   Place the remaining ½ cup bread crumbs in a shallow bowl. Dredge the cakes in the bread crumbs to coat, gently shaking off the excess.

4   Coat a large no-stick skillet with no-stick spray. Warm the skillet over medium heat. Add the cakes and cook for 3 minutes on each side, or until golden brown.

Makes **8** crab cakes.

nutrition at a glance

per crab cake

0.8 g.	total fat
0.2 g.	saturated fat
105	calories
13 mg.	cholesterol
201 mg.	sodium
7.4 g.	protein
16.6 g.	carbohydrates
0.8 g.	dietary fiber

Fisherman's Casserole

This is pure comfort food and quite easy to make. Vary the dish, if you like, by adding a bit of peas, corn or diced carrots, potatoes, or tomatoes.

Lynn's Lore
Flounder is a member of an extremely large species of flatfish, which have evolved into odd-looking sea creatures with both eyes located on the upper side. Dab, English sole, and plaice are also types of flounder.

1½	cups chopped celery
5	ounces button mushrooms, sliced
1	cup chopped green peppers
½	cup chopped onions
¼	cup dry sherry or 2 teaspoons sherry extract
1	cup skim milk
¼	cup all-purpose flour
½	cup water
⅔	cup drained sliced canned water chestnuts
1½	teaspoons Dijon mustard
½	teaspoon Old Bay seasoning
	Several dashes of hot-pepper sauce
	Ground black pepper
	Salt (optional)
6	ounces flounder fillets, cut into ½" chunks
4	ounces medium shelled shrimp
3	tablespoons fat-free Parmesan topping
1	tablespoon chopped fresh parsley

1   Preheat the oven to 350°F. Coat a 2-quart baking dish with no-stick spray.

2   Coat a large no-stick skillet with no-stick spray. Add the celery, mushrooms, green peppers, and onions. Mist with no-stick spray. Cover and cook over medium heat, stirring often, for 5 minutes, or until the onions are golden.

3   Add the sherry or sherry extract and bring to a boil over medium-high heat. Cook for 2 minutes. Add the milk. Reduce the heat to medium, and bring almost to a boil.

4 Place the flour in a small bowl. Gradually whisk in the water until smooth. Stir into the skillet. Cook, whisking constantly, for 3 to 4 minutes, or until the sauce thickens.

5 Add the water chestnuts, mustard, Old Bay seasoning, and hot-pepper sauce. Season to taste with the black pepper and salt (if using). Reduce the heat to low, cover, and cook for 2 minutes.

6 Remove from the heat. Stir in the fish, shrimp, and 2 tablespoons of the Parmesan. Pour the mixture into the prepared baking dish. Dust the top with the remaining 1 tablespoon Parmesan.

7 Bake for 25 minutes, or until hot and bubbly. Sprinkle with the parsley.

Makes **6** servings.

nutrition at a glance	
per serving	
0.9 g.	total fat
0.2 g.	saturated fat
128	calories
43 mg.	cholesterol
402 mg.	sodium
13.4 g.	protein
16 g.	carbohydrates
2.7 g.	dietary fiber

Breton Seafood Stew

quick and easy

This seafood stew is quick to make but special enough to serve to guests. Serve it over tiny new potatoes, rice, quinoa, or orzo and accompany it with bread, salad, and a steamed green vegetable.

1   cup water
2   stalks celery, thinly sliced
2   medium carrots, thinly sliced
1   leek, white part only, thinly sliced
2¾ cups defatted fish stock or vegetable stock (page 93)
2   tablespoons all-purpose flour
¼   cup dry vermouth or apple cider
3   plum tomatoes, diced
1   tablespoon freshly squeezed lemon juice
1   teaspoon grated lemon rind
1   teaspoon grated orange rind
3   cloves garlic, minced
1   sprig fresh thyme
¼   teaspoon saffron threads
8   ounces cod fillet, cut into 1" cubes
3   ounces squid rings or small shelled shrimp

1 In a no-stick Dutch oven over medium-high heat, bring the water to a boil. Add the celery, carrots, and leeks. Reduce the heat to medium, partially cover, and cook, stirring occasionally, for 5 minutes. Add the stock.

2 Place the flour in a small bowl. Gradually whisk in the vermouth or apple cider until smooth. Stir into the pan. Cook, stirring, until thickened.

3 Add the tomatoes, lemon juice, lemon rind, orange rind, garlic, thyme, and saffron. Simmer, stirring occasionally, for 15 minutes. Add the cod and squid or shrimp. Simmer for 5 minutes, or until the cod is cooked. (Check by inserting the tip of a sharp knife in the center.)

Makes **4** servings.

Photograph on page 147

Photograph on page 147

Lynn's Lore

Cut into rings or strips, squid is often fried, which adds an enormous amount of fat. Better to enjoy its mild flavor in fat-free soups or salads. When cooked quickly, as it is here, squid remains tender.

---

nutrition at a glance

per serving
- 0.9 g. total fat
- 0.2 g. saturated fat
- 141 calories
- 64 mg. cholesterol
- 83 mg. sodium
- 11.8 g. protein
- 18.4 g. carbohydrates
- 3 g. dietary fiber

Greek Salad (page 104)

Asian Coleslaw (page 107)

Mexicali Pasta Salad (page 98)

Spicy Shrimp (page 131)

Breton Seafood Stew (page 142)

Scallop Risotto Primavera (page 134)

Cod with Ginger-Orange Sauce (page 124)

Fiesta Chili (page 186)

Garden Pita Pizza (page 177)

Couscous-Stuffed Peppers (page 188)

Moroccan Vegetable Medley (page 190)

Spaghetti with Sun-Dried Tomato Sauce (page 176)

Southwestern Polenta (page 33)

Turkey Cutlets Tarragon (page 165)

Italian Stuffed Artichokes (page 191)

Wild Mushroom Moussaka (page 194)

Main Dishes

Not long ago, a meal without a huge piece of meat

anchoring the plate seemed incomplete. Today, nu-

trient-dense low-fat grains, legumes, and vegetables

are the stars of the plate, alongside moderate

portions of lean poultry and meat.

Meat and skin-on poultry are two of the highest

sources of fat, particularly saturated fat, in the

American diet. Because a diet that is too high in sat-

urated fat is linked to heart disease, diabetes,

and some forms of cancer, it makes perfect sense to reduce the amounts of these foods. Notice that I said *reduce*, not eliminate.

Meals with Meat

I have developed wonderful main dishes using boneless, skinless turkey breast. In addition to being the leanest animal protein around (at 1 gram of fat per 3-ounce cooked portion), turkey breast never met a seasoning that it didn't like. Prepared so many different ways, it's like eating a different meat each time.

Turkey Cutlets Tarragon, for instance, are delicate, in contrast to the vibrant seasonings in Turkey and Black Bean Stew. And exotic Sweet-and-Sour Turkey is worlds away from the American classic Turkey-Broccoli Divan.

Lean beef top round, trimmed of all visible fat, is also a reasonable meat choice (at 3.4 grams of fat per 3-ounce cooked portion). Try my Beef and Mushroom Fajitas and Vegetable Stew with Beef to see how flavorful this cut really is.

Meat-Free Meals

Main dishes made from fiber-filled vegetables, fruits, and grains are earthy, simple, and inexpensive. You'll feel good—and energetic—after you eat them.

Garden Pita Pizza, Spaghetti with Sun-Dried Tomato Sauce, Couscous-Stuffed Peppers, and Wild Mushroom Moussaka won't leave anyone in your family asking, "Where's the beef?"

Soybean meat substitutes such as texturized vegetable protein mimic the texture and appearance of ground beef but are low in saturated fat and contain no cholesterol. Try my White Chili and Fiesta Chili to see what I mean. Look for texturized vegetable protein (TVP) in health food stores and some supermarkets.

Tofu—pressed soybean curd—is also versatile, easy to use, and very low in saturated fat. It's renowned as a carrier of spicy flavors.

Every serving of my main dishes contains less than 1 gram of fat. Of course, the number of servings that you'll eat may vary. If you're a petite woman, you might choose one serving and accompany it with several fat-free or low-fat side dishes to round out the meal. If you're a six-foot-plus man with greater calorie needs, you may need to eat two or even three servings. But these dishes are so lean that your total fat intake will still be extremely low—so eat hearty!

Turkey Teriyaki Kabobs

For this Japanese-style dish, you use long wooden or metal skewers. Serve with rice and crisp steamed asparagus or broccoli.

1	pound boneless, skinless turkey breast, trimmed of all visible fat
2	tablespoons low-sodium soy sauce
2	teaspoons grated fresh ginger
2	teaspoons sugar
1	large clove garlic, minced
8	large button mushrooms
1	medium eggplant, cut into 16 cubes
16	snow peas
4	scallions, cut into 4 pieces each
16	yellow pear tomatoes or cherry tomatoes

1 If using wooden skewers, submerge 8 long ones in cold water for 30 minutes.

2 Cut the turkey into 1" cubes. In a medium bowl, combine the soy sauce, ginger, sugar, and garlic. Add the turkey and mushrooms. Cover and refrigerate for 20 minutes, stirring occasionally.

3 Bring a medium saucepan of water to a boil. Add the eggplant; cook for 2 minutes. Add the snow peas and scallions; cook for 1 minute. Drain, then plunge the vegetables into a big bowl of ice water. Let stand for 30 seconds; drain and pat dry.

4 Preheat the oven broiler or prepare a charcoal grill.

5 Divide the turkey, mushrooms, eggplant, snow peas, scallions, and tomatoes among 8 skewers. Brush well with the marinade; reserve the marinade.

6 Broil or grill 4" from the heat for 2 to 3 minutes. Turn the skewers and brush with the marinade. Cook for 2 to 3 minutes, or until the turkey cubes are no longer pink in the center when tested with the point of a sharp knife. Discard the remaining marinade.

Makes **8** kabobs.

Lynn's Kitchen Tip

Vegetables are sometimes parboiled—cooked briefly in boiling water—to partially cook them before use in a stir-fry, grilled recipe, or other quick-cooking dish. After parboiling, drain the vegetables, then plunge them into a large bowl of ice water to stop the cooking. Drain and pat dry for use in the recipe.

nutrition at a glance
per kabob

0.8 g.	total fat
0.2 g.	saturated fat
96	calories
39 mg.	cholesterol
181 mg.	sodium
15 g.	protein
7.3 g.	carbohydrates
1.9 g.	dietary fiber

Orange-Rosemary Turkey

For a tasty variation, substitute dried sage for the rosemary and 1 tablespoon lemon juice for the orange juice. Sprinkle with fat-free Parmesan topping before serving.

4	boneless, skinless turkey breast cutlets (3 ounces each)
¼	cup orange juice
2	teaspoons dried rosemary, crumbled
1	large clove garlic, minced
	Ground black pepper
	Salt (optional)
1	teaspoon finely chopped fresh parsley

1 Use a meat mallet to flatten the turkey cutlets to ¼" thickness.

2 In a nonaluminum 12" x 8" baking dish, combine the orange juice, rosemary, and garlic. Add the turkey and turn to coat both sides. Cover and refrigerate for 1 hour, turning the turkey once during this time.

3 Preheat the oven broiler or prepare a charcoal grill. Coat a broiler pan or barbecue the grill rack with no-stick spray.

4 Remove the turkey from the marinade; reserve the marinade. Broil or grill the turkey 4" from the heat, basting once with the reserved marinade, for 2 minutes, or until lightly browned at the edges. Turn and cook, basting once with the reserved marinade, for 2 minutes, or until the turkey is no longer pink in the center when tested with the point of a sharp knife. Discard any remaining marinade.

5 Season the turkey to taste with the pepper and salt (if using). Sprinkle with the parsley.

Makes **4** servings.

nutrition at a glance

per serving

0.9 g.	total fat
0.3 g.	saturated fat
102	calories
58 mg.	cholesterol
38 mg.	sodium
20 g.	protein
1.6 g.	carbohydrates
0.2 g.	dietary fiber

20 Fast and Tasty Turkey Cutlets

Sprinkled with fresh herbs or spices, splashed with flavored vinegar or citrus juice, or topped with a dollop of a savory condiment, boneless, skinless turkey breast cutlets are the fastest fat-free entrée in town. To make, coat a large no-stick skillet with no-stick spray. Warm the pan over medium heat. Add ¼"-thick turkey cutlets and cook for 2 minutes, or until browned on the bottom. Flip and cook for 2 to 3 minutes, or until the cutlets are no longer pink in the center when tested with the point of a sharp knife. Top as desired. Here are some tasty fat-free suggestions.

* Balsamic vinegar
* Cajun spice blend
* Caramelized Onion Compote (page 301)
* Chicken Gravy (page 293)
* Chopped fresh dill
* Chutney
* Cranberry sauce
* Curry powder
* Dijon mustard
* Finely chopped scallions
* Ground cumin
* Hoisin sauce
* Horseradish
* Orange juice
* Rémoulade Sauce (page 300)
* Roasted Garlic (page 304)
* Salsa
* Thinly sliced fresh basil
* Teriyaki sauce
* White-wine Worcestershire sauce

Sweet-and-Sour Turkey

quick and easy

For a bit of spicy heat, stir in ¼ teaspoon crushed red-pepper flakes just before serving. Serve with cooked white or brown rice. Increasing the turkey in the recipe to 1 pound will increase the fat only slightly—to 1.4 grams per serving.

1	large onion, coarsely chopped
1	green pepper, cut into 1" pieces
2	carrots, sliced
1	clove garlic, minced
10	ounces boneless, skinless turkey breast, trimmed of all visible fat and cut into ½" cubes
1½	tablespoons cornstarch
3	tablespoons white-wine vinegar or cider vinegar
3	tablespoons packed brown sugar
2	tablespoons water
2	teaspoons low-sodium soy sauce
1	can (20 ounces) pineapple chunks (packed in juice)

1 Coat a large no-stick skillet with no-stick spray. Warm over medium heat. Add the onions, peppers, carrots, and garlic. Cover and cook, stirring occasionally, for 6 to 8 minutes, or until the onions are golden. If necessary, add 1 to 2 teaspoons water to prevent sticking. Remove from the pan.

2 Add the turkey to the skillet. Cook over medium heat, stirring occasionally, for 3 to 4 minutes, or until no longer pink.

3 Place the cornstarch in a medium bowl. Add the vinegar and stir to dissolve the cornstarch. Add the brown sugar, water, and soy sauce; stir to dissolve the brown sugar.

4 Drain the pineapple, reserving ¾ cup of the juice. Set aside the pineapple. Add the juice to the bowl and stir the mixture into the skillet. Cook, stirring, for 1 to 2 minutes, or until the mixture thickens. Stir in the pineapple and the reserved onion mixture. Cook for 1 minute to heat.

Makes **4** servings.

nutrition at a glance	
per serving	
0.9 g.	total fat
0.2 g.	saturated fat
269	calories
48 mg.	cholesterol
153 mg.	sodium
18.7 g.	protein
48.1 g.	carbohydrates
2.7 g.	dietary fiber

Turkey Cutlets Tarragon

quick and easy

If your market doesn't sell turkey breast cutlets, buy a skinless turkey breast half and have the meat cutter thinly slice it.

4	boneless, skinless turkey breast cutlets (3 ounces each)
¼	cup fat-free mayonnaise
2	teaspoons dried tarragon
½	teaspoon Dijon mustard

1 Use a meat mallet to flatten the turkey cutlets to ¼" thickness.

2 In a small bowl, mix the mayonnaise, tarragon, and mustard. Divide half of the mixture among the cutlets and spread evenly over the top side of each.

3 Coat a large no-stick skillet with no-stick spray. Warm the pan over medium heat. Add the turkey, seasoned side down, and cook for 2 minutes, or until browned on the bottom. Flip the cutlets.

4 Spread with the remaining mayonnaise mixture. Cover and cook for 2 to 3 minutes, or until the turkey is no longer pink in the center when tested with the point of a sharp knife.

Makes **4** servings.

Photograph on page 156

Photograph on page 156

Lynn's Lore

Turkey cutlets are conveniently packaged slices of boneless, skinless turkey breast that are in the supermarket poultry case. If cutlets are unavailable in your store, or if you want to save a bit on the cost, it's easy to cut your own. Remove all skin and fat from a partially frozen boneless turkey breast half. With a sharp knife, cut crosswise into ½"-thick slices.

nutrition at a glance

per serving

0.9 g.	total fat
0.3 g.	saturated fat
106	calories
58 mg.	cholesterol
147 mg.	sodium
20.5 g.	protein
2.2 g.	carbohydrates
0 g.	dietary fiber

Peking Turkey and Vegetables

quick and easy

This colorful wok dish is quick to get on the table. The secret to success in Chinese stir-frying is having all the ingredients cut and measured before you turn on the stove. Doubling the amount of turkey in the recipe to 12 ounces will increase the total fat to only 1.3 grams per serving. Serve with basmati, long-grain white, or brown rice.

2	teaspoons cornstarch
1	tablespoon rice vinegar
⅓	cup hoisin sauce
1	tablespoon grated fresh ginger
2	teaspoons sugar
1	cup water or defatted chicken stock (page 94)
6	ounces boneless, skinless turkey breast, trimmed of all visible fat and cut into ¼" strips
1	cup chopped onions
½	sweet red pepper, cut into thin strips
2	cloves garlic, minced
¾	cup diagonally sliced carrots
1½	cups broccoli florets
½	cup snow peas
½	cup sliced water chestnuts
1	tablespoon chopped fresh cilantro

1 Place the cornstarch in a small bowl. Add the vinegar and stir to dissolve the cornstarch. Stir in the hoisin sauce, ginger, sugar, and ½ cup of the water or stock. Set aside.

2 Coat a no-stick wok or large no-stick skillet with no-stick spray. Warm over medium-high heat. Add the turkey and cook, tossing frequently, for 2 minutes, or until no longer pink. Transfer to a bowl and set aside.

3 Add the onions, peppers, and garlic to the pan. Remove the pan from the heat and mist the vegetables with no-stick spray. Cover and cook over medium-high heat, stirring occasionally, for 3 to 4 minutes, or until the onions are golden. Add to the turkey and set aside.

4 Add the remaining ½ cup water or stock to the pan; bring to a simmer. Add the carrots; cook for 2 minutes. Add the broccoli; cook for 4 minutes, stirring occasionally. Add the snow peas; cook for 1 to 2 minutes, or until the broccoli is barely tender.

5 Add the water chestnuts and cilantro. Add the reserved hoisin-sauce mixture and turkey mixture. Cook, stirring, for 2 to 3 minutes, or until the sauce thickens.

Makes **4** servings.

Photograph on page 241

Turkey-Broccoli Divan

Our male taste testers were crazy about this dish. You can serve it over fat-free crumpets, toast, English muffins, pasta, rice, or potatoes. Or just enjoy it on its own, as our tasters did.

2	cups broccoli florets cut into 1½ " lengths
8	ounces button mushrooms, cut in half
1	large onion, coarsely chopped
1¾	cups diced cooked turkey breast
2½	tablespoons all-purpose flour
½	cup fat-free liquid creamer
1	cup defatted vegetable stock (page 93) or chicken stock (page 94)
2	tablespoons dry white wine or nonalcoholic white wine (optional)
¼	teaspoon ground black pepper
	Salt (optional)
3	tablespoons fat-free Parmesan topping

1 Preheat the oven to 350°F.

2 In a large no-stick skillet over medium-high heat, bring ¼ " water to a boil. Add the broccoli. Cover and return to a boil. Cook for 2 minutes, or until the broccoli is bright green. Drain and place in a 12" x 8" baking dish.

(continued)

Lynn's Lore

Turkey is native to the Americas and was domesticated by the Aztecs. Today, most American turkeys come from a Dutch breed that's prized for its plumpness.

3 Coat the skillet with no-stick spray. Add the mushrooms and onions. Cover and cook over medium-high heat for 1 to 2 minutes, or until the mushrooms start to release some liquid. Uncover and cook, stirring often, for 1 to 2 minutes, or until the onions are softened. Spread over the broccoli. Cover with the turkey.

4 Place the flour in a small saucepan. Gradually whisk in the creamer until smooth. Add the stock, wine (if using), and pepper. Cook over medium heat, whisking constantly, for 4 minutes, or until thickened. Season to taste with the salt (if using). Pour over the turkey. Sprinkle with the Parmesan.

5 Cover with foil and bake for 15 minutes. Uncover and bake for 15 minutes, or until bubbly and golden. Let stand for 10 minutes.

Makes **6** servings.

Photograph on page 242

nutrition at a glance
per serving
0.9 g.	total fat
0.3 g.	saturated fat
138	calories
45 mg.	cholesterol
91 mg.	sodium
19.6 g.	protein
12.6 g.	carbohydrates
1.8 g.	dietary fiber

Turkey and Black Bean Stew

Increasing the turkey to 1 pound will raise the fat per serving to a mere 1.2 grams. Serve with cooked rice and chopped scallions and lime wedges for garnish.

1	cup dry black beans
1	medium onion, chopped
1	carrot, shredded
½	green pepper, cut into 1" squares
½	sweet red pepper, cut into 1" squares
2	teaspoons ground oregano
1½	teaspoons ground cumin
4	cloves garlic, minced
4	cups water or defatted chicken stock (page 94)
8	ounces boneless, skinless turkey breast, trimmed of all visible fat and cut into 1" cubes
2	plum tomatoes, coarsely chopped
2	jalapeño peppers, minced (wear plastic gloves when handling)
1	tablespoon vinegar
½	teaspoon salt (optional)
2	tablespoons thinly sliced fresh basil

1   Place the beans in a large saucepan and cover with cold water. Bring to a boil over medium-high heat. Remove from the heat and set aside for 1 hour.

2   Meanwhile, coat a no-stick Dutch oven with no-stick spray. Warm over medium-high heat. Add the onions, carrots, green peppers, sweet red peppers, oregano, cumin, and garlic.

3   Reduce the heat to medium. Cook, stirring, for 4 to 6 minutes, or until the onions start to soften. Remove the vegetables and set aside.

4   Drain and rinse the beans. Add the beans to the Dutch oven. Add the water or stock. Bring to a boil over medium-high heat. Reduce the heat to medium-low. Partially cover and simmer, stirring occasionally, for 1½ hours, or until the beans are nearly tender.

5   Add the reserved vegetables. Simmer for 30 minutes, or until the beans are tender.

6   Add the turkey, tomatoes, jalapeño peppers, vinegar, and salt (if using). Simmer for 5 minutes, or until the turkey is cooked. Remove from the heat and stir in the basil. Let stand for 5 minutes to allow the flavors to blend.

Makes **8** servings.

nutrition at a glance	
per serving	
0.9 g.	total fat
0.2 g.	saturated fat
144	calories
19 mg.	cholesterol
26 mg.	sodium
13.5 g.	protein
21.3 g.	carbohydrates
7 g.	dietary fiber

Turkey and Potato Curry

Serve with rice, a steamed vegetable, and Cuke and Zuke Raita (page 105). Doubling the amount of turkey to 12 ounces will increase the total fat to only 1.2 grams per serving.

1	large onion, chopped
3	cloves garlic, minced
½	teaspoon curry powder
2	large potatoes, cut into ½" cubes
6	ounces boneless, skinless turkey breast, trimmed of all visible fat and cut into ½" cubes
⅓	cup raisins
1	tablespoon minced fresh ginger
1	tablespoon cornstarch
1	teaspoon freshly squeezed lemon juice or lime juice
¾	cup fat-free plain yogurt
1	cup defatted chicken stock (page 94)
½	cup thawed frozen peas
1	tablespoon chopped fresh cilantro

1   Preheat the oven to 350°F.

2   Coat a large ovenproof no-stick skillet with no-stick spray. Add the onions, garlic, and curry powder. Cover and cook over medium heat, stirring occasionally, for 4 to 5 minutes, or until the onions start to soften. If necessary, add 1 to 2 teaspoons water to prevent sticking.

3   Add the potatoes, turkey, raisins, and ginger. Remove from the heat.

4   Place the cornstarch in a small bowl. Add the lemon juice or lime juice and stir to dissolve the cornstarch. Whisk in the yogurt. Gradually whisk in the stock until smooth. Add to the skillet. Stir gently to combine.

5   Cover and bake for 45 to 50 minutes, or until the potatoes are tender when pierced with a knife. Remove from the oven.

6   Sprinkle with the peas. Cover and let stand for 2 minutes to heat the peas. Sprinkle with the cilantro.

Makes **4** servings.

> **Lynn's Fat-Free Flavor**
>
> Fat-free plain yogurt adds tangy flavor and creamy texture to dishes without contributing fat. And you can make a marvelous soft cheese from yogurt (page 304) that requires virtually no work.

nutrition at a glance

per serving

0.8 g.	total fat
0.2 g.	saturated fat
225	calories
30 mg.	cholesterol
85 mg.	sodium
16.4 g.	protein
39.3 g.	carbohydrates
3.4 g.	dietary fiber

Beef and Mushroom Fajitas

Starting in the Southwest and spreading throughout the country, fajitas are on more and more dinner tables. This delightful fat-free version is sure to become a family favorite. Doubling the amount of beef in this recipe to 1 pound raises the total fat to only 1.8 grams per fajita. Garnish each fajita with chopped fresh cilantro, fat-free sour cream, and hot-pepper sauce to taste.

¼   cup lime juice
1½   teaspoons chili powder
1   teaspoon dried oregano
1   teaspoon sugar
3   cloves garlic, minced
8   ounces lean beef top round, trimmed of all visible fat and cut into thin strips
4   ounces portobello mushrooms or shiitake mushroom caps, cut into ½" slices
½   Spanish onion, cut into ½" slices
½   sweet red pepper, cut into ½" strips
½   yellow pepper, cut into ½"strips
    Ground black pepper
    Salt (optional)
8   fat-free flour tortillas (7" diameter), heated

1   In a resealable plastic bag, mix the lime juice, chili powder, oregano, sugar, and garlic. Add the meat and mushrooms, seal the bag, and press gently to coat the meat with the marinade. Place in the refrigerator and marinate for 30 minutes.

2   Coat a large no-stick skillet with no-stick spray. Warm over medium-high heat. Add the meat, mushrooms, and 2 tablespoons of the marinade. Cook, stirring frequently, for 4 to 5 minutes, or until the meat is cooked. Remove and set aside.

3   Wash and dry the skillet. Coat with no-stick spray. Warm over medium-high heat. Add the onions, red peppers, and yellow peppers.

(continued)

Cover and cook for 1 to 2 minutes, or until the onions start to release moisture. Uncover and cook, stirring frequently, for 4 to 5 minutes, or until the onions are golden. If necessary, add 1 to 2 teaspoons water to prevent sticking. Season to taste with the black pepper and salt (if using).

4   Place the tortillas on a work surface. Divide the beef mixture among them, spooning it down the middle. Top with the onions and peppers. Fold the tortillas to enclose the filling.

Makes **8** fajitas.

Photograph on page 240

Vegetable Stew with Beef

This stew tastes so meaty that no one would ever guess it has only 4 ounces lean beef—and less than 1 gram of fat per serving. Doubling the amount of beef to 8 ounces increases the fat to only 1.5 grams per serving.

4	ounces lean beef top round, trimmed of all visible fat
1	medium potato, cut into 1" x ½" strips
1	medium onion, coarsely chopped
1	cup sliced carrots
1	cup sliced button mushrooms
2	stalks celery, cut into 1" pieces
½	cup all-purpose flour
1	cup apple cider
1	cup water
¼	cup chopped fresh parsley
1	teaspoon dried rosemary, crumbled
1	teaspoon dried thyme
1	teaspoon dried basil
¼	teaspoon dried tarragon
3	cloves garlic, thinly sliced
¼	teaspoon ground black pepper
1	beef bouillon cube
1	vegetable bouillon cube
	Salt (optional)

Lynn's Kitchen Tip

When buying beef, use your eyes to gauge the amount of visible fat. Even if meat is labeled lean, judge for yourself. For a stew, select the leanest top round with no marbling. Trim away all visible fat before cooking.

1 Preheat the oven to 350°F.

2 Cut the beef into ¼"-thick slices, then into 1" x ½" strips. Place in a 3-quart baking dish. Scatter the potatoes, onions, carrots, mushrooms, and celery over the meat.

3 Place the flour in a medium bowl. Gradually whisk in the apple cider and water until smooth. Add the parsley, rosemary, thyme, basil, tarragon, garlic, and pepper. Pour over the vegetables. Add the beef bouillon cube and the vegetable bouillon cube.

4 Cover and bake for 1½ hours, or until the meat and vegetables are tender. Season to taste with the salt (if using). Stir gently before serving.

Makes **6** servings.

Photograph on page 239

Photograph on page 239

nutrition at a glance
per serving
0.9 g.	total fat
0.3 g.	saturated fat
132	calories
12 mg.	cholesterol
218 mg.	sodium
7.3 g.	protein
24 g.	carbohydrates
2.3 g.	dietary fiber

Soufflé Primavera

This soufflé is delightful for brunch or lunch or as part of a light dinner. For a formal meal, it's smashing served as a side dish with fish. Don't be intimidated by this French classic—I've included several tips to ensure that your soufflé gets a great liftoff.

4	cups water
1½	cups finely chopped carrots
1½	cups finely chopped broccoli florets
1	cup skim milk
½	cup chopped leeks
½	cup finely chopped onions
3	tablespoons all-purpose flour
½	cup fat-free egg substitute
½	teaspoon ground black pepper
⅛	teaspoon ground nutmeg
	Pinch of salt (optional)
9	tablespoons fat-free Parmesan topping
5	egg whites, at room temperature
	Dash of freshly squeezed lemon juice or cream of tartar

1   Preheat the oven to 425°F.

2   Place the water in a large saucepan and bring to a boil over medium-high heat. Add the carrots and broccoli. Reduce the heat to low and simmer for 5 minutes, or until the carrots are crisp-tender. Drain, reserving the cooking liquid. Transfer the vegetables to a medium bowl and set aside.

3   Add the milk to the saucepan. Bring almost to a boil, stirring occasionally, over medium heat. Pour into a small heatproof bowl and set aside.

4   Add 1 cup of the reserved cooking liquid to the saucepan; bring to a boil over medium-high heat. Add the leeks and onions; cook for 5 to 7 minutes.

5   Sprinkle the flour over the leek mixture. Whisk constantly for 3 minutes. Pour in the milk and cook, whisking constantly, for 3 minutes, or until thickened. Remove from the heat.

6 Gradually whisk in the egg substitute. Stir in the pepper, nutmeg, salt (if using), the reserved vegetables and 4 tablespoons of the Parmesan.

7 Place the egg whites in a large bowl. Beat with an electric mixer until foamy. Add the lemon juice or cream of tartar. Beat until stiff peaks form.

8 Add about one-third of the whites to the vegetable mixture. Carefully fold in with a rubber spatula. Do not overmix; some streaks of white can remain. Add the remaining whites and fold them in until just incorporated.

9 Coat a 1½-quart soufflé dish with no-stick spray. Add 4 tablespoons of the remaining Parmesan to the dish and coat the bottom and sides of the dish with the Parmesan. Spoon the soufflé mixture into the dish. Sprinkle with the remaining 1 tablespoon Parmesan.

10 Place the dish in the oven. Reduce the heat to 375°F. Bake for 20 minutes without opening the oven. Bake an additional 10 minutes, or until the soufflé jiggles slightly in the center when gently shaken. Bake for 5 minutes more, if desired, to cook until firm.

Makes **4** servings.

nutrition at a glance	
per serving	
0.7 g.	total fat
0.2 g.	saturated fat
222	calories
1 mg.	cholesterol
478 mg.	sodium
23.8 g.	protein
32.7 g.	carbohydrates
5.6 g.	dietary fiber

Spaghetti with Sun-Dried Tomato Sauce

This satisfying spaghetti was one of our tasters' top picks. Serve it with Artichoke Salad (page 103) and Italian bread spread with Roasted Garlic (page 304).

(page 103) ... (page 304)

½   cup hot water
1   teaspoon chopped dry-pack sun-dried tomatoes
½   medium onion, sliced
1   large clove garlic, minced
1   can (16 ounces) tomato juice
4   large cherry tomatoes, chopped
¼   cup thinly sliced fresh basil
2   teaspoons dried oregano
    Pinch of sugar
    Ground black pepper
    Salt (optional)
8   ounces low-fat spaghetti (0.5 g. fat per 2-ounce serving)
4   tablespoons fat-free Parmesan topping

1   In a small bowl, combine the water and sun-dried tomatoes. Let stand for 10 minutes, or until the tomatoes are softened. Transfer the tomatoes and water to a large no-stick skillet.

2   Add the onions and garlic. Cook over medium heat, stirring occasionally, for 8 minutes. Stir in the tomato juice, cherry tomatoes, basil, oregano, and sugar. Cover and simmer over low heat, stirring occasionally, for 20 minutes. Season to taste with the pepper and salt (if using).

3   Meanwhile, cook the spaghetti according to the package directions. Drain and serve topped with the sauce. Sprinkle with the Parmesan.

Makes **4** servings.

Photograph on page 154

Photograph on page 154

Lynn's Kitchen Tip

Choose sun-dried tomatoes that are dry-packed in cellophane. They have barely any fat, as opposed to sun-dried tomatoes packed in olive oil.

nutrition at a glance

per serving

0.8 g.	total fat
0 g.	saturated fat
290	calories
0 mg.	cholesterol
634 mg.	sodium
14.2 g.	protein
56.4 g.	carbohydrates
3 g.	dietary fiber

Garden Pita Pizza

quick and easy

Pita pizzas are so easy and so satisfying. For terrific flavor, I sauté the vegetables before they go on the pizza. It takes just a few minutes and makes a huge difference in the taste. This recipe multiplies perfectly, so you can make it for one or a party of ten. Garnish with crushed red-pepper flakes.

⅓ cup thinly sliced button mushrooms
⅓ cup thinly sliced zucchini
⅛ teaspoon garlic powder
¼ cup tomato sauce
1 fat-free whole-wheat or white pita (6" diameter)
2 tablespoons finely chopped scallions
1 tablespoon slivered fresh basil
¼ teaspoon dried oregano
1 large pitted black olive, chopped
2 tablespoons shredded fat-free mozzarella cheese
1 tablespoon fat-free Parmesan topping

1 Preheat the oven to 425°F.

2 Place the mushrooms and zucchini in a large no-stick skillet. Coat with no-stick spray. Cover and cook over medium-high heat for 2 to 3 minutes, or until the mushrooms start to release their juice. Remove the cover and cook, stirring occasionally, for 1 to 2 minutes, or until the mushrooms and zucchini are golden. Stir in the garlic powder and 2 tablespoons of the tomato sauce. Set aside.

3 Place the pita bread on a baking sheet. Bake for 1 minute to crisp. Remove from the oven and spread with the remaining 2 tablespoons tomato sauce. Spoon on the mushroom mixture. Sprinkle with the scallions, basil, oregano, olives, mozzarella, and Parmesan.

4 Bake for 8 to 10 minutes, or until the cheese melts and is golden.

Makes **1** pita pizza.

Photograph on page 151

nutrition at a glance
per pita pizza
0.9 g. total fat
0.1 g. saturated fat
183 calories
1 mg. cholesterol
414 mg. sodium
15.4 g. protein
32 g. carbohydrates
3.4 g. dietary fiber

Polenta Italiana

This open-faced polenta and vegetable sandwich is really a stacked tower of vegetable power. Serve with ripe melon, a couple strips of fat-free ham, roasted sweet red peppers, and a tossed salad with Creamy Italian Dressing (page 115).

Polenta

1½	cups vegetable stock (page 93)
½	cup yellow cornmeal
1	small onion, finely chopped
2	cloves garlic, minced
	Pinch of salt
¼	cup fat-free Parmesan topping

Sun-Dried Tomato Sauce

4	teaspoons cornstarch
1	cup vegetable stock (page 93)
8	dry-packed sun-dried tomato halves, cut into small pieces
½	cup dry red wine or apple cider
2	tablespoons balsamic vinegar
1	teaspoon finely chopped fresh rosemary
2	cloves garlic, minced
	Ground black pepper
	Salt (optional)

Vegetable Filling

4	round eggplant slices (1" thick)
4	tomato slices (¾ " thick)
	Ground black pepper
	Salt (optional)

1 *To make the polenta:* Line a baking sheet with foil and coat it with no-stick spray. Set aside.

2 In a medium saucepan, combine the stock, cornmeal, onions, garlic, and salt. Bring to a boil over medium-high heat, stirring constantly. Reduce the heat to medium and cook, stirring occasionally, for 12 to 15 minutes, or until the polenta is thick enough to hold a spoon upright.

3 Pour the polenta onto the baking sheet; spread it evenly into an 8" x 8" square, about ¾ " thick.

4   Cover loosely with plastic wrap and place in the refrigerator to chill for at least 4 hours, or until firm. Cut diagonally from corner to corner to make 4 triangles. Sprinkle with the Parmesan.

5   *To make the sun-dried tomato sauce:* Place the cornstarch in a small saucepan. Gradually whisk in the stock to dissolve the cornstarch. Add the tomatoes, wine or apple cider, vinegar, rosemary, and garlic. Stir over medium-high heat for 2 to 3 minutes, or until thickened. Season to taste with the pepper and salt (if using). Cover and keep warm.

6   *To make the vegetable filling:* Preheat the oven to 425°F. Coat a large baking sheet with no-stick spray.

7   Place the eggplant and tomatoes on the baking sheet and mist with no-stick spray. Sprinkle with the pepper and salt (if using). Cover loosely with foil and bake for 10 minutes. Remove the foil.

8   Place the polenta in a single layer on the baking sheet with the eggplant and tomatoes. Bake for 10 minutes, or until the eggplant and tomatoes are tender and the polenta is crisp.

9   Top each polenta triangle with 1 eggplant slice and 1 tomato slice. Reheat the sun-dried tomato sauce if needed. Spoon over the sandwiches.

Makes **4** servings.

Sicilian Calzone

quick and easy

This savory pizza turnover makes a terrific dinner with my Tossed Antipasto Salad (page 97).

4	ounces thawed frozen French bread dough
2	cups chopped spinach leaves, blanched, drained, and squeezed dry
2	plum tomatoes, diced
1	cup fat-free ricotta cheese
¼	cup finely chopped scallions
1	tablespoon finely chopped fresh basil
½	teaspoon dried oregano
1	clove garlic, minced
¼	teaspoon ground black pepper
	Pinch of salt (optional)
1	tablespoon shredded fat-free mozzarella cheese
½	cup tomato sauce with Italian seasonings

1 Position the oven rack in the lower third of the oven. If desired, place a baking stone on the rack. Preheat the oven to 425°F.

2 On a lightly floured work surface, roll the dough into a 10" circle. Cover and let rest while making the filling.

3 In a medium bowl, combine the spinach, tomatoes, ricotta, scallions, basil, oregano, garlic, pepper, and salt (if using). Spoon the mixture over half of the dough circle to within ½" of the edge. Fold the dough over the filling to enclose. Crimp the edges to seal.

4 With a large spatula, transfer the calzone to a baking sheet or to the baking stone in the oven. Sprinkle the top with the mozzarella. Bake for 20 to 25 minutes, or until the crust browns. Cut in half.

5 Heat the tomato sauce in a small saucepan. Serve with the calzone.

Makes **2** servings.

nutrition at a glance

per serving

0.9 g.	total fat
0.1 g.	saturated fat
264	calories
10 mg.	cholesterol
852 mg.	sodium
21.5 g.	protein
39.5 g.	carbohydrates
4 g.	dietary fiber

Black Bean and Rice Cakes

Serve with Tomato Relish (page 299) or, if you're pressed for time, with jarred salsa spiked with a bit of freshly squeezed lime juice and chopped fresh basil.

1	cup water
½	cup white rice
	Pinch of salt (optional)
1	can (15 ounces) black beans, rinsed and drained
½	cup fresh bread crumbs (from 40-calorie-per-slice bread)
1	stalk celery, finely chopped
¼	cup finely chopped sweet red peppers
¼	cup fat-free egg substitute
¼	teaspoon ground black pepper

1   Preheat the oven to 375°F. Coat a baking sheet with no-stick spray and set aside.

2   In a medium no-stick saucepan, combine the water, rice, and salt (if using). Bring to a boil over medium-high heat. Reduce the heat to low. Cover and cook for 20 minutes, or until the rice is tender and the water has been absorbed.

3   Remove from the heat. Stir in the beans, bread crumbs, celery, red peppers, egg substitute, and black pepper.

4   Coat a ½-cup metal or plastic measuring cup with no-stick spray. Pat one quarter of the rice mixture firmly into the cup and then turn it out onto the baking sheet by rapping the cup lightly on the sheet. Press to flatten to a ¾"-thick cake. Repeat with remaining mixture to form 4 cakes.

5   Bake for 20 minutes, or until heated through.

Makes **4** cakes.

Photograph on page 320

nutrition at a glance

per cake

0.7 g.	total fat
0.2 g.	saturated fat
213	calories
0 mg.	cholesterol
232 mg.	sodium
10.1 g.	protein
42 g.	carbohydrates
5.2 g.	dietary fiber

Garden and Grain Loaf

This moist, satisfying loaf—delicately seasoned with an herb mixture from the south of France—can be served with Roasted Pepper Sauce (page 291), Chicken Gravy (page 293), Marinara Sauce (page 288), or Mushroom Sauce (page 294). Paper-thin carrot curls, cut with a vegetable peeler, make a pretty garnish.

½	cup quick-cooking rolled oats
⅓	cup Grape-Nuts cereal
12	ounces button mushrooms, finely chopped
1	large onion, finely chopped
1	large carrot, finely shredded
1	medium zucchini, shredded
3	cloves garlic, minced
2	cups fresh whole-grain bread crumbs (from 40-calorie-per-slice bread)
¼	cup fat-free egg substitute
1	tablespoon Dijon mustard
1	tablespoon tomato paste
1½	teaspoons dried herbes de Provence
1	teaspoon low-sodium Worcestershire sauce
¼	teaspoon ground black pepper
	Pinch of salt (optional)

1 Preheat the oven to 350°F. Coat an 8" x 4" loaf pan with no-stick spray.

2 Line a baking sheet with foil. Place the oats and Grape-Nuts in separate piles on the sheet; spread each pile into a thin layer. Bake for 12 to 15 minutes, or until golden; stir occasionally and keep the oats and cereal separate. Let cool for a few minutes. Transfer the Grape-Nuts to a blender or food processor and grind coarsely; set aside. Do not turn off the oven.

3 Coat a large no-stick skillet with no-stick spray. Add the mushrooms, onions, carrots, zucchini, and garlic. Mist the vegetables with no-stick spray. Stir-fry over medium-high heat for 5 minutes. Remove from the heat. Stir in the bread crumbs and the reserved oats and Grape-Nuts.

4   In a small bowl, combine the egg substitute, mustard, tomato paste, herbes de Provence, Worcestershire sauce, pepper, and salt (if using). Whisk to combine. Add to the skillet and mix well.

5   Spoon the mixture into the prepared loaf pan. Smooth the top with the back of a spoon.

6   Bake for 40 to 45 minutes, or until browned on top and firm to the touch. Remove from the oven and let stand for 10 minutes. Run a knife around the edge. Unmold and slice.

Makes **8** servings.

nutrition at a glance
per serving

0.9 g.	total fat
0.1 g.	saturated fat
99	calories
0 mg.	cholesterol
167 mg.	sodium
5 g.	protein
21.2 g.	carbohydrates
4.5 g.	dietary fiber

Black Bean Tamale Pie

This hearty Southwestern-style casserole is a perfect buffet entrée. Everything but the topping can be made ahead of time and stored in the refrigerator. Serve with a green vegetable, a salad, and fat-free vanilla ice cream topped with orange slices.

Black Beans

1	dried chipotle pepper (wear plastic gloves when handling)
½	cup hot water
2	cups vegetable stock (page 93)
2½	cups chopped onions
1½	cups tomato sauce
4	cloves garlic, minced
1	tablespoon chili powder
1	tablespoon tomato paste
2	teaspoons dried oregano
1	teaspoon ground cumin
1	teaspoon sugar
	Pinch of salt (optional)
2	cups cooked black beans
¼	cup chopped fresh cilantro

Cornbread Topping

½	cup all-purpose flour
¼	cup yellow cornmeal
1½	teaspoons baking powder
	Pinch of salt (optional)
⅓	cup canned creamed-style corn
⅓	cup canned chopped mild green chili peppers
2	tablespoons skim milk
½	tablespoon sugar
1	egg white

1 *To make the black beans:* In a small bowl, combine the pepper and the water. Let soak for 30 minutes, or until softened. Split the pepper and discard the seeds and stem. Puree the pepper and the liquid in a blender or food processor. Set aside.

2 Meanwhile, in a large saucepan over medium-high heat, bring the stock to a boil. Add the onions, tomato sauce, garlic, chili powder, tomato paste, oregano, cumin, sugar, and salt (if using). Reduce the heat to medium-low and simmer for 1 hour, or until the mixture thickens.

3 Add the beans and 1 to 2 teaspoons of the chipotle puree (reserve the remainder for another use). Simmer for 15 minutes. Remove from the heat and stir in the cilantro.

4 Pour into a 12" x 8" baking dish. Set aside.

5 *To make the cornbread topping:* Preheat the oven to 400°F.

6 In a small bowl, mix the flour, cornmeal, baking powder, and salt (if using).

7 In a large bowl, combine the corn, peppers, milk, and sugar.

8 Place the egg white in a medium bowl. Beat with an electric mixer until soft peaks form. Fold into the corn mixture. Stir in half of the flour mixture just until incorporated, then add the remaining flour mixture and stir just until the dry ingredients are moistened.

9 Spoon over the bean mixture; spread with the back of a spoon to cover. Bake for 20 minutes, or until a toothpick inserted in the center of the cornbread topping comes out clean.

Makes **8** servings.

nutrition at a glance
per serving
0.9 g.	total fat
0.2 g.	saturated fat
168	calories
0 mg.	cholesterol
756 mg.	sodium
7.6 g.	protein
34.1 g.	carbohydrates
6.7 g.	dietary fiber

Fiesta Chili

I like to use chipotle peppers (dried smoked jalapeños) to add a complex smoky note to this chili, but a fresh jalapeño pepper works fine, too.

1	cup dry red beans
1	can (16 ounces) tomatoes, chopped (with juice)
2	cups tomato juice
1	large tomato, coarsely chopped
1	cup orange juice
1	large onion, coarsely chopped
1	sweet red pepper, cut into 1" cubes
1	cup granulated texturized vegetable protein (optional)
½	carrot, shredded or finely diced
1	dried chipotle pepper, cut into small pieces (wear plastic gloves when handling)
3	cloves garlic, minced
2	tablespoons chili powder
1	tablespoon dried basil
2	teaspoons grated orange rind
2	teaspoons vinegar
1	teaspoon ground cumin
1	teaspoon dried oregano
1	teaspoon packed brown sugar or 2 tablespoons raisins
	Ground black pepper
	Salt (optional)
1	cup shredded fat-free mozzarella cheese

1 Place the beans in a large no-stick Dutch oven. Cover generously with cold water. Bring to a boil over medium-high heat. Remove from the heat, cover, and allow to stand for 1 hour. Discard the soaking water. Rinse the beans and return to the pot.

2 Add the canned tomatoes, tomato juice, chopped tomatoes, orange juice, onions, red peppers, texturized vegetable protein (if using), carrots, chipotle peppers, garlic, chili powder, basil, orange rind, vinegar, cumin, oregano, and brown sugar or raisins. Mix well.

Lynn's Fat-Free Flavor

There are dozens of varieties of kidney beans, several of them variegated in color. You can use any of the kidney-shaped beans in chili, soups, salads, side dishes, and appetizers. The darker beans are more robustly flavored and firmer in texture than the lighter beans.

3 Simmer over medium heat, stirring occasionally, for 1½ hours, or until the beans are tender. Season to taste with the black pepper and salt (if using). Serve sprinkled with the mozzarella.

Makes **8** servings.

Photograph on page 150

White Chili

quick and **easy**

Sometimes just the aroma of cooking chili tickles the nose and starts the hunger pangs. I guarantee that you will love this unique stew. You can easily add 1 cup granulated texturized vegetable protein with the amount of water called for on the package directions to make the chili seem meaty.

1	Spanish onion, chopped
½	cup diced yellow peppers
2	cloves garlic, minced
2½	cups water
1	can (15 ounces) navy beans or cannellini beans, rinsed and drained
1	cup diced tomatoes
⅓	cup white whole-kernel corn
2	tablespoons diced canned mild green chili peppers
½	teaspoon chopped jalapeño peppers (wear plastic gloves when handling)
½	teaspoon ground cumin
½	teaspoon chili powder
½	teaspoon vinegar
⅛	teaspoon ground red pepper (optional)
	Salt (optional)
½	cup shredded fat-free Swiss cheese

1 In a large no-stick pot, combine the onions, yellow peppers, garlic, and ½ cup of the water. Stir over medium-high heat for 5 minutes, or until the peppers are nearly cooked and the water has evaporated.

Lynn's Fat-Free Flavor

Instead of complaining that winter tomatoes don't taste as sweet and juicy as summer's red beauties, I developed this chili recipe to take advantage of pale varieties. When cooked, they add a delightful tart sweetness to this unusual dish. Green tomatoes or tomatillos also work beautifully, as do slightly underripe yellow tomatoes.

(continued)

2 Add the beans, tomatoes, corn, mild chili peppers, jalapeño peppers, cumin, chili powder, vinegar, ground red pepper (if using), and the remaining 2 cups water. Cover and cook over medium-low heat, stirring occasionally, for 15 minutes. Season to taste with the salt (if using). Serve sprinkled with the Swiss.

Makes **4** servings.

Couscous-Stuffed Peppers

For this very colorful entrée, you can use a mixture of colored peppers. The varieties most often available are purple, green, red, orange, yellow, and white. Garnish with slivers of orange rind.

1½	cups canned diced recipe-ready tomatoes
2	cloves garlic, minced
4	yellow peppers
¼	cup chopped onions
2	dried apricot halves, slivered
2	dates, chopped
2	tablespoons raisins
2	vegetable bouillon cubes
½	teaspoon dried thyme
¼	teaspoon grated orange rind
1	cup couscous
2	tablespoons chopped fresh parsley
2	tablespoons thinly sliced fresh basil
	Ground black pepper
	Salt (optional)

1 In a small no-stick saucepan, combine the tomatoes and garlic. Cover and simmer over medium heat for 10 minutes. Coat an 8" x 8" baking dish with no-stick spray. Cover the bottom of the dish with the tomatoes and garlic. Set aside.

Lynn's Kitchen Tip
You don't need a citrus zester to make julienne slivers of orange rind. First, scrub the fruit with warm, soapy hot water. Rinse well, then dry. With a paring knife or vegetable peeler, take off ½"-wide strips of rind, with as little white pith attached as possible. Cut the strips into slivers.

2 Bring a large pot of water to a boil over high heat. Cut the tops off the yellow peppers; discard the membranes and seeds. Drop the peppers and the tops into the pot. Boil for 2 minutes. Using tongs, remove the tops and set aside to drain. Boil the peppers for 2 to 3 minutes more, or until partially cooked. Using tongs, remove the peppers and rinse under cold water. Drain upside down in a colander. Reserve 2¾ cups of the cooking water.

3 Pour 2½ cups of the reserved cooking water into a medium saucepan. Bring to a boil over medium heat. Add the onions, apricots, dates, raisins, bouillon cubes, thyme, and orange rind. Reduce the heat to low and simmer for 15 minutes.

4 Remove from the heat and stir in the couscous. Cover and let stand for 5 minutes. Fluff with a fork. Sprinkle with the parsley, basil, black pepper and salt (if using). Mix lightly.

5 Preheat the oven to 350°F.

6 Divide the couscous mixture among the peppers. Stand the peppers in the baking dish. Drizzle the remaining ¼ cup cooking water over the peppers. Top with the reserved pepper tops.

7 Cover loosely with foil. Bake for 30 minutes, or until the peppers are tender.

Makes **4** servings.

Photograph on page 152

nutrition at a glance
per serving
0.8 g. total fat
0.1 g. saturated fat
279 calories
0 mg. cholesterol
265 mg. sodium
8.3 g. protein
62.3 g. carbohydrates
7.3 g. dietary fiber

Moroccan Vegetable Medley

This beautifully spiced vegetable entrée was a hit with our taste testers. Serve each portion over 1 cup steamed couscous, which will raise the fat content by only 1 gram.

6	cups water or vegetable stock (page 93)
4	sprigs fresh cilantro
4	cloves garlic
1	tablespoon chopped fresh parsley
1	teaspoon curry powder
¾	teaspoon ground cumin
¼–½	teaspoon crumbled saffron threads
	Pinch of ground cinnamon
	Pinch of salt (optional)
3	carrots, halved lengthwise and cut into 1" pieces
2	small russet potatoes, cut into large pieces
½	medium onion, cut into quarters
1	medium zucchini, quartered lengthwise and cut into 1" pieces
½	cup canned chick-peas, rinsed and drained
¼	cup raisins
2	tablespoons chopped fresh cilantro

1 In a large pot, combine the water or stock, cilantro sprigs, garlic, parsley, curry powder, cumin, saffron, cinnamon, and salt (if using). Bring to a boil over medium-high heat. Add the carrots, potatoes, and onions. Return to a boil. Reduce the heat to medium. Partially cover and simmer for 25 to 30 minutes, or until the potatoes are almost tender.

2 Add the zucchini, chick-peas, and raisins; stir gently so the vegetables don't break up. Simmer for 10 to 12 minutes, or until the zucchini is tender. Sprinkle with the chopped cilantro.

Makes **4** servings.

Photograph on page 153

Photograph on page 153

Lynn's Fat-Free Flavor

Only a few varieties of grapes are dried to make raisins. The Thompson seedless, the tiny Zante, and the Muscat are the most common. Both dark and golden raisins can be made from Thompson seedless grapes. The dark raisins are sun-dried for several weeks. The golden are treated with sulfur dioxide to prevent them from darkening.

nutrition at a glance
per serving
- 0.9 g. total fat
- 0.1 g. saturated fat
- 140 calories
- 0 mg. cholesterol
- 87 mg. sodium
- 4.6 g. protein
- 30.8 g. carbohydrates
- 4.7 g. dietary fiber

Italian Stuffed Artichokes

Artichoke lovers, this lush and elegant main course is for you. The savory stuffing gives way to the tender artichoke heart.

4	medium artichokes, cleaned, bottom trimmed flat
1	cup chopped button mushrooms
1	small leek, white and some green stem, chopped
¼	yellow pepper, finely chopped
1	stalk celery, finely chopped
¼	cup water
1½	cups fresh bread crumbs (from 40-calorie-per-slice bread)
¼	cup fat-free egg substitute
2	tablespoons chopped fresh parsley
1	clove garlic, minced
¼	teaspoon ground black pepper
3	tablespoons freshly squeezed lemon juice

1   Place the artichokes, stem side down, in a deep no-stick saucepan wide enough to hold them tightly in a single layer. Add 2" of water. Cover and bring to a boil over medium-high heat. Reduce the heat to medium-low and cook for 30 to 40 minutes, or until an outer leaf pulls off easily. Add more water to the pan, if necessary, during cooking.

2   Drain the artichokes and set aside to cool. Preheat the oven to 375°F.

3   While the artichokes are cooling, coat a large no-stick skillet with no-stick spray. Warm over medium-high heat. Add the mushrooms, leeks, yellow peppers, celery, and water. Cook, stirring, for 4 minutes. Remove from the heat. Stir in the bread crumbs, egg substitute, parsley, garlic, black pepper, and 1 tablespoon of the lemon juice. Mix well.

4   Divide the stuffing among the artichokes, spooning it into the center cavity and also between a few of the inner leaves.

5   Place in a single layer in an 8" x 8" baking dish. Add ¼" of water and the remaining 2 tablespoons lemon juice to the bottom of the dish. Bake for 30 minutes, or until the stuffing is hot.

Makes **4** servings.

Photograph on page 157

nutrition at a glance

per serving

0.9 g.	total fat
0.2 g.	saturated fat
132	calories
0 mg.	cholesterol
253 mg.	sodium
8.5 g.	protein
27.9 g.	carbohydrates
9.6 g.	dietary fiber

Gingered Vegetables with Bulgur

quick and easy

**This colorful entrée with crisp-cooked vegetables in a savory sauce
has plenty of variety and nutrients. Serve with Asian Coleslaw
(page 107) or a crisp salad with Ranch Dressing (page 118).**

4	teaspoons cornstarch
1	tablespoon apricot preserves
1	cup vegetable stock (page 93)
1	tablespoon low-sodium soy sauce
2	teaspoons grated fresh ginger
2	cloves garlic, minced
1	cup baby carrots, cut in quarters lengthwise
2	tablespoons chopped onions
2	cups cauliflower cut into 1" pieces
1	cup sliced button or portobello mushrooms
1	small sweet red pepper, cut into strips
1	small yellow pepper, cut into strips
8	asparagus spears, cut into 1" lengths
½	cup broccoli florets
1	cup cooked bulgur
½	cup cubed low-fat firm tofu
¼	teaspoon toasted sesame seeds

1 In a small bowl, whisk the
cornstarch and preserves to mix. Whisk in the stock,
soy sauce, ginger, and garlic. Set aside.

2 Pour ¼" water into a large
no-stick skillet. Add the carrots and onions. Cook over
medium-high heat, stirring, for 3 minutes. Add the cauliflower and mushrooms; add a little more water if the
pan is dry. Cover and cook for 2 minutes. Add the red
peppers, yellow peppers, asparagus, and broccoli; cover
and cook for 2 minutes. Pour off any excess water.

3 Add the reserved stock mix-
ture. Cook over medium-high heat, stirring constantly,
for 2 minutes, or until thickened. Stir in the bulgur.
Cook for 1 to 2 minutes, or until hot.

4 Remove from the heat.
Gently stir in the tofu. Sprinkle with the sesame seeds.

Makes **4** servings.

nutrition at a glance

per serving

0.9 g.	total fat
0.1 g.	saturated fat
143	calories
0 mg.	cholesterol
400 mg.	sodium
7.2 g.	protein
28.9 g.	carbohydrates
6.8 g.	dietary fiber

Greek Stuffed Peppers

This simple old favorite, with an updated stuffing, is colorful and a breeze to make. Briefly microwaving the peppers before stuffing cuts down on the baking time.

3	sweet red, yellow, or green peppers
2	stalks celery, finely chopped
1	medium onion, finely chopped
2	cloves garlic, minced
1	tablespoon water
1	cup cooked white or brown rice
1½	cups cooked navy beans or chick-peas, lightly mashed
1	tablespoon freshly squeezed lemon juice
1	teaspoon finely chopped fresh mint (optional)
½	teaspoon dried oregano
	Salt (optional)
	Hot-pepper sauce (optional)

1 Preheat the oven to 400°F.

2 Cut the peppers in half lengthwise. Remove and discard the stems, membranes, and seeds. Place the peppers, cut side up, on a microwaveable tray. Microwave on high power for 5 minutes.

3 Transfer the peppers to a 12" x 8" baking dish, arranging them cut side up in a single layer. Set aside.

4 Coat a medium no-stick saucepan with no-stick spray. Add the celery, onions, and garlic. Cover and cook over medium heat for 2 to 3 minutes, or until the onions start to brown. Add the water and cook, stirring, until the water evaporates.

5 Remove the saucepan from the heat. Add the rice, beans or chick-peas, lemon juice, mint (if using), and oregano. Season to taste with the salt (if using) and hot-pepper sauce (if using). Stir to combine. Spoon into the pepper cavities.

6 Cover with foil and bake for 40 to 45 minutes, or until the peppers are tender and the stuffing is hot.

Makes **6** servings.

Lynn's Kitchen Tip

Instead of throwing out those small amounts of leftover cooked grains, start saving them for stuffing. Cool your leftover cooked rice, barley, bulgur, or millet, and then spread it out in a thin layer on a small baking sheet. Freeze for about one hour, or until the grains are firm. With your fingers, crumble the grains into a freezer bag or plastic container. (The grains will stay separate and can easily be measured later without thawing.) Keep adding leftover grains, and soon you'll have a gourmet mix to stuff into peppers, tomatoes, eggplant, or zucchini.

nutrition at a glance
per serving

0.5 g.	total fat
0.1 g.	saturated fat
131	calories
0 mg.	cholesterol
121 mg.	sodium
5.6 g.	protein
26.8 g.	carbohydrates
5.3 g.	dietary fiber

Wild Mushroom Moussaka

Instead of ground lamb in this classic Greek eggplant casserole, I use a mixture of cultivated and wild mushrooms. They lighten the dish and add sophistication. You can prepare the mushroom-eggplant filling up to a day in advance. Cover tightly with plastic wrap and store in the refrigerator. Prepare the luscious fat-free cheese sauce just before baking.

Mushroom-Eggplant Filling

1	cup hot water
½	ounce dried mushrooms
1	medium eggplant
	Salt (optional)
1	large onion, chopped
3	cloves garlic, minced
1	pound button mushrooms, sliced
¼	cup red wine or nonalcoholic red wine (optional)
1	cup canned crushed tomatoes
2	tablespoons tomato paste
½	teaspoon dried oregano
⅛	teaspoon ground cinnamon
¼	cup chopped fresh parsley
1	teaspoon dried basil
	Ground black pepper
2	egg whites

Mornay Sauce

¼	cup all-purpose flour
2	cups skim milk
½	cup fat-free egg substitute
½	cup fat-free sour cream
⅓	cup fat-free Parmesan topping

1 *To make the mushroom-eggplant filling:* In a small bowl, combine the water and dried mushrooms; set aside to soak for 20 minutes. Drain through a fine sieve set over a measuring cup; set aside ½ cup of the liquid. Chop the mushrooms into small pieces and set aside. Preheat the oven to 350°F. Coat a baking sheet with no-stick spray.

2 Cut the eggplant lengthwise into ¼"-thick slices. Season lightly with the salt (if using) on both sides. Place the eggplant on the baking sheet in a single layer. Coat with no-stick spray. Bake for 10 minutes. Turn the slices and bake for 10 minutes, or until tender. Remove from the oven.

3 Coat a large no-stick skillet with no-stick spray. Warm over medium-high heat. Add the onions and garlic. Reduce the heat to medium, cover, and cook, stirring occasionally, for 2 to 3 minutes, or until golden.

4 Add the button mushrooms, the reserved chopped mushrooms, and the reserved mushroom liquid. Cover and cook over medium-high heat, stirring occasionally, for 5 minutes, or until the mushrooms are wilted.

5 Uncover and cook, stirring occasionally, for 5 to 6 minutes, or until most of the liquid evaporates. Add the wine (if using) and cook, stirring occasionally, for 5 minutes, or until most of the liquid evaporates.

6 Add the crushed tomatoes, tomato paste, oregano, and cinnamon. Cover and cook over medium-low heat for 5 minutes. Stir in the parsley, basil, and pepper to taste. Remove from the heat.

7 Place the egg whites in a medium bowl. Beat with an electric mixer until soft peaks form. Fold the egg whites into the mushroom mixture and set aside.

8 Place half of the eggplant slices in a 12" x 8" baking dish. Top with the mushroom mixture and remaining eggplant slices.

9 *To make the Mornay sauce:* Place the flour in a medium no-stick saucepan; whisk in ½ cup of the milk until smooth. Whisk in the remaining 1½ cups milk. Cook over medium heat, stirring constantly, for 5 to 6 minutes, or until thickened. Remove from the heat.

10 Whisk in the egg substitute, sour cream, and Parmesan. Pour over the eggplant. Bake for 45 to 50 minutes, or until the mixture bubbles at the sides of the pan. Remove from the oven and let stand for 5 minutes before cutting.

Makes **8** servings.

Photograph on page 158

nutrition at a glance	
per serving	
0.8 g.	total fat
0.2 g.	saturated fat
155	calories
1 mg.	cholesterol
249 mg.	sodium
10.7 g.	protein
26.9 g.	carbohydrates
4 g.	dietary fiber

Ratatouille with Saffron Custard

Ratatouille is a rustic Mediterranean vegetable stew that simmers the best of the summer garden—zucchini, eggplant, onions, and tomatoes—into a savory mélange. I've added a rich saffron-scented custard to make it even more special.

Ratatouille

1	green pepper
1	sweet red pepper
1	can (16 ounces) stewed tomatoes, chopped (with juice)
1	medium onion, chopped
4	cloves garlic, minced
1	small eggplant, cubed
1	small zucchini, cubed
1	small yellow squash, cubed
2	tablespoons dry red wine or nonalcoholic red wine (optional)
½	cup tomato sauce
1	tablespoon tomato paste
½	teaspoon dried oregano
¼	teaspoon dried rosemary, crumbled
¼	teaspoon ground black pepper
	Pinch of salt (optional)
1	tablespoon thinly sliced fresh basil
2	teaspoons chopped fresh parsley

Saffron Custard

⅛	teaspoon saffron threads
3	tablespoons hot water
1	cup fat-free ricotta cheese
½	cup fat-free egg substitute
⅓	cup fat-free Parmesan topping
¼	cup skim milk
¼	teaspoon ground black pepper

1   *To make the ratatouille:*
Line a baking sheet with foil. Cut the green pepper and red pepper in half lengthwise; discard the stems, mem-

branes, and seeds. Place the peppers, cut side down, on the baking sheet and flatten with the palm of your hand. Broil 4" from the heat for 10 to 12 minutes, or until the peppers are blackened. Remove from the oven and wrap the foil tightly around the peppers. Set aside for 10 minutes. Peel off and discard the skin. Cut into ¼" strips.

2   Pour the stewed tomatoes into a sieve placed over a medium bowl. Pour the juice from the bowl into a large no-stick skillet; reserve the tomatoes. Bring the juice to a boil over medium-high heat. Add the onions and garlic; cook for 2 minutes.

3   Add the eggplant, zucchini, squash, wine (if using), tomato sauce, tomato paste, oregano, rosemary, black pepper, salt (if using), and the reserved tomatoes. Bring to a boil.

4   Reduce the heat to medium-low and simmer, stirring occasionally, for 20 minutes. Add the roasted peppers and simmer for 10 minutes, or until all the vegetables are tender and excess liquid evaporates. Stir in the basil and parsley.

5   Coat a 12" x 8" baking dish with no-stick spray. Pour the mixture into the dish; set aside.

6   *To make the saffron custard:* Preheat the oven to 350°F.

7   Combine the saffron and water in a medium bowl. Set aside to soak for 5 minutes.

8   Whisk in the ricotta, egg substitute, Parmesan, milk, and pepper. Pour over the vegetables.

9   Bake for 40 minutes, or until lightly browned. Remove from the oven and let stand for 5 minutes before serving.

Makes **6** servings.

nutrition at a glance
per serving
0.6 g. total fat
0.1 g. saturated fat
144 calories
4 mg. cholesterol
580 mg. sodium
12.3 g. protein
23.1 g. carbohydrates
4.8 g. dietary fiber

Grain Casserole with Green Salsa

This hearty casserole is a great way to use up small amounts of rice. Or you can make it with one of the unseasoned blended-rice mixes now in the supermarkets. If you don't have tomatillos, use 2 green tomatoes. You can prepare the salsa ahead and keep it in the refrigerator for a few days.

Rice Mixture

2¼	cups vegetable stock (page 93)
¼	cup wild rice
¼	cup basmati rice
¼	cup jasmine or white rice
⅔	cup canned hominy, rinsed and drained
½	cup chopped celery
½	cup chopped carrots
1	teaspoon low-sodium soy sauce

Green Salsa

6	tomatillos
½	cup finely chopped red onions
2	serrano chili peppers, finely chopped (wear plastic gloves when handling)
2	tablespoons chopped fresh cilantro
1	clove garlic, minced
½	teaspoon white-wine vinegar
¼	teaspoon sugar
	Salt (optional)

Vegetables

1½	cups broccoli florets
1¼	cups cauliflower florets
2	large plum tomatoes, thinly sliced

1 *To make the rice mixture:* Bring the stock to a boil in a medium no-stick saucepan over medium-high heat. Add the wild rice. Reduce the heat to medium, cover, and simmer for 25 minutes. Stir in the basmati rice and jasmine or white rice; cover and simmer for 15 to 20 minutes, or until the wild rice is tender.

2 Add the hominy, celery, carrots, and soy sauce. Stir to combine.

3 Coat a 12" x 8" baking dish with no-stick spray. Spread the rice mixture evenly in the dish.

4 *To make the green salsa:* While the rice is cooking, remove and discard the papery skins from the tomatillos. Bring a medium saucepan of water to a boil over high heat. Add the tomatillos. Reduce the heat to medium. Simmer for 20 minutes, or until the tomatillo skins split. Drain and peel off the skins. Cut the flesh into quarters.

5 Place the tomatillos in a blender or food processor; process until pureed. Add the onions, peppers, cilantro, garlic, vinegar, and sugar. Pulse several times to combine. Season to taste with the salt (if using). Spoon over the grain mixture.

6 *To make the vegetables:* Preheat the oven to 350°F.

7 Bring 3 cups water to a boil in a large no-stick skillet over medium-high heat. Add the broccoli and cauliflower. Reduce the heat to medium, cover, and cook for 8 minutes, or until just tender. Drain and spread over the salsa. Top with the tomatoes. Bake for 20 minutes, or until heated through.

Makes **6** servings.

nutrition at a glance	
per serving	
0.9 g.	total fat
0.1 g.	saturated fat
144	calories
0 mg.	cholesterol
258 mg.	sodium
4.5 g.	protein
28.9 g.	carbohydrates
3.3 g.	dietary fiber

Stuffed Potatoes

Steaming hot and heaped with an irresistible creamy vegetable filling, these baked potatoes are very satisfying. Our taste testers loved them. One of these potatoes is almost a meal in itself, sided with a Tossed Antipasto Salad (page 97).

4	large russet potatoes
2	cups small broccoli florets
2	large tomatoes, diced
4	scallions, thinly sliced
2	tablespoons water
1½	cups fat-free sour cream
4	teaspoons fat-free Parmesan topping
¼	cup chopped fresh parsley

1 Preheat the oven to 350°F.

2 Wash and gently scrub the potatoes, but don't dry. Place at least 4" apart on the oven rack and bake for 1 hour, or until tender. Remove from the oven.

3 Coat a large no-stick skillet with no-stick spray. Add the broccoli, tomatoes, scallions, and water. Cook over medium-high heat, stirring occasionally, for 4 to 6 minutes, or until the broccoli is bright green and crisp-tender. Remove from the heat and stir in the sour cream.

4 Cut a 1"-deep cross in each potato. Squeeze the ends to open the cut and push up the potato flesh slightly. Spoon the filling over the potatoes. Sprinkle with the Parmesan and parsley.

Makes **4** servings.

nutrition at a glance
per serving

0.9 g.	total fat
0.2 g.	saturated fat
539	calories
0 mg.	cholesterol
155 mg.	sodium
17.3 g.	protein
117.3 g.	carbohydrates
11.7 g.	dietary fiber

Vegetable Side Dishes

You may have noticed that there are more recipes in

this chapter than in any other chapter in this

cookbook. The reason is clear: Vegetables are

essential for a healthy low-fat eating plan.

Vegetables, along with fruits, are practically

perfect foods. With a few exceptions, most are close

to fat-free in their natural state. Vegetables provide a

density of nutrients—high quantities of vitamins such

as A, C, and sometimes B, plus various minerals.

Vegetables also contain powerful substances called antioxidants, which may destroy the free radicals that can lead to cancer, heart disease, and premature aging. All vegetables contain fiber, and many are terrific sources of the complex carbohydrates that give you a nice full feeling.

Cultivating the Vegetable Habit

Vegetables add excitement to cooking and eating: vivid colors, textures from crisp to creamy, a field of flavors from sweet to sharp. Vegetable variety is exceptional.

Get into the habit of trying at least one new vegetable a week. By year's end, you'll have 52 stalwart friends that will support your good health efforts.

Cooking with Flavor, Not Fat

Most vegetables are low in fat, so you don't want to undo all of nature's good work by pouring on the fat during cooking.

The secret to sautéing leeks, onions, mushrooms, peppers, zucchini, crookneck squash, or celery without oil is to start the cooking in a covered no-stick skillet that's coated with no-stick spray. The water-filled vegetables will "sweat" their sweet juices, which caramelize on the bottom of the pan and create that wonderful browned flavor that we associate with fat-added cooking.

After the caramelization starts, uncover and continue cooking. Stir occasionally, adding just a teaspoon or two of water to prevent sticking and to loosen those tasty browned bits.

For steamed or microwaved vegetables, try these flavor enhancers.

❊ Asparagus, broccoli, broccoflower, cauliflower: Steam or microwave with citrus juice mixed with an equal amount of vegetable stock or water. Add herbs, spices, ginger, onions, or garlic.

❊ Carrots, sweet potatoes, winter squash: Steam or microwave in apricot juice or orange juice. Add a pinch of cinnamon, nutmeg, or Cajun spice blend.

❊ Greens, kale, spinach, or Swiss chard: Steam or microwave in vinegar or lemon juice combined with an equal amount of vegetable stock or water.

Peas and Leeks with Cilantro

quick and easy

Fresh cilantro and dark sesame oil add a bit of Asian intrigue to a simple dish of leeks and peas.

2   leeks, white and some green stem, sliced
1   tablespoon water
2   cups fresh or frozen peas
1   tablespoon chopped fresh cilantro
    Dark sesame oil in a spray bottle

1   Coat a large skillet with no-stick spray. Add the leeks. Cover and cook over medium-high heat, stirring occasionally, for 3 to 4 minutes, or until the leeks start to release liquid. Uncover and reduce the heat to medium. Cook, stirring occasionally, for 2 to 3 minutes, or until golden. Add a few drops of the water if the mixture starts to stick.

2   Add the peas. Cover and cook over low heat for 3 to 5 minutes, or until tender. Sprinkle with the cilantro and spray lightly with the oil. Toss to coat.

Makes **4** servings.

nutrition at a glance
per serving
0.6 g. total fat
0.1 g. saturated fat
99   calories
0 mg.   cholesterol
15 mg. sodium
4.6 g. protein
19.6 g. carbohydrates
5.3 g. dietary fiber

Sugar Snap Peas with Mint

quick and easy

This delicate fresh glaze is an easy and simple embellishment for crispy steamed sugar snaps.

1   pound sugar snap peas
1   tablespoon freshly squeezed lemon juice
1   tablespoon honey
1   tablespoon finely chopped fresh mint

1   Bring 1 cup water to a boil in a large saucepan over high heat. Add the peas; cover and cook for 2 to 3 minutes, or until the peas are bright green and crisp-tender. Drain and return to the saucepan. Add the lemon juice, honey, and mint. Stir to coat the peas.

Makes **4** servings.

nutrition at a glance

per serving

0.3 g.	total fat
0 g.	saturated fat
66	calories
0 mg.	cholesterol
8 mg.	sodium
3.9 g.	protein
12.9 g.	carbohydrates
3.4 g.	dietary fiber

Tomatoes with Herbed Crumbs

quick and easy

In the South, some cooks stew tomatoes for at least 2 hours over very low heat until they are almost syrupy. In many areas, day-old bread cubes are added just before serving. My version is quicker and retains the fresh appeal of vine-ripened tomatoes. These are excellent served over fat-free mashed potatoes.

4	medium tomatoes, cut into quarters
1	cup tomato juice
2	stalks celery, finely chopped
2	teaspoons red-wine vinegar
1½	teaspoons sugar
½	teaspoon dried oregano
	Ground black pepper
	Salt (optional)
¼	cup fresh bread crumbs (from 40-calorie-per-slice bread)
2	tablespoons chopped fresh parsley
2	tablespoons fat-free Parmesan topping

1 In a large no-stick saucepan, combine the tomatoes, tomato juice, celery, vinegar, sugar, and oregano. Bring to a boil over medium-high heat. Reduce the heat to medium and simmer for 15 to 18 minutes, or until the tomatoes are very soft. If thicker tomatoes are desired, boil for 2 to 3 minutes longer. Season to taste with the pepper and salt (if using).

2 In a small bowl, combine the bread crumbs, parsley, and Parmesan. Sprinkle over the tomatoes just before serving.

Makes **4** servings.

Lynn's Kitchen Tip:

Italian, or flat-leaf, parsley is more intensely flavored than the common curly-leaf variety, but the two types are interchangeable in cooking. Parsley is a self-seeding biennial that can easily be grown in a home garden.

nutrition at a glance

per serving
- 0.7 g. total fat
- 0.1 g. saturated fat
- 74 calories
- 0 mg. cholesterol
- 332 mg. sodium
- 3.8 g. protein
- 15.8 g. carbohydrates
- 2.6 g. dietary fiber

Florida Beets with Greens

quick and easy

Orange brings out the natural sweetness of fresh beets. Make this dish when you have beets with fresh-looking tops.

5   red beets with greens attached
1   cup freshly squeezed orange juice
2   tablespoons grated orange rind
1   clove garlic, minced
     Salt (optional)

1   Cut the leafy greens from the beet stems. Stack the leaves, roll into a cylinder, and cut into thin slices. Place the leaves in a large no-stick pot.

2   Trim the bulbs from the remaining stems; discard the stems. Scrub the beets well and trim the stem and root ends. Peel the beets, if desired. Thinly slice the beets and set aside.

3   Add the orange juice and orange rind to the pot. Cover and bring to a boil over medium-high heat. Cook for 3 to 5 minutes, or until the leaves are wilted. Remove the greens with a slotted spoon or tongs (so the liquid remains in the pot). Set the greens aside.

4   Add the beets and garlic to the pot. Cover and cook over medium heat for 10 minutes, or until the beets are crisp-tender. Season to taste with the salt (if using).

5   If necessary, microwave the greens on high power for 1 minute to reheat. Arrange the greens on a serving platter. Top with the beets. Spoon some of the cooking liquid over the beets and greens.

Makes **4** servings.

nutrition at a glance

per serving
0.3 g.   total fat
0 g.   saturated fat
74   calories
0 mg.   cholesterol
210 mg.   sodium
3.1 g.   protein
16.7 g.   carbohydrates
4.3 g.   dietary fiber

Beets with Pineapple Sauce

This beet dish is so versatile, it can be served hot or cold, as a side dish to any meat entrée, or as a salad on a bed of greens. Scrub the beets well, but don't peel them before roasting.

4	medium beets
1	teaspoon cornstarch
1	tablespoon red-wine vinegar
½	cup crushed pineapple
¼	cup pineapple juice
1	teaspoon grated fresh ginger
½	teaspoon sugar
¼	teaspoon grated orange rind

1 Preheat the oven to 375°F.

2 Individually wrap the beets in foil. Place on a baking sheet and bake for 45 minutes, or until tender when pierced with a sharp knife. Set aside until cool enough to handle.

3 Peel off the beet skins. Trim off the stem and root ends; discard. Cut each beet into 8 wedges; set aside.

4 Place the cornstarch in a medium saucepan. Add the vinegar and stir to dissolve the cornstarch. Add the pineapple, pineapple juice, ginger, sugar, and orange rind. Bring to a boil over medium heat. Cook, stirring constantly, for 1 minute, or until the mixture thickens. Add the beets and stir to coat with the sauce. Cook for 1 minute. Serve hot or cold.

Makes **4** servings.

nutrition at a glance

per serving

0.1 g.	total fat
0 g.	saturated fat
55	calories
0 mg.	cholesterol
39 mg.	sodium
1 g.	protein
13.3 g.	carbohydrates
1.1 g.	dietary fiber

Sweet-and-Spicy Carrots

quick and easy

Spicy and slightly sweet, Jamaican jerk seasoning brings carrots alive. Our tasters raved about them.

1   pound carrots, sliced
1   cup water
2   tablespoons packed brown sugar
1   teaspoon hot-pepper sauce
1   teaspoon freshly squeezed lemon juice
1   teaspoon ground cumin
2   cloves garlic, minced
½   teaspoon chili powder
     Ground black pepper
     Salt (optional)

1   In a medium no-stick saucepan, combine the carrots and water. Bring to a boil over medium-high heat. Cook, stirring occasionally, for 10 minutes, or until the carrots are tender but still firm. Drain the carrots well and transfer to a bowl.

2   Dry the saucepan and coat with no-stick spray. Add the brown sugar, hot-pepper sauce, lemon juice, cumin, garlic, and chili powder. Cook, stirring, for 2 to 3 minutes, or until the sugar bubbles and the spices are fragrant. Add the carrots. Toss or stir to coat the carrots with the sauce. Season to taste with the black pepper and salt (if using).

Makes **4** servings.

Lynn's Kitchen Tip

Store carrots, celery, asparagus, and radishes unwashed in resealable plastic bags in the refrigerator. If they get limp, rehydrate them by sprinkling a little water into the bag. Reseal and refrigerate for several hours. Pour out any excess water within 12 hours and then use the vegetables as soon as possible.

nutrition at a glance
per serving
    0.4 g. total fat
    0.1 g. saturated fat
    78   calories
    0 mg.   cholesterol
    76 mg. sodium
    1.4 g. protein
    18.7 g. carbohydrates
    2.8 g. dietary fiber

Carrots in Sour Cream

quick and easy

These rich-tasting carrots are delicious with grilled pork tenderloin, catfish, or turkey breast cutlets.

1	pound baby carrots
1	small onion or shallot, chopped
2	tablespoons water
1	tablespoon frozen apple juice concentrate
1	teaspoon Dijon mustard
⅓	cup fat-free sour cream or fat-free plain yogurt
1	tablespoon chopped fresh parsley

1 Place the carrots in a steamer basket. Steam over boiling water in a covered saucepan for 10 minutes, or until crisp-tender.

2 In a large no-stick skillet, combine the onions or shallots, water, and apple juice concentrate. Cover and bring to a boil over medium-high heat. Reduce the heat to medium and cook for 2 to 3 minutes. Add the carrots and mustard. Toss over medium-high heat for 1 to 2 minutes, if necessary, to evaporate excess liquid.

3 Remove from the heat. Add the sour cream or yogurt and toss to coat. Sprinkle with the parsley.

Makes **4** servings.

nutrition at a glance

per serving

0.8 g.	total fat
0.1 g.	saturated fat
82	calories
0 mg.	cholesterol
87 mg.	sodium
2.5 g.	protein
16.9 g.	carbohydrates
3.9 g.	dietary fiber

Easy Seasonings
for Cooked Vegetables

Bottled condiments, herbs, spices, and fat-free dairy products offer a wealth of effortless enhancements for simply cooked vegetables. For times when you want to up the flavor ante from a spritz of butter-flavored spray and a squeeze of lemon juice, cash in with these easy seasonings.

Asparagus, Broccoli, and Cauliflower

* Drizzle with lemon juice or balsamic vinegar. Top with a swirl of fat-free Cheddar topping from a squeeze bottle or a sprinkling of fat-free Parmesan topping.
* Sprinkle with toasted herbed bread crumbs and ground black pepper.
* Drizzle with a spoonful of honey mustard.

Green Beans

* Sprinkle with diced raw sweet red peppers or diced bottled roasted peppers and a few drops of hot-pepper sauce.
* Toss with soy sauce or Worcestershire sauce and a smidgen of minced garlic or garlic salt.
* Toss with mirin (sweet rice wine), a pinch of brown sugar, and hot-pepper flakes.
* Toss with chopped fresh savory, chopped scallions, diced tomatoes, and lemon juice or lime juice.

Beets

* Toss with lime juice and chopped fresh cilantro.
* Mix cider vinegar, sugar, and a small amount of cornstarch. Toss with the beets in a saucepan over low heat to thicken.

❋ Toss with lemon juice, brown sugar, a pinch of ground ginger, and a pinch of dry mustard.

❋ Mix orange juice and grated orange rind with a small amount of cornstarch. Toss with the beets in a saucepan over low heat to thicken.

❋ Drizzle with cider vinegar and add a dollop of fat-free sour cream, yogurt, or yogurt cheese. Toss to coat. Sprinkle with chopped fresh dill.

Leafy Greens

❋ Drizzle with cider vinegar, balsamic vinegar, or lemon juice and diced fat-free ham.

❋ Toss with a spoonful of salsa and fat-free sour cream.

Carrots

❋ Toss with finely chopped fresh mint and honey.

❋ Drizzle with soy sauce and a sprinkle of ground ginger or chopped pickled ginger.

❋ Sprinkle lightly with brown sugar and a dollop of fat-free yogurt, yogurt cheese, or sour cream. Toss to combine.

❋ Toss with toasted bread crumbs and a pinch of ground cumin.

Green or Sweet Red Peppers

❋ Sprinkle with capers.

❋ Drizzle red-wine vinegar and a sprinkling of fresh basil or dried oregano over roasted peppers.

❋ Sprinkle fat-free Parmesan topping over baked, grilled, or roasted pepper strips.

Baked Citrus Carrots

Either chopped flat-leaf parsley or cilantro is a tasty addition to these sunny carrots.

1   pound carrots, cut into 3"-long sticks
2   tablespoons chopped fresh chives or scallions
2   tablespoons freshly squeezed lemon juice
2   tablespoons freshly squeezed orange juice
½   teaspoon grated orange rind
2   tablespoons fresh bread crumbs (from 40-calorie-per-slice bread), optional

1   Preheat the oven to 350°F.

2   In an 8" x 8" baking dish, combine the carrots, chives or scallions, lemon juice, orange juice, and orange rind. Cover with foil and bake for 45 minutes, or until tender.

3   Remove the foil. Sprinkle with the bread crumbs (if using). Coat with no-stick spray. Broil 4" from the heat for 1 to 2 minutes, or until the crumbs are golden.

Makes **4** servings.

nutrition at a glance

per serving
0.2 g.   total fat
0 g.   saturated fat
53   calories
0 mg.   cholesterol
69 mg.   sodium
1.3 g.   protein
12.5 g.   carbohydrates
2.7 g.   dietary fiber

Bayou Green Beans

quick and easy

Our testers loved these spicy, bright green beans studded with nubbins of sautéed garlic. I leave the beans whole, but you can cut them in smaller pieces if you like.

1   medium onion, finely chopped
4   cloves garlic, minced
1   teaspoon Cajun spice blend
1   pound green beans
2   tablespoons water
    Dash of liquid smoke

1   Coat a large no-stick skillet with no-stick spray. Add the onions, garlic, and Cajun spice blend. Cover and cook over medium-high heat, stirring often, for 3 to 4 minutes, or until the onions are golden.

2   Add the beans, water, and liquid smoke. Cover and cook for 6 to 7 minutes, or until the beans are crisp-tender.

Makes **4** servings.

nutrition at a glance
per serving
0.4 g.   total fat
0.1 g.   saturated fat
55   calories
0 mg.   cholesterol
49 mg.   sodium
2.6 g.   protein
12.3 g.   carbohydrates
3.9 g.   dietary fiber

Green Beans and Mushrooms

quick and easy

This is a simple dish with gentle flavors. It is just right with comfort foods such as baked or mashed potatoes topped with fat-free gravy. A modest serving of fish, turkey, or chicken breast will complete the homey meal.

1   small onion, finely chopped
4   tablespoons water
8   ounces large button mushrooms, sliced
2   cups defatted chicken stock (page 94)
1   pound green beans
2   tablespoons cornstarch
    Ground black pepper
    Salt (optional)

1 Coat a large no-stick saucepan with no-stick spray. Add the onions and 2 tablespoons of the water. Cook over medium heat, stirring, for 4 minutes, or until the onions are translucent. Add the mushrooms. Cook for 4 minutes, or until the mushrooms are cooked through.

2 Add the stock and bring to a boil. Simmer for 10 minutes to reduce the stock. Add the beans; cover and cook for 5 minutes, or until the beans are crisp-tender.

3 Place the cornstarch in a cup. Add the remaining 2 tablespoons water and stir to dissolve the cornstarch. Add to the saucepan. Cook, stirring constantly, for 2 to 3 minutes, or until thickened. Season to taste with the pepper and salt (if using).

Makes **4** servings.

nutrition at a glance
per serving
0.6 g. total fat
0.1 g. saturated fat
78   calories
0 mg. cholesterol
15 mg. sodium
3.4 g. protein
17.6 g. carbohydrates
5 g. dietary fiber

Creamed Pearl Onions

quick and **easy**

Creamed-onion lovers, take heart. This is the flavorful fat-free recipe that you've been waiting for. If pearl onions are not available, this recipe is also delicious with coarsely chopped onions, shallots, or leeks.

1   pound pearl onions or 1 package (16 ounces) frozen pearl onions
1   cup water
2   tablespoons dry sherry or 1 teaspoon sherry extract
3   tablespoons all-purpose flour
2   cups fat-free liquid creamer or evaporated skim milk
¼   teaspoon ground black pepper
    Pinch of ground nutmeg
    Pinch of salt (optional)
1   tablespoon chopped fresh parsley
    Paprika

1   In a medium no-stick saucepan, combine the onions, water, and sherry or sherry extract. Cover and bring to a boil over medium-high heat. Reduce the heat to medium and cook for 10 minutes, or until the onions are tender. Drain. If using fresh onions, peel them. Set aside.

2   Wipe the saucepan dry. Add the flour. Gradually whisk in the creamer or evaporated milk to make a smooth mixture. Add the pepper, nutmeg, and salt (if using). Cook over medium-high heat, whisking constantly, for 3 minutes, or until the mixture thickens.

3   Add the onions and cook for 1 minute to reheat them. Sprinkle with the parsley and paprika just before serving.

Makes **4** servings.

Photograph on page 243

nutrition at a glance

per serving

0.3 g.	total fat
0 g.	saturated fat
161	calories
0 mg.	cholesterol
266 mg.	sodium
2.2 g.	protein
32.5 g.	carbohydrates
2 g.	dietary fiber

Dilled Squash with Mushrooms

Baking accents the natural sweetness of this delicate summer squash. Fresh dill is essential for the flavor of this dish.

1	pound crookneck squash, cut into thin diagonal slices
4	ounces button mushrooms, sliced
1	large onion, sliced
1	orange or yellow pepper, sliced
¼	cup chopped fresh dill
2	tablespoons chopped fresh chives
1	large clove garlic, minced
¼	teaspoon ground black pepper
	Pinch of salt (optional)
½	cup fat-free Parmesan topping

1   Preheat the oven to 350°F. Coat a 12" x 8" baking dish with no-stick spray.

2   In a large bowl, combine the squash, mushrooms, onions, sliced peppers, dill, chives, garlic, black pepper, and salt (if using). Toss to mix. Spread evenly in the prepared dish. Sprinkle with the Parmesan.

3   Cover with foil. Bake for 25 to 30 minutes, or until the squash is tender.

Makes **6** servings.

Lynn's Fat-Free Flavor

Chives are a mild member of the onion family. Both their slender stems and their springtime lavender blossoms are edible. Chives grow easily in window gardens as well as outdoors. Chop or snip chives for cooking or for use in salads. A crisscross of long chive stems makes an elegant garnish on rice, vegetables, chicken, or fish.

nutrition at a glance

per serving
0.4 g.	total fat
0.1 g.	saturated fat
61	calories
0 mg.	cholesterol
132 mg.	sodium
5.4 g.	protein
10.8 g.	carbohydrates
1.8 g.	dietary fiber

Sweet-and-Sharp Spaghetti Squash

quick and easy

Here's a simple, savory way to prepare spaghetti squash. If you like a slightly less tangy mustard flavor, use a combination of fat-free mayonnaise and Dijon mustard.

1	spaghetti squash
½	cup diced plum tomatoes
¼	cup currants or raisins
2	teaspoons Dijon mustard
2	teaspoons dry sherry or ½ teaspoon sherry extract
1	tablespoon water
1	teaspoon white-wine vinegar
1	teaspoon chopped fresh thyme
½	teaspoon sugar

1 Microwave the squash on high power for 2 minutes to make cutting easier. Cut the squash in half lengthwise. Wrap each half in wax paper. Microwave each half on high power for 5 to 5½ minutes. Let stand for 3 minutes. Scoop out and discard the seeds and attached stringy membranes.

2 With a fork, pull out the strands of squash and place in a large no-stick skillet. Add the tomatoes, currants or raisins, mustard, sherry or sherry extract, water, vinegar, thyme, and sugar. Toss to combine.

3 Cook over medium heat, tossing frequently, for 3 to 4 minutes, or until hot.

Makes **4** servings.

Lynn's Fat-Free Flavor

Although the pulp of spaghetti squash resembles the pasta for which it's named, it has a mild flavor that can easily be overpowered by tomato-based sauces. It is best simply spritzed with butter-flavored spray and a sprinkling of salt and ground black pepper. For a dressier treatment, toss with a simple white sauce (page 294) flavored with dill.

---

nutrition at a glance

per serving

0.9 g.	total fat
0.1 g.	saturated fat
98	calories
0 mg.	cholesterol
103 mg.	sodium
2 g.	protein
21.9 g.	carbohydrates
3.9 g.	dietary fiber

Summer Succotash

Fresh flavors shine through in this traditional American dish. Diced summer squash or zucchini can also be added.

¾   cup defatted chicken stock (page 94)
1   large onion, chopped
1   green pepper, chopped
1   medium potato, diced
1   large clove garlic, minced
10   ounces fresh lima beans or 1 package (10 ounces) frozen baby lima beans, thawed
½   cup fresh whole-kernel corn or thawed frozen whole-kernel corn
1   small tomato, diced
2   tablespoons chopped fresh dill
2   tablespoons chopped fresh parsley
     Ground black pepper
     Salt (optional)

1   Coat a large no-stick saucepan with no-stick spray. Add the stock, onions, peppers, potatoes, and garlic. Cook over medium-high heat, stirring occasionally, for 10 minutes.

2   Reduce the heat to medium. Add the beans; cover and cook for 5 minutes. Add the corn; cover and cook for 5 minutes. Add the tomatoes; cook, stirring, for 5 minutes. Stir in the dill and parsley. Season to taste with the pepper and salt (if using).

Makes **6** servings.

Lynn's Kitchen Tip

Corn, potatoes, and onions all contain natural starches that thicken with cooking, making a tasty natural sauce. Cook for at least 15 minutes to release the starches. You can add several tablespoons of liquid, such as defatted chicken stock, vegetable stock, or water, to increase the saucing property of these vegetables.

nutrition at a glance

per serving

0.8 g.	total fat
0.1 g.	saturated fat
107	calories
0 mg.	cholesterol
23 mg.	sodium
5 g.	protein
21.5 g.	carbohydrates
4.2 g.	dietary fiber

Asian Vegetable Stir-Fry

quick and easy

The secret to good stir-fries is to cut all your vegetables before you begin cooking. For this recipe, feel free to vary the vegetables. Try bok choy, cabbage, green beans, asparagus, or thinly sliced sweet potatoes. To heat things up, add crushed red-pepper flakes. Garnish with chopped scallions or sprouts.

1	tablespoon cornstarch
½	cup vegetable stock (page 93)
	Dark sesame oil in a spray bottle
2	large carrots, cut into thin diagonal slices
2–3	cloves garlic, minced
2	teaspoons grated fresh ginger
2	teaspoons low-sodium soy sauce
5	scallions, cut into 1" diagonal slices
1	can (6 ounces) sliced water chestnuts or bamboo shoots, drained
2	teaspoons dry sherry or ½ teaspoon sherry extract
6	ounces snow peas
½	teaspoon sugar
½	teaspoon sesame seeds or crushed red-pepper flakes (optional)

1 Place the cornstarch in a cup. Add ¼ cup of the stock and stir to dissolve the cornstarch. Set aside.

2 Coat a large no-stick skillet or wok with a spritz of the oil. Add the carrots, garlic, ginger, 1 teaspoon of the soy sauce and 2 tablespoons of the remaining stock. Cook over medium-high heat, stirring, for 2 minutes.

3 Add the scallions, water chestnuts or bamboo shoots, sherry or sherry extract, and the remaining 2 tablespoons stock. Cook, stirring and tossing, for 2 minutes.

4 Add the snow peas, sugar, the remaining 1 teaspoon soy sauce, and the cornstarch mixture. Cook, tossing, for 1 minute, or until thickened. Spoon onto 4 dinner plates. Sprinkle with the sesame seeds or red-pepper flakes (if using).

Makes **4** servings.

nutrition at a glance
per serving
0.7 g.	total fat
0.1 g.	saturated fat
72	calories
0 mg.	cholesterol
128 mg.	sodium
2.4 g.	protein
14.7 g.	carbohydrates
3.6 g.	dietary fiber

Scalloped Potatoes and Fennel

The buttery-rich flavor of yellow-fleshed potatoes is seductive. Look for this wonderful variety, which is sold under a number of names, including Yukon Gold and Finnish Yellow. The gentle flavor of fresh fennel beautifully complements the potatoes.

3	large yellow-fleshed potatoes, very thinly sliced
1	medium leek, white and some green stem, thinly sliced
1½	cups thinly sliced fennel
4	tablespoons all-purpose flour
	Ground black pepper
	Salt (optional)
1½	cups vegetable stock (page 93)
¼	cup fat-free Parmesan topping
	Paprika

1 Coat a 10" glass pie plate with no-stick spray. Add half of the potatoes in an even layer. Top with half of the leeks and half of the fennel. Sprinkle with 2 tablespoons of the flour and a dusting of pepper and salt (if using). Repeat to use the remaining vegetables, flour, pepper and salt.

2 Pour the stock into the pie plate. Cover tightly with plastic wrap; slit the wrap twice with a sharp knife. Microwave on high power for a total of 12 to 15 minutes; rotate the pie plate after 6 minutes.

3 Carefully remove the plastic and discard. Sprinkle the top of the mixture with the Parmesan and paprika.

4 Preheat the oven to 425°F.

5 Bake for 30 to 35 minutes, or until the top is browned. Remove and let stand for 5 minutes before cutting into wedges.

Makes **8** servings.

Photograph on page 244

---

nutrition at a glance

per serving

0.2 g.	total fat
0 g.	saturated fat
115	calories
0 mg.	cholesterol
70 mg.	sodium
4.1 g.	protein
25.1 g.	carbohydrates
2.9 g.	dietary fiber

10 Terrific Toppers for Baked Potatoes

A russet potato, baked in its skin, is a good source of potassium and fiber, yet it contains only a trace amount of fat. For an easy satisfying meal, cut open a baked spud and spoon on one of these tasty accompaniments.

* Fat-free sour cream or fat-free ricotta mixed with chopped fresh chives, parsley, tarragon, basil, or dill, herbes de Provence, Cajun spice blend, or ground black pepper
* Barbecue sauce, fat-free sour cream, and finely chopped scallions
* Julienned fat-free ham and shredded fat-free Cheddar cheese. Broil briefly to melt the cheese.
* Curried Vegetable-Turkey Sauce (page 289)
* Fat-free Chicken Gravy (page 293) or fat-free commercial gravy with fat-free sautéed mushrooms
* Salsa (heated in the microwave, if desired), fat-free plain yogurt, and chopped fresh cilantro
* Lightly steamed corn kernels, chopped onions, chopped carrots, and chopped sweet red peppers mixed in Basic White Sauce (page 294)
* Steamed broccoli florets topped with fat-free marinara sauce or fat-free Cheddar topping from a squeeze bottle
* Fiesta Chili (page 186) or canned fat-free chili
* Sauerkraut (rinsed, drained, and heated)

Potato-Carrot Mash

quick and **easy**

Dietitian Chris Louden told me of this recipe, which is pure comfort food. Sprinkle with chopped parsley and a whisper of ground nutmeg for a garnish.

4   medium russet potatoes, peeled and diced
3   cups diced carrots
1   teaspoon salt (optional)
1   cup fat-free liquid creamer
     Ground black pepper

1   In a medium saucepan, combine the potatoes, carrots, and enough cold water to cover them. Add the salt (if using). Bring to a boil over medium-high heat. Reduce the heat to medium and cook at a brisk simmer for 25 minutes, or until the carrots are tender.

2   Drain the potatoes and carrots and return to the saucepan. Mash with a potato masher, leaving some small lumps of carrots visible.

3   In a small saucepan over medium heat, warm the creamer. Add to the vegetables and stir to combine. Season to taste with the pepper.

Makes **4** servings.

Lynn's Fat-Free Flavor

Making luscious fat-free mashed potatoes is easy. Start with baked russets (my preference) or boiled red or white potatoes; peel. (For a mellow, nutty accent, add a few peeled garlic cloves to the potatoes as they cook. Mash the garlic along with the potatoes.) Mash with a potato masher or press the potatoes through a ricer or food mill. Stir in a few tablespoons skim milk, fat-free creamer, buttermilk, fat-free ricotta, fat-free sour cream, or plain yogurt. You can add chopped fresh chives, dill, tarragon, or basil.

nutrition at a glance

per serving
0.9 g.   total fat
0.2 g.   saturated fat
160   calories
0 mg.   cholesterol
134 mg.   sodium
1.9 g.   protein
35.8 g.   carbohydrates
5.6 g.   dietary fiber

Western Fries

Use the best chili powder for these potatoes because the seasoning is important. I often add wedges of scrubbed unpeeled sweet potatoes and yuca, a root vegetable available in Hispanic food stores and many large supermarkets.

3	very large russet potatoes
¼	teaspoon sugar
	Salt (optional)
2–3	teaspoons chili powder
1	teaspoon Cajun spice blend (optional)

1 Preheat the oven to 400°F. Cover a large baking sheet with foil.

2 Slice the potatoes lengthwise into eighths. Pat dry with paper towels. Place on the baking sheet. Coat all sides of the potatoes with no-stick spray. Sprinkle evenly with the sugar and a little salt (if using). Sprinkle with the chili powder and Cajun spice blend (if using). Use your fingers to coat the potatoes evenly.

3 Place the potatoes in the oven. Lower the heat to 350°F and bake for 30 to 40 minutes, or until the potatoes are crisp on the outside and tender when pierced with a sharp knife.

Makes **4** servings.

Photograph on page 247

Lynn's Kitchen Tip

Slicing potatoes into wedges is safe and easy when you keep your potato steady and your knife pointed toward the cutting board. Here's how: Place the potato, flattest side down, on a cutting board. With your non-cutting hand, hold the potato steady with your fingertips tucked toward the palm of your hand. Cut the potato in half lengthwise. Position both halves, cut side down; cut each in half lengthwise. You now have quarters. Position each quarter, skin side down, and cut in half to make 2 wedges. You will have 8 long wedges from each potato.

---

nutrition at a glance

per serving

0.5 g.	total fat
0.1 g.	saturated fat
208	calories
0 mg.	cholesterol
34 mg.	sodium
4.5 g.	protein
47.7 g.	carbohydrates
5 g.	dietary fiber

Sweet-and-Sour Red Cabbage

quick and easy

This dish keeps well and is especially good after the sauce has permeated the cabbage. In cold weather, it's nice to have some on hand in the refrigerator to reheat as a topper for baked or boiled potatoes.

½   medium head red cabbage, thinly sliced
2   tart apples, chopped or shredded
1   small onion, chopped
¼   cup packed brown sugar
2   tablespoons apple-cider vinegar
2   tablespoons freshly squeezed lemon juice
½   teaspoon grated lemon rind (optional)
     Pinch of salt (optional)
1   tablespoon cornstarch
2   tablespoons water

1   In a large no-stick saucepan, combine the cabbage, apples, onions, brown sugar, vinegar, lemon juice, lemon rind (if using), and salt (if using). Cover and cook over low heat, stirring occasionally, for 15 minutes, or until the cabbage is tender.

2   Place the cornstarch in a cup. Add the water and stir to dissolve the cornstarch. Stir into the saucepan.

3   Increase the heat to medium. Cook, stirring constantly, for 2 minutes, or until thickened.

Makes **6** servings.

Lynn's Lore

It is reported that the Greek philosopher Diogenes said to a young courtier, "If you lived on cabbage, you would not be obliged to flatter the powerful." The young man retorted, "If you flattered the powerful, you would not be obliged to live on cabbage."

nutrition at a glance
per serving
0.3 g. total fat
0.1 g. saturated fat
88 calories
0 mg. cholesterol
10 mg. sodium
1 g. protein
22.3 g. carbohydrates
3 g. dietary fiber

Creamed Kale

quick and easy

Creamed spinach has been a favorite for decades. I've updated it with super-nutritious curly-leafed kale. (Of course, you can also make this dish with spinach, if you prefer.) Serve it as a side dish, a stuffing for baked potatoes or tomatoes, or as a bed for poached fish. It can even be chilled and pureed for a dip.

2	small cloves garlic, minced
2	tablespoons all-purpose flour
1½	cups skim milk
6	tablespoons fat-free sour cream
2	tablespoons low-fat sour cream
¼	cup fat-free Parmesan topping
	Dash of ground nutmeg
	Salt (optional)
1	cup water
1¼	pounds kale, stems removed, coarsely chopped
	Ground black pepper

1　Place the garlic in a large no-stick skillet. Coat with no-stick spray. Sauté over medium heat, stirring occasionally, for 1 to 2 minutes, or until the garlic is golden. Add the flour. Slowly whisk in the milk to form a smooth mixture.

2　Cook over medium heat, stirring constantly, for 4 minutes, or until thickened. Stir in the fat-free sour cream, low-fat sour cream, Parmesan, and nutmeg. Season to taste with the salt (if using). Turn off the heat.

3　Meanwhile, place the water in a large no-stick pot. Bring to a boil over high heat. Add the kale. Cover and cook over medium-high heat for 7 to 9 minutes, or until the kale is crisp-tender. Drain and add to the cream sauce. Stir to combine. Cook over low heat for 1 to 2 minutes to reheat the sauce. Season to taste with the pepper.

Makes **4** servings.

nutrition at a glance

per serving

0.9 g.	total fat
0.4 g.	saturated fat
100	calories
3 mg.	cholesterol
136 mg.	sodium
7.4 g.	protein
16.2 g.	carbohydrates
2.1 g.	dietary fiber

Greek-Style Cauliflower

quick and easy

Tender cauliflower takes to this zesty tomato sauce sparked with cinnamon, a signature spice in Greek cuisine. Garnish with some crumbled low-fat feta cheese if you like.

½	large onion, chopped
2	cloves garlic, minced
1	teaspoon dried oregano
½	teaspoon crushed fennel seeds
¼	teaspoon ground cinnamon
1	medium head cauliflower, broken into florets
½	cup tomato sauce
1	tablespoon freshly squeezed lemon juice
	Ground black pepper
	Salt (optional)
¼	teaspoon crushed red-pepper flakes (optional)

1 Coat a large no-stick skillet with no-stick spray. Add the onions, garlic, oregano, fennel seeds, and cinnamon. Cover and cook over medium-high heat for 3 to 4 minutes, or until the onions are golden. If necessary, add 1 to 2 teaspoons water to prevent sticking.

2 Add the cauliflower, tomato sauce, and lemon juice. Season with the black pepper and salt (if using). Bring the mixture to a boil. Cover and reduce the heat to medium. Cook for 8 minutes, or until the cauliflower is tender. Sprinkle with the red-pepper flakes (if using).

Makes **4** servings.

nutrition at a glance
per serving
- 0.6 g. total fat
- 0.2 g. saturated fat
- 39 calories
- 1 mg. cholesterol
- 212 mg. sodium
- 2.2 g. protein
- 7.7 g. carbohydrates
- 2 g. dietary fiber

Cauliflower Puree with Garlic

quick and easy

If you keep pureed Roasted Garlic (page 304) on hand in the refrigerator or freezer, you can make this earthy cauliflower dish in minutes. For a variation, pour the puree into a baking dish, dust with fat-free Parmesan topping, and broil until the topping is golden.

1½ cups vegetable stock (page 93)
1   medium head cauliflower, broken into florets
½   cup chopped onions
2   tablespoons pureed Roasted Garlic (page 304)
    Ground black pepper
    Salt (optional)
1   tablespoon thinly sliced fresh basil

1 In a large no-stick saucepan over medium-high heat, bring the stock to a boil. Add the cauliflower and onions. Reduce the heat to medium, cover, and simmer for 20 minutes, or until the vegetables are very tender. Drain in a colander (if desired, save the stock for soup or other uses).

2 Place the vegetables in a blender or food processor. Add the garlic. Season with the pepper and salt (if using). Puree until smooth. Stir in the basil. If desired, return to the saucepan to reheat gently for 2 to 3 minutes.

Makes **4** servings.

nutrition at a glance

per serving

0.8 g.	total fat
0.1 g.	saturated fat
59	calories
0 mg.	cholesterol
27 mg.	sodium
3.7 g.	protein
11.6 g.	carbohydrates
3.2 g.	dietary fiber

Hungarian Broccoli and Mushrooms

quick and easy

The broccoli is cooked al dente, making the color a glorious bright green. If you prefer it more tender, simply cook it a little longer.

1	pound broccoli
8	ounces button mushrooms, sliced
½	cup finely chopped shallots
1½	tablespoons all-purpose flour
1	teaspoon paprika
1½	cups vegetable stock (page 93)
	Ground black pepper
	Ground red pepper
	Salt (optional)

1 Cut the florets from the broccoli stems. Peel the stems, then cut into ¼"-thick rounds.

2 In a large no-stick saucepan over high heat, bring 1 cup water to a boil. Add the broccoli stems; cover and cook for 2 minutes. Add the florets. Cover and cook for 3 to 4 minutes, or until crisp-tender. Drain and set aside.

3 Dry the saucepan. Coat it with no-stick spray. Add the mushrooms and shallots. Cover and cook over medium-high heat for 3 to 4 minutes, or until the mushrooms release some liquid. Uncover and reduce the heat to medium. Cook, stirring, for 2 to 3 minutes, or until the mushrooms are lightly browned. Remove the mixture from the pan. Set aside.

4 Off heat, place the flour and paprika in the saucepan. Gradually whisk in ¼ cup of the stock to form a smooth paste. Whisk in the remaining 1¼ cups stock. Cook over medium-high heat, whisking constantly, for 3 to 4 minutes, or until thick.

5 Add the mushroom mixture and the reserved broccoli; cook for 2 minutes, or until heated through. Season to taste with the black pepper, red pepper, and salt (if using).

Makes **4** servings.

nutrition at a glance

per serving

0.7 g.	total fat
0.1 g.	saturated fat
70	calories
0 mg.	cholesterol
41 mg.	sodium
5.2 g.	protein
14 g.	carbohydrates
5 g.	dietary fiber

Sicilian Broccoli

quick and **easy**

Sweet raisins play beautifully off the sharp, earthy flavor of broccoli. This is an attractive dish to serve, and it's simple to make. It even tastes great the next day as a salad.

1 pound broccoli
2 plum tomatoes, chopped
4 cloves garlic, minced
2 tablespoons raisins
2 tablespoons thinly sliced fresh basil
   Salt (optional)
2 tablespoons chopped toasted pine nuts (optional)

1 Cut the florets from the broccoli stems. Peel the stems, then cut into ¼"-thick rounds.

2 Bring 1 cup water to a boil in a large no-stick saucepan over high heat. Add the broccoli stems; cover and cook for 2 minutes. Add the florets. Cover and cook for 3 to 4 minutes, or until crisp-tender. Drain and set aside.

3 In the same saucepan, combine the tomatoes, garlic, and raisins. Cook over medium heat, stirring frequently, for 4 to 5 minutes, or until the tomatoes soften. Add the basil and the broccoli. Cook, stirring, for 1 to 2 minutes, or until the broccoli is heated through. Season to taste with the salt (if using). Sprinkle with the pine nuts (if using).

Makes **4** servings.

Photograph on page 248

Photograph on page 248

Lynn's Kitchen Tip

Cooking broccoli can be problematic, because the tender florets often overcook before the stem is tender. But both parts can cook in almost the same time with this method: Cut off the florets where they join the stem; separate them into equal-size florets. Slice the stem into ¼"-thick rounds. Cook the stem pieces by blanching, stir-frying, or steaming for 2 minutes. Add the florets and continue cooking for 3 to 4 minutes, or until the stems are crisp-tender.

---

nutrition at a glance

per serving

0.5 g.	total fat
0.1 g.	saturated fat
55	calories
0 mg.	cholesterol
32 mg.	sodium
3.8 g.	protein
11.5 g.	carbohydrates
3.8 g.	dietary fiber

Mediterranean Vegetables

quick and easy

This lemony Mediterranean mélange is particularly good with grilled fish. Serve it topped with fat-free plain yogurt.

1	onion, chopped
2	large cloves garlic, minced
1	teaspoon ground cumin
1	teaspoon dried oregano
1	small plum tomato, diced
½	cup cooked chick-peas
8	ounces spinach leaves, thinly sliced
¼	cup diced jarred roasted red peppers or pimentos
2	tablespoons freshly squeezed lemon juice
	Salt (optional)
	Crushed red-pepper flakes (optional)

1 In a large no-stick saucepan, combine the onions, garlic, cumin, and oregano. Cover and cook over medium-low heat, stirring occasionally, for 5 minutes, or until the onions are golden. If necessary, add 1 to 2 teaspoons water to prevent sticking.

2 Stir in the tomatoes and chick-peas. Cook for 2 to 3 minutes, or until the tomatoes soften.

3 Add the spinach, roasted peppers or pimentos, and lemon juice. Cook over medium-high heat, stirring constantly, for 1 minute, or until the spinach wilts and excess moisture evaporates. Season to taste with the salt (if using) and red-pepper flakes (if using.)

Makes **4** servings.

Lynn's Fat-Free Flavor

Few condiments bring out the natural flavors of foods as well as fresh lemon juice and grated lemon rind. Choose bright yellow fruit that's unblemished, firm, and heavy for its size (a sign of juiciness). Store fresh lemons in a plastic bag in the refrigerator vegetable crisper for up to two weeks. Scrub lemons just before using if you're grating the rind.

nutrition at a glance

per serving

0.9 g.	total fat
0.1 g.	saturated fat
68	calories
0 mg.	cholesterol
92 mg.	sodium
4 g.	protein
12.8 g.	carbohydrates
2.9 g.	dietary fiber

Orange-Kissed Turnip Custards

It's fun to give the lowly turnip the Cinderella treatment with these elegant individual baked custards. They make a special side dish for Thanksgiving or Christmas dinner.

1   can (6 ounces) mandarin oranges
1½   cups vegetable stock (page 93)
1   teaspoon low-sodium soy sauce
1   teaspoon packed brown sugar
¼   teaspoon minced fresh ginger
2   cups sliced turnips
¾   cup fat-free egg substitute
½   cup evaporated skim milk
     Ground black pepper

1   Coat four ¾-cup ovenproof custard cups with no-stick spray.

2   Drain the oranges, reserving ½ cup of the juice. Place the juice in a medium no-stick saucepan. Set the oranges aside.

3   To the saucepan with the juice, add the stock, soy sauce, brown sugar, and ginger. Bring to a boil over medium-high heat. Add the turnips. Cover, reduce the heat to medium, and simmer for 15 minutes, or until tender. Drain well.

4   Preheat the oven to 350°F.

5   Place the turnip mixture in a blender or food processor. Puree until smooth. Add the egg substitute and milk. Process just to combine. Season to taste with the pepper.

6   Spoon into the prepared custard cups, tapping each one lightly. Smooth the tops and place in an 8" x 8" baking dish. Add hot water so that it comes halfway up the sides of the custard cups. Bake for 20 minutes, or until a knife inserted in the center comes out clean.

7   Carefully remove the baking dish from the oven. Gently remove the cups from the water. Garnish with the reserved oranges.

Makes **4** servings.

Photograph on page 245

Photograph on page 245

Lynn's Kitchen Tip

These custards are especially nice when unmolded. Run a knife around the inside of each cup. Place on a hot pad on a heatproof surface to cool for 3 minutes. Set a small plate atop each cup. Hold the cup to the plate tightly and invert both. Tap the custard cup and plate on a towel-lined counter, then gently lift off the custard cup.

nutrition at a glance
per serving
0.1 g. total fat
0.1 g. saturated fat
85 calories
1 mg. cholesterol
220 mg. sodium
8 g. protein
14 g. carbohydrates
1.6 g. dietary fiber

Sweet Potato Pudding

This luscious Louisiana pudding is hard to resist. I like to make it with dark-fleshed garnet sweet potatoes whenever I find them in the market. You can omit the ginger, but it does give the pudding a special flavor boost.

2	medium sweet potatoes
1	cup fat-free liquid creamer
¼	cup fat-free egg substitute
2	tablespoons packed brown sugar
1	tablespoon minced candied ginger (optional)
1	teaspoon grated lemon rind
1	teaspoon ground cinnamon
¼	teaspoon ground nutmeg
¼	teaspoon ground black pepper
	Pinch of ground allspice
	Pinch of salt (optional)
2	egg whites

1   Preheat the oven to 350°F. Coat a 1-quart baking dish with no-stick spray.

2   Pierce the sweet potatoes several times with a fork. Microwave on high power, rotating once, for 7 to 10 minutes, or until soft. (The sweet potatoes can also be baked directly on the oven rack at 400°F for 1 hour, or until soft.) Set aside to cool slightly.

3   Peel the sweet potatoes and press through a ricer or fine sieve into a medium bowl. Add the creamer, egg substitute, brown sugar, ginger (if using), lemon rind, cinnamon, nutmeg, pepper, allspice, and salt (if using). Stir to combine.

4   Place the egg whites in a medium bowl. Beat with an electric mixer until stiff peaks form. Fold into the sweet potato mixture.

5   Pour into the prepared baking dish. Cover with foil and bake for 45 minutes. Remove the foil and bake for 15 minutes, or until a knife inserted in the center comes out clean. Serve hot or cold.

Makes **4** servings.

Lynn's Fat-Free Flavor

Candied ginger is fresh ginger that has been poached in sugar syrup and coated in coarse sugar. The process tames ginger's heat, making it a wonderful addition to both savory and sweet dishes. It's expensive in supermarkets but can often be purchased much cheaper in bulk-food stores. Store tightly sealed in a cool, dry place. It keeps well for months.

nutrition at a glance

per serving

0.1 g.	total fat
0 g.	saturated fat
143	calories
0 mg.	cholesterol
61 mg.	sodium
4.3 g.	protein
29.6 g.	carbohydrates
2.1 g.	dietary fiber

Twice-Baked Sweet Potatoes

These sweet potatoes are rich and filling. Because the sweet potato skin is delicate, be sure to leave ¼" layer of flesh next to the skin when scooping out the flesh. Garnish with a dusting of nutmeg.

3   medium sweet potatoes
¼   cup drained canned apricots, peaches, or pears
½   teaspoon grated orange rind
⅛   teaspoon ground cinnamon
2   tablespoons packed brown sugar
    Salt (optional)
12 miniature marshmallows (optional)

1   Preheat the oven to 400°F.

2   Pierce the sweet potatoes several times with a fork. Place on a baking sheet and bake for 1 hour, or until tender. Allow to cool for several minutes.

3   Cut each sweet potato in half lengthwise. Carefully scoop out most of the flesh from 4 of the halves, leaving ¼" shell. Place the shells on the baking sheet and set aside. Scoop the flesh completely from the remaining 2 halves; discard the skins.

4   Place the flesh in a medium bowl. Add the apricots, peaches, or pears. Mash the mixture. Add the orange rind, cinnamon, and 1 tablespoon of the brown sugar. Season to taste with the salt (if using). Stir or mash to combine.

5   Spoon the filling into the reserved shells, mounding it above the tops of the shells. Sprinkle with the remaining 1 tablespoon brown sugar. Dot with the marshmallows (if using).

6   Bake for 2 to 3 minutes, or until the filling is hot.

Makes **4** servings.

nutrition at a glance
per serving

0.1 g.	total fat
0 g.	saturated fat
128	calories
0 mg.	cholesterol
12 mg.	sodium
1.6 g.	protein
31.2 g.	carbohydrates
2.7 g.	dietary fiber

Brussels Sprouts with Apples

quick and easy

I like my Brussels sprouts bright and a bit crunchy. In this recipe, sweet apple juice balances the bite of the miniature cabbages. The sprouts are quartered to both speed cooking and enable them to absorb more apple flavor. The toasted walnuts are a wonderful complement and will add only about 1 gram of fat per serving.

½	cup apple juice
½	teaspoon dried rosemary, crushed
1	pound Brussels sprouts, cut into quarters
2	small tart apples, cut into quarters and sliced
1	teaspoon cornstarch
1	tablespoon water
	Ground black pepper
	Salt (optional)
1	tablespoon finely chopped toasted walnuts (optional)

1   In a large no-stick skillet, combine the apple juice and rosemary. Bring to a boil over medium-high heat. Add the Brussels sprouts. Cover, reduce the heat to medium, and cook for 6 minutes. Add the apples.

2   Place the cornstarch in a cup. Add the water and stir to dissolve the cornstarch. Add to the skillet. Cook, stirring gently but constantly, for 3 minutes, or until a glaze forms. Season to taste with the pepper and salt (if using). Stir in the walnuts (if using).

Makes **4** servings.

nutrition at a glance
per serving

0.9 g.	total fat
0.2 g.	saturated fat
97	calories
0 mg.	cholesterol
27 mg.	sodium
3.3 g.	protein
23 g.	carbohydrates
6.8 g.	dietary fiber

Oven-Glazed Rutabagas

Roasting really brings out the natural sweetness in rutabagas as well as other root vegetables. Try this technique with turnips, carrots, or sweet potatoes.

4	rutabagas, ends trimmed
1	medium onion, coarsely chopped
¼	teaspoon ground black pepper
	Pinch of salt (optional)
1½	tablespoons packed brown sugar
1	small clove garlic, minced

1 Preheat the oven to 375°F.

2 Microwave the rutabagas on high power for 4 minutes, turning the rutabagas once, to make peeling easier. Allow to stand until cool enough to handle. Peel and cut into 1" cubes.

3 Coat a no-stick baking sheet with no-stick spray. Place the rutabagas and onions on the sheet. Mist with no-stick spray. Sprinkle with the pepper and salt (if using). Toss to coat. Spread in an even layer.

4 Bake for 35 minutes, stirring twice during baking time. Sprinkle evenly with the brown sugar and garlic. Bake for 10 minutes, or until the vegetables are tender and golden.

Makes **4** servings.

nutrition at a glance
per serving
- 0.3 g. total fat
- 0.1 g. saturated fat
- 72 calories
- 0 mg. cholesterol
- 24 mg. sodium
- 1.7 g. protein
- 16.9 g. carbohydrates
- 2.2 g. dietary fiber

Roast Vegetables for Fabulous Flavor

Roasting brings out the sweet side of many vegetables. Good candidates include celery, fennel, leeks, onions, carrots, potatoes, zucchini, tomatoes, peppers, winter squash, cauliflower, broccoli, eggplant, broccoflower, turnips, kohlrabi, beets, and sweet potatoes.

Some combinations are naturals. One of my favorites is onions, potatoes, and carrots coated lightly with no-stick spray and a sprinkling of crushed fennel seeds or ground cumin.

To roast vegetables, cut them in like-size pieces (no smaller than 1" cubes) and place in a foil-lined baking dish. Lightly coat with no-stick spray. Season with ground spices, finely chopped herbs, minced garlic, or salt. Toss and bake at 375°F, stirring occasionally, for 45 minutes to 1 hour, or until the vegetables are tender and browned. If the vegetables start to brown too quickly, cover them loosely with foil and continue baking until tender.

Roasted vegetables are tasty as side dishes or as a main course accompanied by a grain pilaf. You can also puree them in a blender or food processor to use as a base for sauces and soups.

Acorn Squash with Cranberries

quick and easy

A mulled cider mix makes a super seasoning for sweet acorn squash. This presentation is particularly attractive for a Thanksgiving feast. Choose dark green acorn squash with a touch of orange or use one of the new golden acorn squash. You can also substitute small halved butternut squash.

2	acorn squash
½–¾	cup apple juice or apple cider, heated
¼	cup dried cranberries
2	tablespoons packed brown sugar
½	teaspoon ground cinnamon
	Dash of ground allspice

1   Pierce each squash several times with a fork. Place side by side in a microwave. Microwave on high power for 10 minutes. Turn the squashes over and microwave for 8 to 10 minutes, or until a sharp knife can pierce the flesh. Let stand for 5 minutes.

2   Cut each squash in half lengthwise. Scoop out and discard the seeds. Place the squash, cut side up, on a baking sheet. Fill the cavities with the juice or cider and the cranberries.

3   In a small bowl, mix the brown sugar, cinnamon, and allspice. Sprinkle evenly over the squash. Broil 4" from the heat for 1 to 2 minutes, or until the sugar melts.

Makes **4** servings.

Photograph on page 246

nutrition at a glance

per serving

0.3 g.	total fat
0.1 g.	saturated fat
160	calories
0 mg.	cholesterol
10 mg.	sodium
1.8 g.	protein
41 g.	carbohydrates
7.7 g.	dietary fiber

Parsnips with Pearl Onions

quick and easy

Pearl onions, tomatoes, olives, and thyme liven up mild parsnips.

1	cup vegetable stock (page 93)
12	ounces parsnips, cut into ½" pieces
1	cup frozen pearl onions, thawed
2	plum tomatoes, diced
½	teaspoon dried thyme
1	teaspoon chopped pitted green olives or tiny capers
	Ground black pepper
	Salt (optional)

1 In a large no-stick skillet over high heat, bring the stock to a boil. Add the parsnips; cover and cook for 4 to 5 minutes. Add the onions; cover and cook for 4 to 5 minutes.

2 Reduce the heat to medium-high. Add the tomatoes and thyme. Cook, stirring, until most of the liquid is absorbed. Add the olives or capers. Season to taste with the pepper and salt (if using).

Makes **4** servings.

Lynn's Kitchen Tip

To easily peel pearl onions, boil the unpeeled onions in water to cover for 15 to 20 minutes. Drain and rinse with cold water. Squeeze the root end to pop the onion out of its skin.

nutrition at a glance
per serving

0.5 g.	total fat
0.1 g.	saturated fat
96	calories
0 mg.	cholesterol
35 mg.	sodium
1.9 g.	protein
22.7 g.	carbohydrates
4.5 g.	dietary fiber

Vegetable Stew with Beef (page 172)

Beef and Mushroom Fajitas (page 171)

Peking Turkey and Vegetables (page 166)

Turkey-Broccoli Divan (page 167)

Creamed Pearl Onions (page 215)

Scalloped Potatoes and Fennel (page 220)

Orange-Kissed Turnip Custards (page 231)

Acorn Squash with Cranberries (page 237)

Western Fries (page 223)

Sicilian Broccoli (page 229)

Herbed Bulgur Pilaf (page 282)

Mediterranean Beans (page 262)

Tubetti with Tomato and Ham (page 269)

Orzo with Asparagus (page 271)

Broccoli Alfredo Sauce (page 287) with fettuccine

Nectarine Salsa (page 303) on chicken

Beans, Pasta, Rice, and Grains

Going with the grains is great advice for anyone concerned with healthful eating. The U.S. Department of Agriculture Food Guide Pyramid of healthy eating guidelines rests solidly on a base of grains—and with good reason.

Grains, rice, and pasta provide complex carbohydrates, which are an important source of energy in any healthful eating plan. They also contain fiber, vitamins, and minerals. The Food Guide Pyramid suggests 6 to 11 servings of these foods each day.

Explore Grains

If your grain vocabulary extends no further than whole-wheat bread and oatmeal, it's time to get acquainted with the wonderful universe of grain products right on your supermarket shelves. Rice, cornmeal, bulgur, quinoa, millet, wild rice, and barley are all waiting for you.

For a chart on cooking the grains featured in this chapter, see "Grains: A Cook's Guide" on page 281. Most of them can be cooked in double batches and the extras frozen to microwave for instant side dishes.

When you're really in a hurry, turn to couscous—tiny grains of precooked semolina—which rehydrates in hot water or stock in about 5 minutes. Whole-wheat couscous is sold in natural foods stores.

Benefit from Beans

Dry legumes mesh so well with grains because they, too, are integral to healthy low-fat eating. Dry beans, lentils, and peas are excellent sources of fiber, vitamins, and minerals. Among the many choices are navy, kidney, pinto, cannellini, Great Northern, lima, and black beans; chick-peas, green and yellow split peas; and lentils in shades of green, red, and brown.

Like red meat, beans are loaded with protein. But unlike red meat, beans are light on fat, particularly saturated fat. Compare 1½ cups cooked black beans with 3 ounces broiled beef top sirloin (choice grade). The beans contain 23 grams of protein, 1 gram of total fat, and 0.4 gram of saturated fat. By contrast, the beef contains 25 grams of protein but also 10 grams of total fat and 4 grams of saturated fat.

For convenience, you can cook dry beans in a big batch, then freeze them in recipe-ready portions (see page 259). Cook beans in plain water or defatted stock with no seasonings. That way, you'll be able to adapt these plain beans to the seasonings in any recipe.

For real speed, start with canned beans. They're as nutritious as dry beans cooked from scratch, but they cost a bit more. They also contain more sodium, so be sure to rinse them with cold water and drain before adding to a recipe. One can (15 ounces) yields about 2 cups beans.

The more you eat beans, grains, and other high-fiber foods, the better your body will feel.

Curried Lentils with Fruit

These mildly spiced lentils, tossed with tart apples and sweet dried fruit, are a nice change from typical heavy lentil dishes. If you prefer a less sweet dish, reduce the dried fruit to 2 tablespoons.

2   cups vegetable stock (page 93)
1   cup dry green lentils
2   stalks celery with leafy tops, diced
½   teaspoon curry powder
1   tart apple, diced
¼   cup dried currants or diced dried apricots
2   teaspoons grated fresh ginger
    Salt (optional)

1   In a medium no-stick saucepan, combine the stock, lentils, celery, and curry powder. Bring to a boil over medium-high heat. Reduce the heat to medium-low, cover, and cook for 30 minutes, or until the lentils are soft but not mushy.

2   Add the apples, currants or apricots, and ginger. Cover and cook for 5 minutes. Season to taste with the salt (if using).

Makes **4** servings.

nutrition at a glance
per serving
0.7 g. total fat
0.1 g. saturated fat
201 calories
0 mg. cholesterol
28 mg. sodium
12.2 g. protein
39.2 g. carbohydrates
7.5 g. dietary fiber

Boston Baked Beans

This classic sweet-and-smoky American bean dish is perfect for a picnic or any other informal gathering. You may use canned beans or cook dry navy beans from scratch (start with about 2½ cups).

5	cups cooked navy beans
1	medium onion, coarsely chopped
1	stalk celery with leafy tops, coarsely chopped
½	cup dark molasses
½	cup packed dark brown sugar
2	teaspoons dry mustard
1	teaspoon liquid smoke
1	bay leaf
	Salt (optional)

1   Preheat the oven to 350°F.

2   In a 2-quart baking dish, combine the beans, onions, celery, molasses, brown sugar, mustard, liquid smoke, and bay leaf. Cover and bake for 1½ hours. Season to taste with the salt (if using.) Remove and discard the bay leaf before serving.

Makes **8** servings.

nutrition at a glance

per serving
- 0.9 g. total fat
- 0.2 g. saturated fat
- 278 calories
- 0 mg. cholesterol
- 19 mg. sodium
- 10.3 g. protein
- 59.1 g. carbohydrates
- 10.4 g. dietary fiber

Beans: A Cook's Guide

Cooking dry beans isn't difficult. It's an easy kitchen project that takes little actual work on a stay-at-home day. Cook up 1 or 2 pounds of beans at a time as the basis for many fabulous fat-free dishes. Simply freeze the cooked beans in recipe-ready portions, so you have them on hand for quick meals.

Cooking times for dry beans vary depending on the variety, the size, and the age of the beans. Generally, soaked dry beans take from 1½ to 3 hours to cook. For best results, follow the cooking directions on the package.

Lentils and dry split peas cook more quickly than other beans. And they do not need soaking before cooking. Dry beans, however, benefit from soaking. Soaking softens the tough skin and starts the rehydration process. Additionally, it helps decrease the flatulence-producing compounds in the beans. You can cook beans without soaking them first, but they'll take longer.

Before cooking beans, pick out and discard any stones, broken beans, or other debris. Wash the beans well with cold water. Place in a large bowl and cover generously with cold water. Let stand for at least 3 hours—or overnight. (Alternatively, for a quicker method, place the beans in a large pot and cover generously with cold water. Bring to a boil over high heat. Remove from the heat, cover, and allow to stand for 1 hour.) Discard the soaking water and rinse the beans. Cook according to the package directions or recipe instructions.

Mexican Beans

If you want to cook your own beans, be sure to make extra for other uses. Start with 1 pound dry beans; soak and cook as usual. Refrigerate or freeze the extras for other side dishes, soups, or salads.

1	large red onion, coarsely chopped
2	cloves garlic, minced
1	teaspoon chili powder
1	teaspoon ground cumin
3	cups canned navy beans, rinsed and drained
½	cup water or defatted chicken stock (page 94)
1	plum tomato, finely diced
½	cup chopped scallions
1	tablespoon chopped fresh cilantro
	Hot-pepper sauce (optional)

1 Coat a large no-stick saucepan with no-stick spray. Add the onions; mist with no-stick spray. Cover and cook over medium-high heat for 2 minutes, or until the onions start to release moisture. Uncover and cook, stirring occasionally, for 2 to 3 minutes, or until browned. If necessary, add 1 to 2 teaspoons water to prevent sticking.

2 Add the garlic, chili powder, and cumin. Cook, stirring, for 2 minutes.

3 Add the beans and water or stock. Stir to mix well. Cover and simmer for 10 minutes. Add the tomatoes, scallions, and cilantro. Stir to combine. Season with the hot-pepper sauce (if using).

Makes **6** servings.

nutrition at a glance

per serving

0.7 g.	total fat
0.1 g.	saturated fat
130	calories
0 mg.	cholesterol
9 mg.	sodium
8.3 g.	protein
23.8 g.	carbohydrates
8.3 g.	dietary fiber

Puerto Rican Black Beans

This traditional Caribbean bean dish is usually served with rice, a sprinkling of chopped raw onions, hot-pepper sauce, and a squirt of fresh lime juice.

1	cup dry black beans
1	Spanish onion, chopped
1	carrot, shredded
1	stalk celery with leafy top, finely chopped
1	tomato, chopped
3	cloves garlic, minced
1	teaspoon ground cumin
½	teaspoon dried basil
¼	teaspoon dried thyme
¼–½	teaspoon finely chopped jalapeño peppers (wear plastic gloves when handling)
1	bay leaf
3	cups water
	Salt (optional)

1 Place the beans in a large no-stick pot and cover generously with cold water. Bring to a boil over medium-high heat. Remove from the heat, cover, and allow to stand for 1 hour. Drain; discard the soaking water and rinse the beans. Return to the pot.

2 Add the onions, carrots, celery, tomatoes, garlic, cumin, basil, thyme, peppers, bay leaf, and water. Bring to a boil over medium-high heat.

3 Reduce the heat to medium-low, cover, and simmer for 1½ to 2 hours, or until the beans are tender. Remove and discard the bay leaf.

4 Transfer half of the mixture to a blender and puree. Return the mixture to the pot. (The beans can also be partially pureed in the pot with a hand blender.) Season to taste with the salt (if using).

Makes **4** servings.

nutrition at a glance

per serving
- 0.9 g. total fat
- 0.2 g. saturated fat
- 190 calories
- 0 mg. cholesterol
- 29 mg. sodium
- 11.6 g. protein
- 35.2 g. carbohydrates
- 11.7 g. dietary fiber

Mediterranean Beans

quick and easy

These robust legumes are a great match for a big Romaine salad, a small serving of grilled swordfish, and crusty bread.

1	medium onion, coarsely chopped
1½	tablespoons finely diced fat-free smoked ham or Canadian bacon
1	carrot, sliced
1	stalk celery, sliced
2	cloves garlic, minced
1	can (15 ounces) cannellini or Great Northern beans, rinsed and drained
½	cup defatted chicken stock (page 94)
2	tablespoons thinly sliced fresh basil
1	teaspoon dried oregano
10	cherry tomatoes, cut into quarters
¼	cup Marsala wine (optional)
	Ground black pepper
	Salt (optional)

1 Coat a large no-stick saucepan with no-stick spray. Add the onions and ham or bacon; mist with no-stick spray. Cover and cook over medium-high heat for 2 to 3 minutes, or until the onions start to release moisture. Uncover and cook, stirring occasionally, for 2 to 3 minutes, or until the onions are browned. If necessary, add 1 to 2 teaspoons water to prevent sticking.

2 Add the carrots, celery, and garlic. Cook, stirring occasionally, for 7 minutes. Add the beans, stock, basil, and oregano. Bring to a boil. Reduce the heat to medium-low and cook, stirring occasionally, for 8 to 10 minutes, or until the liquid is almost evaporated.

3 Add the tomatoes and wine (if using). Bring to a boil over medium heat. Cook for 2 minutes. Season to taste with the pepper and salt (if using).

Makes **4** servings.

Photograph on page 250

Photograph on page 250

Lynn's Fun Food Fact

Cannellini are large, white Italian kidney beans with a mild, earthy flavor. If unavailable, other white beans—such as Great Northern or navy—can be substituted.

nutrition at a glance

per serving

0.6 g.	total fat
0 g.	saturated fat
96	calories
1 mg.	cholesterol
229 mg.	sodium
4.7 g.	protein
18.5 g.	carbohydrates
4.5 g.	dietary fiber

French White Beans

quick and **easy**

Use Great Northern, cannellini, or navy beans for this easy side dish that's dotted with sweet roasted peppers. Leftovers are excellent served at room temperature, sprinkled with lemon juice or balsamic vinegar.

1   large leek, white and some green stem, thinly sliced
1   cup thinly sliced fennel
½   cup water
1   can (15 ounces) white beans, rinsed and drained
1   cup fresh or thawed frozen peas
1   cup diced jarred roasted sweet red peppers
½   teaspoon vinegar
¼   teaspoon chopped fresh thyme
    Ground black pepper

1   In a large no-stick skillet, combine the leeks, fennel, and water. Cover and cook over medium heat for 5 minutes, or until the fennel is crisp-tender. Drain and return the vegetables to the skillet.

2   Add the beans, peas, red peppers, vinegar, and thyme. Cook for 4 to 5 minutes, or until hot. Season to taste with the black pepper.

Makes **4** servings.

nutrition at a glance

per serving

0.5 g.	total fat
0.1 g.	saturated fat
175	calories
0 mg.	cholesterol
238 mg.	sodium
10.6 g.	protein
33.8 g.	carbohydrates
8.5 g.	dietary fiber

Tex-Mex Pinto Beans

quick and easy

Fresh corn makes this simple dish really special. It's great with spicy turkey fillets, a large green salad, and apple pie.

½	cup water
1	medium onion, diced
1	stalk celery, diced
	Kernels from 1 ear corn
1	can (15 ounces) pinto beans, rinsed and drained
2	cloves garlic, minced
1	teaspoon dried oregano
½	teaspoon ground cumin
	Hot-pepper sauce
1	tablespoon chopped fresh cilantro (optional)

1 In a large no-stick skillet, bring the water to a boil over medium-high heat. Add the onions and celery. Cover and cook for 5 minutes. Add the corn and cook for 2 minutes. Drain and return the vegetables to the skillet.

2 Add the beans, garlic, oregano, and cumin. Cook over medium heat, stirring occasionally, for 5 minutes, or until the beans are hot. Season to taste with the hot-pepper sauce. Sprinkle with the cilantro (if using).

Makes **4** servings.

nutrition at a glance

per serving

0.8 g.	total fat
0.1 g.	saturated fat
143	calories
0 mg.	cholesterol
197 mg.	sodium
7.6 g.	protein
28.2 g.	carbohydrates
7.8 g.	dietary fiber

Confetti Black Beans

quick and easy

Garnish individual portions of this festive side dish with a dollop of fat-free sour cream, chopped lettuce, and fresh cilantro leaves.

1   cup chopped onions
2   large cloves garlic, minced
½   cup water
1   sweet red pepper, diced
2   plum tomatoes, chopped
½   cup whole-kernel corn
1   bay leaf
1   cup cooked black beans
2   tablespoons chopped fresh cilantro
1   tablespoon fresh lime juice
⅛   teaspoon ground red pepper
    Ground black pepper
    Salt (optional)

1   Coat a large no-stick saucepan with no-stick spray and place over medium heat. Add the onions and garlic; stir. Cover and cook for 2 minutes, or until the onions start to release moisture. Uncover and cook, stirring, for 2 to 3 minutes, or until golden. Add the water, diced red peppers, tomatoes, corn, and bay leaf. Cook for 2 minutes. Add the beans.

2   Reduce the heat and simmer for 15 minutes, or until the liquid is almost gone. Add the cilantro, lime juice, and ground red pepper. Season to taste with the black pepper and salt (if using). Cook for 1 minute. Remove and discard the bay leaf.

Makes **4** servings.

nutrition at a glance
per serving
0.7 g.   total fat
0.1 g.   saturated fat
105   calories
0 mg.   cholesterol
8 mg.   sodium
5.4 g.   protein
21.2 g.   carbohydrates
5.5 g.   dietary fiber

Pasta e Fagioli

quick and easy

This simply prepared dish will please both bean and pasta lovers. And it will especially please the youngsters. During one tasting session, the two-year-old daughter of one of our testers ate her mother's entire portion. If you don't have pinto beans, substitute pink or red ones.

1	onion, chopped
1	clove garlic, minced
2	cups water
1	cup canned pinto beans, rinsed and drained
1	tablespoon tomato paste
½	teaspoon honey
6	ounces low-fat miniature shell pasta or tube pasta (0.5 g. fat per 2-ounce serving)
1	tablespoon thinly sliced fresh basil
2	tablespoons chopped fresh parsley
	Ground black pepper
	Salt (optional)
¼	cup fat-free Parmesan topping

1 Coat a large no-stick saucepan with no-stick spray. Add the onions. Cover and cook over medium heat for 5 minutes, or until the onions start to release moisture. Add the garlic. Cook, stirring frequently, for 3 to 4 minutes, or until the onions are golden. If necessary, add 1 to 2 teaspoons water to prevent sticking.

2 Add the water, beans, tomato paste, and honey; stir to combine. Add the pasta and stir. Cover and simmer for 10 to 15 minutes, or until the pasta is tender. Stir in the basil and parsley. Season to taste with the pepper and salt (if using). Serve sprinkled with the Parmesan.

Makes **4** servings.

nutrition at a glance

per serving

0.9 g.	total fat
0.2 g.	saturated fat
238	calories
0 mg.	cholesterol
235 mg.	sodium
11.8 g.	protein
46 g.	carbohydrates
5.6 g.	dietary fiber

Autumn Couscous with Mint

quick and easy

Other types of hard-shell squash or even sweet potatoes can be substituted for the butternut squash in this dish.

1	small McIntosh apple, chopped
1	tablespoon freshly squeezed lemon juice
1	pound butternut squash, peeled, seeded and cut in 1" cubes
½	teaspoon ground cinnamon
1½	cups water
1	cup couscous
2	tablespoons chopped fresh mint
1	tablespoon grated lemon rind
½	teaspoon salt (optional)

1 Place the apples in a small bowl. Sprinkle with the lemon juice and toss to coat. Set aside.

2 Place the squash in a steamer basket. Sprinkle with the cinnamon and toss to coat. Place the basket in a large saucepan. Add 1" of water to the pan, cover, and bring to a boil over medium-high heat. Reduce the heat to medium and steam for 7 to 9 minutes, or until the squash is tender.

3 Meanwhile, in a medium no-stick saucepan over medium-high heat, bring the 1½ cups water to a boil. Stir in the couscous. Cover, remove from the heat, and set aside for 5 minutes.

4 Transfer the couscous to a large bowl; fluff with a fork. Lightly stir in the squash, mint, lemon rind, and salt (if using). Sprinkle with the apples.

Makes **4** servings.

nutrition at a glance
per serving
0.6 g.	total fat
0.1 g.	saturated fat
243	calories
0 mg.	cholesterol
19 mg.	sodium
7.5 g.	protein
53.3 g.	carbohydrates
6.9 g.	dietary fiber

Couscous with Corn and Cumin

quick and easy

This side dish is wonderful in late summer, when fresh corn is at its prime.

1	cup fresh whole-kernel corn or thawed frozen whole-kernel corn
1½	cups water
1	cup couscous
½	jalapeño pepper, seeded and finely chopped (wear plastic gloves when handling)
½	cup chopped sweet red or green peppers
1	clove garlic, minced
½	teaspoon ground cumin
½	teaspoon salt (optional)
2	tablespoons chopped fresh cilantro

1　Place the corn in a small saucepan; add enough cold water to cover. Cook over medium heat for 3 to 4 minutes, or until tender. Drain and set aside.

2　In a medium no-stick saucepan, bring the 1½ cups water to a boil over medium-high heat. Stir in the couscous. Cover, remove from the heat, and set aside for 5 minutes.

3　Coat a large no-stick skillet with no-stick spray. Warm over medium heat for 1 minute. Add the jalapeño peppers and red or green peppers; cook for 3 minutes, or until softened. Add the garlic, cumin, and salt (if using). Cook, stirring, for 1 minute. Stir in the corn.

4　Transfer the couscous to a large bowl; fluff with a fork. Stir in the corn mixture and cilantro.

Makes **4** servings.

nutrition at a glance

per serving

0.9 g.	total fat
0.1 g.	saturated fat
227	calories
0 mg.	cholesterol
16 mg.	sodium
7.5 g.	protein
47.4 g.	carbohydrates
3.7 g.	dietary fiber

Tubetti with Tomato and Ham

quick and easy

Any small dry pasta such as macaroni, shells, or pennetti may be substituted for the tubetti, which are short lengths of tubes. I like to garnish this dish with plenty of chopped parsley.

1½	tablespoons diced fat-free ham or prosciutto trimmed of all visible fat
1	medium onion, chopped
3	cloves garlic, minced
¾	cup diced tomatoes
	Ground black pepper
	Salt (optional)
6	ounces low-fat tubetti pasta (0.5 g. fat per 2-ounce serving)
¼	cup fat-free Parmesan topping

1 In a large no-stick skillet over medium-high heat, cook the ham or prosciutto, stirring occasionally, for 5 minutes, or until browned. Remove from the pan and set aside.

2 Off the heat, coat the skillet with no-stick spray. Add the onions. Cover and cook over medium-high heat, stirring occasionally, for 5 to 6 minutes, or until golden. If necessary, add 1 to 2 teaspoons water to prevent sticking.

3 Add the garlic and cook for 2 to 3 minutes. Add the tomatoes and the reserved ham or prosciutto. Stir to combine. Season to taste with the pepper and salt (if using). Keep warm over low heat.

4 Meanwhile, bring a large pot of water to a boil over high heat. Add the pasta and cook according to the package directions. Reserve ¼ cup of the cooking water, then drain the pasta.

5 Return the pasta to the pot. Add the onion mixture and 1 to 2 tablespoons of the cooking water. Toss to combine. Add a bit more cooking water, if needed, to moisten. Sprinkle with the Parmesan.

Makes **4** servings.

Photograph on page 251

nutrition at a glance

per serving

0.9 g.	total fat
0.1 g.	saturated fat
218	calories
1 mg.	cholesterol
144 mg.	sodium
10.1 g.	protein
42.3 g.	carbohydrates
2.3 g.	dietary fiber

Macaroni and Cheese

quick and easy

Macaroni and cheese is all-American and, unfortunately, usually almost all fat. But this fabulous fat-free adaptation has an added boost of calcium and protein from cottage cheese. For extra color, add ¼ cup pimentos or green peppers and sprinkle on some paprika for garnish.

8	ounces macaroni (0.5 g. fat per 2-ounce serving)
1½	cups fat-free cottage cheese
½	cup buttermilk
1	tablespoon all-purpose flour
1	teaspoon prepared mustard
	Salt (optional)
3	ounces fat-free Cheddar cheese, finely chopped

1 Bring a large pot of water to a boil over high heat. Add the macaroni and cook according to the package directions. Drain and return to the pot. Set aside.

2 Meanwhile, in a blender or food processor, combine the cottage cheese, buttermilk, flour, and mustard. Process for 1 minute, or until very smooth. Season to taste with the salt (if using).

3 Pour the cottage-cheese mixture into a medium no-stick saucepan. Bring to a boil over medium-low heat, stirring constantly. Boil, stirring constantly, for 5 minutes. Remove from the heat. Add the Cheddar and stir until melted. Let stand for 5 minutes to thicken.

4 Pour over the macaroni; toss to combine. Pour into a shallow 1½-quart baking dish. Broil 4" from the heat for 2 to 3 minutes, or until golden brown.

Makes **4** servings.

nutrition at a glance
per serving

0.6 g.	total fat
0 g.	saturated fat
317	calories
10 mg.	cholesterol
436 mg.	sodium
24.9 g.	protein
49.7 g.	carbohydrates
2.1 g.	dietary fiber

Orzo with Asparagus

quick and easy

For a creamed version of this dish, whisk together 1 cup fat-free liquid creamer and 1 tablespoon flour. Cook over medium heat, stirring, until thickened. Add a pinch of ground nutmeg. Omit the cooking water from the final step of the recipe and toss the orzo mixture with the cream sauce.

6	ounces low-fat orzo pasta (0.5 g. fat per 2-ounce serving)
1	cup thinly sliced asparagus
1	medium onion, finely chopped
2	cloves garlic, minced
½	cup drained canned mushroom pieces
1	plum tomato, diced
¼	cup chopped fresh parsley
2	tablespoons diced sweet red peppers
8	fresh basil leaves, thinly sliced
	Ground black pepper
	Salt (optional)

1 Bring a large pot of water to a boil over high heat. Add the orzo and cook according to the package directions; add the asparagus during the last 2 minutes of cooking time. Reserve ½ cup of the cooking water, then drain. Return the orzo and asparagus to the pot. Set aside.

2 Meanwhile, coat a large no-stick skillet with no-stick spray. Add the onions. Cover and cook over medium heat, stirring occasionally, for 5 minutes, or until golden. Add the garlic. Cook for 2 minutes.

3 Add the mushrooms, tomatoes, parsley, red peppers, and basil. Cover and cook for 1 to 2 minutes. Add the orzo and asparagus. Season to taste with the black pepper and salt (if using).

4 Add about ¼ cup of the reserved cooking water; toss to combine. Add a bit more cooking water, if needed, to moisten.

Makes **4** servings.

Photograph on page 252

nutrition at a glance

per serving

0.9 g.	total fat
0.1 g.	saturated fat
188	calories
0 mg.	cholesterol
95 mg.	sodium
7.3 g.	protein
38.2 g.	carbohydrates
3 g.	dietary fiber

Rice and Orzo Pilaf

Look for packages of quick-cooking brown rice in your supermarket that say "cooks in 30 minutes." I prefer the taste and texture of this rice over the instant brown rice that cooks in 10 minutes.

½	cup low-fat orzo pasta (0.5 g. fat per 2-ounce serving)
1	cup chopped onions
½	teaspoon dried marjoram
¼	teaspoon dried rosemary, crumbled
	Pinch of ground turmeric
3¼	cups defatted chicken stock (page 94)
¼	teaspoon ground black pepper
	Pinch of salt (optional)
½	cup quick-cooking brown rice (ready in 30 minutes)
½	cup long-grain white rice

1 Coat a large no-stick skillet with no-stick spray. Add the orzo and mist with the no-stick spray. Cook over medium heat, stirring, for 2 to 3 minutes, or until browned. Add the onions and cook, stirring, for 2 to 3 minutes. Cover and cook for 1 minute.

2 Add the marjoram, rosemary, and turmeric. Cook, stirring constantly, for 1 to 2 minutes. Add the stock, pepper, and salt (if using).

3 Cover and bring to a boil over medium-high heat. Stir in the brown rice. Reduce the heat to medium-low, cover, and simmer for 15 minutes. Add the white rice. Cover and simmer for 20 minutes, or until the rice is tender and the liquid is absorbed. Fluff with a fork.

Makes **6** servings.

nutrition at a glance

per serving

0.9 g.	total fat
0.1 g.	saturated fat
188	calories
0 mg.	cholesterol
13 mg.	sodium
4.9 g.	protein
39.8 g.	carbohydrates
2.5 g.	dietary fiber

Saffron Rice

quick and easy

Moist and creamy saffron rice is a treat fit for guests. You can always use a little more saffron if you like its distinctive flavor. Garnish with chopped fresh parsley or chives.

2 cups defatted chicken stock (page 94) or vegetable stock (page 93)
¼ teaspoon crushed saffron threads
1½ cups chopped leeks
2 cloves garlic, minced
¼ cup white wine (optional)
1 cup long-grain white rice
Pinch of salt (optional)

1 In a microwaveable measuring cup or medium bowl, combine the stock and saffron. Microwave on high power for 2 minutes, or until hot. Remove and set aside for 5 minutes.

2 Coat a medium no-stick saucepan with no-stick spray. Warm over medium heat. Add the leeks and garlic. Cover and cook, stirring occasionally, for 3 minutes, or until golden. Add the wine (if using) and bring to a boil. Stir in the rice.

3 Stir in the saffron stock and salt (if using). Bring to a boil over medium-high heat. Reduce the heat to medium-low, cover, and cook for 20 minutes, or until the rice is tender and the liquid is absorbed. Fluff with a fork.

Makes **4** servings.

nutrition at a glance
per serving
0.6 g. total fat
0.1 g. saturated fat
228 calories
0 mg. cholesterol
19 mg. sodium
4.8 g. protein
47.8 g. carbohydrates
2.2 g. dietary fiber

Spanish Green Rice

quick *and easy*

This savory green rice is terrific with a hot bean soup and a salad. Serve with lemon or lime wedges and hot sauce.

2	cups water or vegetable stock (page 93)
¾	cup long-grain white rice
	Pinch of salt (optional)
¾	cup chopped fresh cilantro
½	cup finely chopped scallions
¼	cup chopped fresh parsley
½	teaspoon finely diced jalapeño peppers (wear plastic gloves when handling)

1 In a medium no-stick saucepan, combine the water or stock, rice, and salt (if using). Bring to a boil over medium-high heat. Reduce the heat to medium-low, cover, and cook for 20 minutes, or until the rice is tender and the liquid is absorbed.

2 Fluff the rice with a fork. Add the cilantro, scallions, parsley, and peppers (if using). Stir with a fork.

Makes **4** servings.

nutrition at a glance
per serving
0.4 g.	total fat
0.1 g.	saturated fat
146	calories
0 mg.	cholesterol
10 mg.	sodium
3.3 g.	protein
31.4 g.	carbohydrates
1.1 g.	dietary fiber

North Woods Wild Rice

If you can't find fresh ripe Bing or yellow Queen Anne cherries, substitute canned or frozen ones. Or use halved seedless tangerine or canned mandarin orange wedges.

1   package (0.35 ounce) dried mushrooms
2   cups boiling water
1   tablespoon molasses
1   bay leaf
1   cup wild rice
¼   cup sweet cherries, pitted and cut into quarters
    Ground black pepper
    Salt (optional)

1   Place the mushrooms in a medium bowl. Add the water and set aside to soak for 10 minutes. Strain through a fine sieve lined with a paper coffee filter or paper towel; reserve the liquid. Chop the mushrooms, discarding any tough stems.

2   Add enough water to the mushroom liquid to equal 2½ cups. Transfer to a large no-stick saucepan. Add the molasses and bay leaf. Bring to a boil over medium-high heat.

3   Add the rice and stir. Reduce the heat to low. Cover and cook for 50 to 55 minutes, or until the rice is tender and most of the liquid is absorbed. Fluff with a fork.

4   Add the cherries. Season to taste with the pepper and salt (if using). Stir to combine. Cook for an additional 1 to 2 minutes, or until the cherries are heated through. Remove and discard the bay leaf.

Makes **4** servings.

nutrition at a glance
per serving
0.8 g.   total fat
0.1 g.   saturated fat
204   calories
0 mg.   cholesterol
7 mg.   sodium
7 g.   protein
44.5 g.   carbohydrates
2.9 g.   dietary fiber

Rice and Vegetable Ring

quick and easy

A rice mold is pretty to serve and easy to make. Prepare it in a no-stick ring mold, a gelatin mold, or a Bundt pan. For variety, replace the broccoli with asparagus cut into ½" pieces.

2	cups long-grain white rice
4½	cups defatted chicken stock (page 94) or vegetable stock (page 93)
	Pinch of salt (optional)
2	cups broccoli florets
1	medium onion, finely chopped
1	cup finely chopped carrots
	Ground black pepper

1 In a large no-stick saucepan, combine the rice, stock, and salt (if using). Bring to a boil over medium-high heat. Reduce the heat to medium-low, cover, and cook for 10 minutes. Add the broccoli, onions, and carrots. Cover and cook for 10 minutes, or until the rice is tender and the liquid is absorbed. Season to taste with the pepper.

2 Coat a 2-quart ring mold with no-stick spray. Spoon the rice and vegetables into the mold, packing it firmly. Cover with foil and let stand for 5 minutes. Invert onto a platter and unmold.

Makes **8** servings.

Lynn's Kitchen Tip

Rice molds are festive for holidays and other special occasions. You can vary the vegetables depending upon the season and your whim. For a party, you can keep the molded ring, covered with foil, in a 200°F oven for 10 to 15 minutes.

nutrition at a glance

per serving

0.6 g.	total fat
0.1 g.	saturated fat
211	calories
0 mg.	cholesterol
24 mg.	sodium
5 g.	protein
45.8 g.	carbohydrates
2.3 g.	dietary fiber

Lemon-Dill Rice

quick and easy

Rice, lemon, and dill are a refreshingly satisfying mix. Cook a double batch so that you have leftovers for rice salad: Toss the cold rice with cooked vegetables, seafood, and your favorite fat-free dressing.

1½ cups defatted chicken stock (page 94)
 1 cup jasmine, basmati, or long-grain white rice
 1 tablespoon grated lemon rind
 ¼ teaspoon ground black pepper
   Pinch of salt (optional)
 1 tablespoon chopped fresh dill or 1 teaspoon dried
 1 tablespoon freshly squeezed lemon juice

1 In a small no-stick saucepan over medium heat, bring the stock to a boil. Stir in the rice, lemon rind, pepper, and salt (if using). Return to a boil. Stir. Reduce the heat to low, cover, and simmer for 20 minutes, or until the rice is tender and the liquid is absorbed.

2 Fluff the rice with a fork. Add the dill and lemon juice. Mix lightly with a fork.

Makes **4** servings.

nutrition at a glance
per serving
 0.4 g. total fat
 0.1 g. saturated fat
 193 calories
 0 mg. cholesterol
 110 mg. sodium
 4.6 g. protein
 41.2 g. carbohydrates
 1 g. dietary fiber

Cajun Red Beans and Rice

quick and easy

Beans and rice are a traditional favorite in many parts of the world. I like to use dark red kidney beans because they have more texture than some other varieties. If you like garnishes, sprinkle cilantro leaves on top for color.

1   cup finely chopped onions
1   cup finely chopped green peppers
1   large clove garlic, minced
1   can (15 ounces) dark red kidney beans, rinsed and drained
1   can (14 ounces) low-sodium chicken broth, defatted
1   cup long-grain white rice
2   ounces fat-free smoked ham or turkey breast, finely chopped
1   bay leaf
½   teaspoon dried thyme
    Salt (optional)

1   In a large no-stick saucepan, combine the onions, peppers, and garlic. Cook over medium heat, stirring often, for 3 minutes. Add the beans, broth, rice, ham or turkey, bay leaf, and thyme. Season to taste with the salt (if using).

2   Bring the mixture to a boil over medium-high heat. Reduce the heat to low, cover, and simmer for 20 minutes, or until the rice is tender and the liquid is absorbed. Fluff the mixture with a fork. Remove and discard the bay leaf.

Makes **4** servings.

nutrition at a glance
per serving

0.6 g.	total fat
0.1 g.	saturated fat
212	calories
3 mg.	cholesterol
314 mg.	sodium
9 g.	protein
41.9 g.	carbohydrates
5.2 g.	dietary fiber

Barley with Mushrooms

Earthy barley acquires even deeper, richer flavor when simmered with hearty dried mushrooms. Brighten this cold-weather side dish with a sprinkling of chopped parsley.

1	package (0.35 ounce) dried mushrooms
2	cups hot water
3	cups sliced fresh button or cremini mushrooms
¾	cup diced carrots
1	medium onion, chopped
2	stalks celery, chopped
2	cloves garlic, minced
½	cup barley
½	teaspoon dried thyme
¼	teaspoon dried rosemary, crumbled
	Pinch of salt (optional)
	Ground black pepper

1　Place the dried mushrooms in a small bowl. Add 1 cup of the water and set aside to soak for 10 minutes. Strain through a fine sieve lined with a paper coffee filter or paper towel; reserve the liquid. Chop the mushrooms, discarding any tough stems; set aside.

2　Meanwhile, coat a large nonstick saucepan with no-stick spray. Add the button or cremini mushrooms, carrots, onions, celery, and garlic. Cover and cook over medium heat, stirring occasionally, for 6 minutes, or until the onions start to brown.

3　Add the barley, thyme, rosemary, and salt (if using). Stir in the remaining 1 cup water, the reserved mushroom liquid, and the soaked mushrooms. Bring to a boil over medium-high heat.

4　Reduce the heat to medium, cover, and cook for 30 minutes, or until the barley is tender and the liquid is absorbed. Fluff with a fork. Season to taste with the pepper.

Makes **4** servings.

nutrition at a glance
per serving
0.9 g.	total fat
0.2 g.	saturated fat
126	calories
0 mg.	cholesterol
36 mg.	sodium
4.6 g.	protein
26.7 g.	carbohydrates
6.7 g.	dietary fiber

Asian Millet with Carrots

Tiny round yellow millet grains look pretty cooked in this pilaflike side dish with carrots, scallions, and cilantro. Serve it with lemon wedges and pass around the crushed red-pepper flakes for those who like things spicy.

1½	cups water or defatted chicken stock (page 94)
1	onion, coarsely chopped
10	baby carrots, diced
⅓	cup millet
2	pieces (4" each) fresh lemongrass (optional)
3	cloves garlic, minced
	Pinch of salt (optional)
3	scallions, chopped
2	tablespoons chopped fresh cilantro
2	teaspoons low-sodium soy sauce
	Ground black pepper

Lynn's Health Watch

Millet is an ancient grain and one that deserves wider use in the United States. Most people know it only as a type of birdseed. But as part of a heart-healthy diet, millet contains complex carbohydrates, fiber, and vegetable protein.

1 In a large no-stick saucepan, combine the water or stock, onions, carrots, millet, lemongrass (if using), garlic, and salt (if using). Cover and bring to a boil over medium-high heat. Reduce the heat to medium, cover, and cook for 35 to 40 minutes, or until the millet is tender and the liquid is absorbed.

2 Stir in the scallions, cilantro, and soy sauce. Season to taste with the pepper. Remove and discard the lemongrass (if using).

Makes **6** servings.

nutrition at a glance
per serving

0.9 g.	total fat
0.2 g.	saturated fat
117	calories
0 mg.	cholesterol
79 mg.	sodium
3.6 g.	protein
23.6 g.	carbohydrates
2 g.	dietary fiber

Grains: A Cook's Guide

Cook grains in water, stock, or vegetable juice in a covered heavy-bottomed pot. Season if you like with herbs, spices, other aromatics, or salt.

Follow the same basic method for all the following grains. Bring the grain and liquid to a boil, then reduce the heat to low so the mixture simmers. Cover and cook for the allotted time. Remove from the heat and set aside, covered, to steam for 5 minutes. Fluff with a fork before serving.

Remember that the amount of liquid and the time listed are approximate. The age of the grain, the weather, and the heat intensity of your stove top can all affect the amount of liquid that the grain absorbs and the time needed to absorb it.

Grain (1 cup)	Liquid (cups)	Cooking Time (min.)
Barley	3	35
Brown rice, quick-cooking	2	30
Brown rice, regular	2	45
Bulgur, medium or coarse	2	20–25
Millet	2½	30
Quinoa	2	15
White rice	2	15
Wild rice	3	45–50

Herbed Bulgur Pilaf

Bulgur is made from wheat berries that have been steamed, dried, and crushed. It's available in fine, medium, and coarse grinds in natural food stores and some supermarkets. I prefer a fine-grind bulgur for this recipe because it cooks quickly.

½   cup chopped scallions
½   cup shredded carrots
1   cup bulgur
½   teaspoon herbes de Provence
2   cups water
¼   cup chopped fresh parsley
    Pinch of salt (optional)
    Ground black pepper
    Fat-free Parmesan topping (optional)

1   Coat a medium no-stick saucepan with no-stick spray. Add the scallions and carrots. Mist with no-stick spray. Cover and cook over medium heat, stirring occasionally, for 4 to 5 minutes, or until the vegetables release moisture.

2   Uncover and cook, stirring, for 3 to 4 minutes, or until the scallions are golden. Add the bulgur and herbes de Provence. Cook, stirring, for 2 to 3 minutes, or until the bulgur is lightly toasted.

3   Add the water, parsley, and salt (if using). Bring to a boil over medium-high heat. Reduce the heat to medium-low, cover, and cook for 18 to 20 minutes, or until the bulgur is tender and the liquid is absorbed.

4   Fluff with a fork. Season to taste with the pepper. Serve sprinkled with the Parmesan (if using).

Makes **4** servings.

Photograph on page 249

nutrition at a glance

per serving

0.6 g.	total fat
0.1 g.	saturated fat
131	calories
0 mg.	cholesterol
18 mg.	sodium
4.8 g.	protein
29.2 g.	carbohydrates
7.3 g.	dietary fiber

Grilled Polenta with Mushrooms

quick and easy

This robust side dish is also good served as an appetizer for a formal fall dinner.

4 slices (½" thick) prepared fat-free polenta in a tube
4 ounces cremini or shiitake mushrooms, sliced
2 cloves garlic, minced
⅓ cup dry white wine or water
2 tablespoons chopped fresh chives or parsley
1 teaspoon fat-free Parmesan topping

1 Coat a barbecue grill rack or stove-top skillet grill with no-stick spray. Prepare a charcoal grill or warm the skillet over high heat.

2 Add the polenta to the rack or skillet. Cook for 4 to 5 minutes on each side.

3 Meanwhile, coat a large no-stick skillet with no-stick spray. Warm over medium heat for 1 minute. Add the mushrooms and cook for 2 to 3 minutes. Add the garlic and cook for 1 minute. Add the wine or water and bring to a boil. Reduce the heat to low. Cook for 2 to 3 minutes, or until the mushrooms are tender. Stir in the chives or parsley and Parmesan. Spoon over the polenta.

Makes **4** servings.

nutrition at a glance
per serving
- 0.2 g. total fat
- 0.1 g. saturated fat
- 83 calories
- 0 mg. cholesterol
- 232 mg. sodium
- 2.3 g. protein
- 15.3 g. carbohydrates
- 2.2 g. dietary fiber

Orange Quinoa with Raisins

quick and easy

The fluffy texture and delicate flavor of quinoa belie its nutritional power. It is one of the finest sources of vegetable protein.

5   scallions
1   large clove garlic, minced
½   teaspoon ground cumin
¼   teaspoon ground cinnamon
1   cup defatted chicken stock (page 94)
½   cup quinoa, rinsed and drained
½   cup golden raisins
    Pinch of salt (optional)
1   teaspoon grated orange rind

1   Cut the green stems from the scallions; chop finely and set aside. Chop the white parts and set aside.

2   Coat a small no-stick saucepan with no-stick spray. Add the white parts of the scallions, garlic, cumin, and cinnamon. Mist with no-stick spray. Cook over medium heat, stirring, for 1 minute.

3   Stir in the stock, quinoa, raisins, and salt (if using). Bring to a boil over medium-high heat. Reduce the heat to low, cover, and cook for 15 minutes, or until the quinoa is tender and the liquid is absorbed.

4   Fluff with a fork. Stir in the orange rind and reserved scallion greens.

Makes **4** servings.

nutrition at a glance	
per serving	
0.9 g.	total fat
0.1 g.	saturated fat
102	calories
0 mg.	cholesterol
55 mg.	sodium
2.9 g.	protein
22 g.	carbohydrates
1.6 g.	dietary fiber

Sauces, Gravies, and Condiments

Judging from the contents of my refrigerator,

sauces, gravies, and condiments are the most

important foods in my kitchen. I have more of these

flavor enhancers—especially condiments—than any

other single item.

I also have a freezer stocked with recipe-ready

portions of sauces and gravies, which I can thaw in

the microwave to top cooked pasta, a baked potato,

steamed zucchini, or pancakes.

Perfect sauces—such as Broccoli Alfredo Sauce and Mushroom and Bacon Sauce—dress up pasta, mashed potatoes, or rice. Dill Sauce on grilled halibut entices even fish phobics. Caramelized Onion Compote or Nectarine Salsa—served with grilled turkey breast—makes a most favorable flavor impression.

Sauce Support

Sauces play an extremely important supporting role in fat-free cooking. With their range of textures and tastes, they keep us from feeling deprived.

Most of my fat-free sauces don't take much time, and many can be made ahead and even frozen. When I'm in the mood, I'll have a sauce-making day and prepare several sauces to freeze in serving portions in plastic bags. So I always have the perfect fat-free sauce when I need it.

With my master Basic White Sauce, which is a simple three-ingredient wonder (five, if you count the salt and pepper), you can make Cheese Sauce, Dill Sauce, Garlic Sauce, Lemon Sauce, Mushroom Sauce, and Onion Sauce.

Serve It Right

How much sauce makes a serving?

✳ My sauces for pasta and rice are ½ cup, which is a good quantity for 1½ cups cooked pasta or rice. (That amount of starch contains less than 1 gram of fat per serving.)

✳ The sauces for poultry and seafood, with the exception of the Spicy Peanut Sauce, are ¼ cup. Because the peanut sauce is both naturally higher in fat and more filling, 3 tablespoons is a good serving size.

✳ The sweet sauces—for cakes, frozen desserts, pancakes, French toast, or cooked cereals—are ¼ cup each.

✳ Condiments tend to have more assertive flavors, so a little bit of each of them will go a long way. Servings of all my condiments—except for the Roasted Garlic—are 2 tablespoons.

I consider both the Roasted Garlic and the Yogurt Cheese to be indispensable condiments. Use Roasted Garlic as a spread, or add it to dips, pureed cooked vegetables, sauces, or grain pilafs. Yogurt cheese, which is made by draining plain fat-free yogurt to release much of the liquid, is a cream-cheese substitute that adds richness and true dairy flavor to dips, spreads, desserts, sauces, and many other dishes.

Broccoli Alfredo Sauce

quick and **easy**

If you're serving the sauce with pasta, the broccoli can be added to the pasta pot instead of being cooked separately.

¼	cup all-purpose flour
2	cups skim milk
1½	cups fat-free liquid creamer
8	ounces fat-free cream cheese
1	ounce low-fat Provolone cheese, shredded
	Pinch of ground nutmeg
1	medium onion, diced
2	tablespoons dry sherry or 1 teaspoon sherry extract
	Pinch of ground red pepper
10	ounces broccoli florets
	Ground black pepper
¼	cup fat-free Parmesan topping

Lynn's Kitchen Tip

To freeze the Alfredo sauce, it's best to prepare it without the broccoli, which will lose some of its bright color in the freezer. At serving time, add the broccoli to the pasta pot a few minutes before the pasta is done cooking. Gently reheat the Alfredo sauce over low heat. Drain the broccoli with the pasta and toss both with the Alfredo sauce to reheat it.

1 Place the flour in a medium no-stick saucepan. Gradually whisk in the milk until smooth. Add the creamer and cream cheese. Cook over medium heat, stirring constantly and breaking the cream cheese into small pieces, for 5 to 7 minutes, or until the mixture thickens.

2 Add the Provolone and nutmeg. Cook, stirring, for 2 minutes, or until the Provolone melts. Reduce the heat to low. Cover and cook, stirring occasionally, for 5 minutes.

3 Meanwhile, coat a large no-stick skillet with no-stick spray. Add the onions and cook, stirring, for 4 to 5 minutes, or until the onions soften. Add the sherry or sherry extract and the red pepper. Cook over medium heat until the sherry evaporates. Add the onions to the saucepan with the Provolone mixture.

4 Bring a medium pot of water to a boil. Add the broccoli; cook for 3 to 4 minutes, or until crisp-tender. Drain and add to the sauce. Season to taste with the black pepper. Stir in the Parmesan.

Makes about **6** cups.

Photograph on page 253

---

nutrition at a glance

per ½ cup

0.9 g.	total fat
0.4 g.	saturated fat
108	calories
5 mg.	cholesterol
265 mg.	sodium
9.8 g.	protein
13.6 g.	carbohydrates
0.9 g.	dietary fiber

Marinara Sauce

quick and easy

This sauce is endlessly versatile. It's good with lasagna or simply spooned over cooked pasta. Sprinkle with a combination of shredded fat-free mozzarella, low-fat mozzarella, and fat-free Parmesan topping before serving.

1	large onion, coarsely chopped
3	cloves garlic, minced
1	can (16 ounces) tomatoes, chopped (with juice)
2	cups tomato juice
2	plum tomatoes, coarsely chopped
¼	cup chopped fresh parsley
1	teaspoon dried oregano
⅛	teaspoon crushed red-pepper flakes (optional)
½	teaspoon sugar (optional)
3	tablespoons thinly sliced fresh basil
	Ground black pepper
	Salt (optional)

1 Coat a large no-stick skillet with no-stick spray. Add the onions and garlic. Mist with no-stick spray. Cook over medium-low heat, stirring, for 5 minutes, or until the onions soften.

2 Add the canned tomatoes (with juice), tomato juice, plum tomatoes, parsley, oregano, red-pepper flakes (if using), and sugar (if using). Cover and simmer over low heat, stirring occasionally, for 15 minutes, or until the tomatoes are softened. With the back of a large spoon, break some of the tomatoes to thicken the sauce.

3 Stir in the basil. Season to taste with the pepper and salt (if using).

Makes about **4** cups.

nutrition at a glance

per ½ cup

0.3 g.	total fat
0 g.	saturated fat
35	calories
0 mg.	cholesterol
316 mg.	sodium
1.5 g.	protein
8 g.	carbohydrates
1.3 g.	dietary fiber

Curried Vegetable-Turkey Sauce

quick and easy

Serve each portion of this creamy sauce over 1½ cups cooked basmati rice, which will add less than 1 gram of fat.

2½	cups water or defatted chicken stock (page 94)
4	ounces boneless, skinless turkey breast, trimmed of all visible fat and cut into bite-size pieces
¼	cup chopped onions
1	teaspoon minced fresh ginger
2	tablespoons all-purpose flour
1	cup skim milk
1	cup chopped carrots
1	tablespoon curry powder
1	cup broccoli florets
1	teaspoon freshly squeezed lemon juice
1½	teaspoons sugar
1	teaspoon cornstarch
1	tablespoon water
	Salt (optional)
½	cup chopped scallions

1   In a large no-stick skillet over medium-high heat, bring 1 cup of the water or stock to a boil. Reduce the heat to medium. Add the turkey and simmer for 2 minutes, or until no longer pink. With a slotted spoon, remove the turkey and set aside.

2   Add the onions and ginger to the skillet. Cook for 1 minute. Sift the flour through a fine sieve into the skillet; cook, stirring constantly, for 1 minute. Slowly add the milk and the remaining 1½ cups water or stock. Cook, stirring constantly, for 1 to 2 minutes, or until the mixture starts to thicken.

3   Add the carrots and curry powder; cook for 5 minutes. Add the broccoli; cook for 3 minutes. Add the lemon juice, sugar, and reserved turkey.

4   Place the cornstarch and water in a cup. Stir to dissolve. Add to the sauce. Cook, stirring constantly, for 1 to 2 minutes. Season to taste with the salt (if using). Stir in the scallions.

Makes about **4** cups.

nutrition at a glance

per ½ cup

0.4 g.	total fat
0.1 g.	saturated fat
53	calories
10 mg.	cholesterol
34 mg.	sodium
5.4 g.	protein
7.4 g.	carbohydrates
1.2 g.	dietary fiber

Mushroom and Bacon Sauce

quick and easy

Big, thick mushroom slices make this pasta sauce taste and look decadent. I use the large stuffer-size button mushrooms, but you can substitute the more earthy portobellos. Capers make a piquant garnish.

1	large onion, chopped
5	cloves garlic, minced
12	ounces large mushrooms, cut into ½"-thick slices
2	stalks celery, sliced
½	cup water or defatted chicken stock (page 94)
1½	teaspoons dried oregano
	Pinch of dried thyme
3	medium tomatoes, coarsely chopped
2	ounces Canadian bacon, cut into matchsticks
½	cup chopped fresh parsley
¼	cup thinly sliced fresh basil
1	tablespoon red-wine vinegar or cider vinegar
	Ground black pepper
	Salt (optional)

1 Coat a large no-stick skillet with no-stick spray. Add the onions and garlic. Cook over medium heat, stirring occasionally, for 5 minutes, or until lightly browned.

2 Add the mushrooms, celery, water or stock, oregano, and thyme. Cook, stirring occasionally, for 20 minutes, or until the sauce is thick and the vegetables are tender.

3 Add the tomatoes, bacon, parsley, basil, and vinegar. Cook, stirring, for 3 to 4 minutes, or until the tomatoes are hot. Season to taste with the pepper and salt (if using).

Makes about **4** cups.

nutrition at a glance

per ½ cup

0.9 g.	total fat
0.2 g.	saturated fat
46	calories
4 mg.	cholesterol
117 mg.	sodium
3.2 g.	protein
7.5 g.	carbohydrates
1.9 g.	dietary fiber

Roasted Pepper Sauce

Here's a pepper-packed sauce for rice, noodles, baked potatoes, sliced braised mushrooms, or turkey cutlets.

1	yellow pepper
1	sweet red pepper
2	tablespoons finely chopped onions
1	small clove garlic, minced
2	tablespoons finely diced tomatoes
1	tablespoon finely chopped celery leaves
1	teaspoon finely chopped fresh parsley
1	can (14 ounces) low-sodium chicken broth, defatted
1½	tablespoons cornstarch
	Ground black pepper
	Salt (optional)

1 Cut the yellow pepper and red pepper in half; discard the stems, membranes, and seeds. Place the peppers, cut side down, on a foil-lined broiler pan. Broil 4" from the heat for 10 to 12 minutes, or until blackened. Remove from the oven and wrap the foil tightly around the peppers. Set aside for 10 minutes. Peel and discard the skin.

2 Finely dice the red peppers. Coarsely dice the yellow peppers; set both aside.

3 Coat a medium no-stick saucepan with no-stick spray. Add the onions and garlic. Cook over medium-low heat for 2 to 3 minutes, or until the onions start to soften. Add the tomatoes, celery, and parsley. Cook, stirring, for 5 minutes. Add the red peppers and 1½ cups of the broth to the saucepan. Pour the mixture into a blender or food processor. Puree. Return the mixture to the saucepan. Cook over medium heat, stirring, until the mixture comes to a boil.

4 Place the cornstarch in a cup. Add the remaining broth and stir to dissolve the cornstarch. Add to the pan. Cook, stirring constantly, for 3 minutes, or until thickened. Add the yellow peppers. Cook for 1 minute. Season to taste with the black pepper and salt (if using).

Makes about **2½** cups.

---

nutrition at a glance
per ½ cup

0.1 g.	total fat
0 g.	saturated fat
39	calories
0 mg.	cholesterol
71 mg.	sodium
3.5 g.	protein
6.3 g.	carbohydrates
1.3 g.	dietary fiber

All-American Barbecue Sauce

quick and easy

Use this thick, dark, basic barbecue sauce for basting skinless poultry, lean pork and beef, seafood, mushrooms, potato wedges, or other vegetables. The sauce will keep, refrigerated, for 2 weeks. If sodium is a concern, you can use low-sodium tomato puree and tomato juice, which will reduce the amount of sodium by about two-thirds.

2	large onions, coarsely chopped
1	tablespoon liquid smoke
2	cups tomato puree
1½	cups tomato juice
½	cup molasses
3	tablespoons Dijon mustard
⅓	cup packed brown sugar
2	tablespoons cider vinegar
1½	tablespoons chili powder
1	teaspoon ground black pepper
½	teaspoon hot-pepper sauce

1 Coat a large no-stick skillet with no-stick spray. Add the onions and ½ tablespoon of the liquid smoke. Cook over medium heat, stirring occasionally, for 6 minutes, or until the onions soften. Add the tomato puree, tomato juice, molasses, mustard, brown sugar, vinegar, chili powder, black pepper, hot-pepper sauce, and the remaining ½ tablespoon liquid smoke. Stir to combine well.

2 Reduce the heat to medium-low. Cook, stirring occasionally, for 20 minutes, or until the sauce is thickened.

Makes about **4** cups.

Lynn's Kitchen Tip

Take a tip from the professional barbecue cooks and baste meat, poultry, or vegetables with barbecue sauce shortly after cooking is completed. You can cook for 1 to 2 minutes more just to heat the sauce. If brushed on too early, the sugar in the sauce will burn.

nutrition at a glance

per ¼ cup

0.5 g.	total fat
0 g.	saturated fat
75	calories
0 mg.	cholesterol
292 mg.	sodium
1.2 g.	protein
18.3 g.	carbohydrates
1.4 g.	dietary fiber

Chicken Gravy

quick and **easy**

You won't find a richer-tasting poultry gravy than this. It can be made with turkey breast instead of chicken. For a smooth version, puree the finished gravy in a blender or food processor.

¼   cup finely chopped onions
¼   cup finely chopped mushrooms
¼   cup finely chopped celery
¼   cup finely chopped carrots
1   small clove garlic, minced
1   ounce skinless, boneless chicken breast, trimmed of all visible fat and finely diced
⅓   cup all-purpose flour
2   cans (14 ounces each) low-sodium chicken broth, defatted
    Pinch of dried thyme
    Pinch of dried rosemary, crumbled
    Pinch of dried sage
    Ground black pepper
    Salt (optional)

1   Coat a large no-stick saucepan with no-stick spray. Add the onions, mushrooms, celery, carrots, and garlic. Cook over medium heat, stirring constantly, for 5 minutes.

2   Add the chicken. Cook, stirring, for 1 to 2 minutes, or until the chicken is no longer pink. Remove the chicken and vegetables; set aside.

3   Add the flour to the pan. Cook over medium heat, stirring, for 5 minutes, or until light tan in color. Remove from the heat and gradually whisk in the broth until smooth. Add the thyme, rosemary, and sage.

4   Cook over medium heat, whisking constantly, for 2 to 3 minutes, or until thick.

5   Add the reserved chicken and vegetables. Reduce the heat to low; simmer for 5 minutes, or until the vegetables are hot. Season to taste with the pepper and salt (if using).

Makes about **4** cups.

nutrition at a glance
per ¼ cup
0.1 g. total fat
0 g. saturated fat
21 calories
1 mg. cholesterol
43 mg. sodium
2.4 g. protein
2.5 g. carbohydrates
0.2 g. dietary fiber

Basic White Sauce with Variations

quick and easy

This versatile "mother sauce" can be used by itself or as a base for many flavored sauces (I've given some variations below to get you started). It stores beautifully in the freezer in recipe-ready portions.

3 tablespoons all-purpose flour
1 cup skim milk
1 cup fat-free liquid creamer
   Pinch of ground black pepper or nutmeg
   Salt (optional)

1 Place the flour in a medium no-stick saucepan. Gradually whisk in the milk until smooth. Add the creamer. Cook over medium heat, whisking constantly, for 4 to 5 minutes, or until the sauce thickens. Add the pepper or nutmeg. Season to taste with the salt (if using).

Makes **2** cups.

Cheese Sauce: To the finished basic sauce, add 2 ounces shredded fat-free Cheddar cheese; whisk over medium-low heat until melted.

Dill Sauce: To the finished basic sauce, add 2 to 3 tablespoons chopped fresh dill.

Garlic Sauce: To the finished basic sauce, add ¼ cup pureed Roasted Garlic (page 304).

Lemon Sauce: To the finished basic sauce, add ¼ cup freshly squeezed lemon juice and ½ teaspoon grated lemon rind.

Mushroom Sauce: To the finished basic sauce, add 8 ounces mushrooms (thinly sliced and sautéed) and 1 small onion (sliced and sautéed).

Onion Sauce: To the finished basic sauce, add ½ cup sautéed chopped onions, 3 ounces shredded fat-free mozzarella cheese, and 2 tablespoons fat-free Parmesan topping.

nutrition at a glance	
per ¼ cup	
0 g.	total fat
0 g.	saturated fat
41	calories
1 mg.	cholesterol
16 mg.	sodium
1.3 g.	protein
7.7 g.	carbohydrates
0 g.	dietary fiber

Spicy Peanut Sauce

quick and easy

This piquant easy-to-make sauce can be served as a hot or cold topper for turkey tenders, chicken tenders, shrimp, fish fillets, or grilled vegetables. Sprinkle the sauce with chopped fresh cilantro just before serving for added color and flavor.

½   cup finely chopped onions
3   tablespoons low-fat peanut butter
1   tablespoon grated fresh ginger
1   teaspoon ground coriander
3   cloves garlic, minced
2   teaspoons packed brown sugar
2   teaspoons low-sodium soy sauce
½   teaspoon crushed red-pepper flakes
1   teaspoon finely chopped jalapeño or serrano peppers (wear plastic gloves when handling)
     Dash of ground cloves
2½ cups defatted chicken stock (page 94)
2   tablespoons cornstarch
2–3 tablespoons freshly squeezed lemon juice or lime juice

1   In a medium no-stick saucepan, combine the onions, peanut butter, ginger, coriander, garlic, brown sugar, soy sauce, red-pepper flakes, jalapeño or serrano peppers, and cloves. Add the stock. Bring to a simmer over medium heat. Reduce the heat to low and cook for 15 minutes, or until the onions are tender.

2   Transfer the mixture to a blender or food processor. Puree until smooth. Return to the saucepan.

3   Place the cornstarch in a cup. Add the lemon juice or lime juice and stir to dissolve the cornstarch. Add to the saucepan. Cook over medium-low heat, stirring constantly, for 2 to 3 minutes, or until thickened.

Makes about **2½** cups.

nutrition at a glance
per 3 tablespoons
0.9 g. total fat
0.2 g. saturated fat
31   calories
1 mg. cholesterol
51 mg. sodium
1.4 g. protein
3.9 g. carbohydrates
0.2 g. dietary fiber

Mexican Sauce

This version of Mexican mole sauce is deeply flavored, slightly sweet, and pleasantly spicy. Pour it over boneless, skinless chicken breasts before baking. Or spoon it over pan-seared turkey cutlets or cooked rice, beans, or even baked potatoes.

1 dried chipotle pepper (wear plastic gloves when handling)
1 onion, finely chopped
1 large clove garlic, minced
1 teaspoon cocoa powder
1 cup defatted chicken stock (page 94)
1 can (8 ounces) tomato sauce
2 teaspoons chili powder
1 teaspoon ground cumin
½ teaspoon sugar
¼ teaspoon ground allspice
¼ teaspoon ground cinnamon
2 teaspoons freshly squeezed lime juice

1 Place the pepper in a small bowl and add hot water to cover. Set aside for 30 minutes, or until softened. Drain.

2 Split the pepper and discard the seeds, membranes and stem. Chop the pepper finely and set aside.

3 Coat a large no-stick saucepan with no-stick spray. Add the onions, garlic, and cocoa. Mist with no-stick spray. Cook over medium heat, stirring, for 8 minutes, or until the onions are softened.

4 Add the reserved peppers. Cook, stirring, for 2 minutes. Add the stock, tomato sauce, chili powder, cumin, sugar, allspice, and cinnamon. Stir well to combine. Reduce the heat to low. Cook for 15 minutes, or until thickened. Add the lime juice and stir well.

Makes about **2** cups.

nutrition at a glance

per ¼ cup

0.3 g.	total fat
0.1 g.	saturated fat
22	calories
0 mg.	cholesterol
181 mg.	sodium
0.8 g.	protein
5 g.	carbohydrates
1.1 g.	dietary fiber

Citrus-Honey Sauce

quick and easy

This smooth sweet-tart sauce is a delight with angel food cake, fat-free pudding, fat-free vanilla ice cream, or fresh ripe berries. For a special treat, make it with limes.

1   tablespoon cornstarch
⅓   cup freshly squeezed lemon juice
½   cup water
¼   cup sugar
2   tablespoons honey
½   teaspoon grated lemon rind
½   teaspoon grated orange rind

1   Place the cornstarch in a medium no-stick saucepan. Add the lemon juice and stir to dissolve the cornstarch. Add the water, sugar, honey, lemon rind, and orange rind. Whisk until smooth.

2   Cook over medium heat, whisking constantly, for 4 to 5 minutes, or until thickened.

Makes about **1** cup.

nutrition at a glance
per ¼ cup
0 g.   total fat
0 g.   saturated fat
94   calories
0 mg.   cholesterol
2 mg.   sodium
0.1 g.   protein
24.8 g.   carbohydrates
0.2 g.   dietary fiber

Blueberry Sauce

quick and easy

Serve this berry good sauce warm with hot cereal, pancakes, or waffles. Or chill it to top fat-free ice cream, fat-free vanilla yogurt, fat-free pudding, angel food cake, or lemon sorbet.

1	tablespoon cornstarch
1	cup water
½	cup sugar
2	tablespoons freshly squeezed lemon juice
2	teaspoons grated lemon rind
1	pint blueberries
1	teaspoon vanilla

1 Place the cornstarch in a cup. Add ¼ cup of the water and stir to dissolve the cornstarch. Set aside.

2 In a medium no-stick saucepan, combine the sugar, lemon juice, lemon rind, and the remaining ¾ cup water. Bring to a boil over medium heat. Reduce the heat to medium-low. Add the blueberries and stir gently. Add the cornstarch mixture. Cook, stirring gently, for 30 seconds, or until thickened. Remove from the heat. Stir in the vanilla.

Makes about **2** cups.

Lynn's Kitchen Tip

Add soft-skinned fruits—such as blueberries, strawberries, raspberries, plums, apricots, and nectarines—to sauces toward the end of the cooking time to reserve their texture and color.

nutrition at a glance

per ¼ cup

0.1 g.	total fat
0 g.	saturated fat
74	calories
0 mg.	cholesterol
3 mg.	sodium
0.3 g.	protein
18.9 g.	carbohydrates
1 g.	dietary fiber

Tomato Relish

quick and easy

The ingredients for this sweet-sharp relish can be chopped and mixed in a wink in a food processor. It's a terrific accompaniment to Black Bean and Rice Cakes (page 181) or nearly any bean recipe. For best results, refrigerate the salsa for several hours to develop the flavor.

2   plum tomatoes, coarsely chopped
2   small scallions, finely chopped
1   small carrot, finely chopped or shredded
1   tablespoon freshly squeezed lemon juice
2   teaspoons candied ginger, minced
2   teaspoons thinly sliced fresh basil
1   clove garlic, minced
    Salt (optional)
    Hot-pepper sauce (optional)

1   In a medium bowl, combine the tomatoes, scallions, carrots, lemon juice, ginger, basil, and garlic. Season to taste with the salt (if using) and hot-pepper sauce (if using). Mix well.

Makes about **1** cup.

Photograph on page 320

nutrition at a glance
per 2 tablespoons
0.1 g. total fat
0 g.   saturated fat
13   calories
0 mg. cholesterol
6 mg. sodium
0.4 g. protein
3 g.   carbohydrates
0.6 g. dietary fiber

Rémoulade Sauce

quick and **easy**

This adaptation of the classic savory New Orleans condiment is superb on chilled cooked turkey, chicken, fish, or shellfish. It's also a fine spread for sandwiches. Make it with a fat-free mayonnaise that's not heavily sweetened.

1   cup fat-free mayonnaise
2   tablespoons chopped fresh parsley
1   tablespoon chopped gherkin or dill pickles
2   teaspoons Dijon mustard
½   teaspoon cider vinegar
½   teaspoon low-sodium Worcestershire sauce
½   teaspoon dried tarragon
1   teaspoon capers, rinsed and drained

1   In a medium bowl, combine the mayonnaise, parsley, pickles, mustard, vinegar, Worcestershire sauce, and tarragon. Chop the capers and add to the bowl. Mix well.

Makes about **1** cup.

---

nutrition at a glance

per 2 tablespoons

0.1 g.	total fat
0 g.	saturated fat
21	calories
0 mg.	cholesterol
248 mg.	sodium
0.2 g.	protein
3.9 g.	carbohydrates
0 g.	dietary fiber

Caramelized Onion Compote

quick and easy

The flavor of this sweet-and-sour condiment will really develop if it is refrigerated for a few days after cooking. Serve with cooked poultry, beef, beans, or grilled vegetables.

2   large onions, chopped
¼   cup finely chopped yellow peppers
½   teaspoon minced garlic
2   tablespoons chopped raisins
2   tablespoons sugar
2   teaspoons brewed coffee
¾   cup white wine or nonalcoholic white wine
1   teaspoon dried thyme
½   teaspoon dried rosemary, crumbled
      Ground black pepper
      Salt (optional)

1   Coat a large no-stick saucepan with no-stick spray. Add the onions, peppers, and garlic. Mist with no-stick spray. Cover and cook over medium heat, stirring occasionally, for 4 to 5 minutes, or until the onions start to release moisture. Uncover and reduce the heat to medium-low. Cook, stirring occasionally, for 5 to 6 minutes, or until golden. If necessary, add 1 to 2 teaspoons water to prevent sticking.

2   Add the raisins, sugar, and coffee. Cook over low heat for 2 minutes, or until the sugar dissolves. Add the wine. Cook over medium heat, stirring occasionally, for 5 minutes, or until the liquid has nearly evaporated.

3   Add the thyme and rosemary. Cook over low heat for 5 minutes. Season to taste with the pepper and salt (if using).

Makes about **2** cups.

nutrition at a glance

per 2 tablespoons
0.1 g.	total fat
0 g.	saturated fat
20	calories
0 mg.	cholesterol
1 mg.	sodium
0.3 g.	protein
3.6 g.	carbohydrates
0.3 g.	dietary fiber

Pinto Bean Salsa with Chipotle

A quicker version of this salsa—different but still delicious—can be made by combining all the ingredients raw.

1 small dried chipotle pepper (wear plastic gloves when handling)
3 medium tomatoes
2 cloves garlic, unpeeled
½ jalapeño pepper (wear plastic gloves when handling)
1 teaspoon dried oregano
¼ teaspoon cumin seeds, crushed
1 cup cooked pinto beans
1 small onion, chopped
2 tablespoons finely chopped green peppers
2 tablespoons freshly squeezed lime juice
1 tablespoon chopped fresh parsley
Salt (optional)

1 Place the chipotle pepper in a small bowl and add hot water to cover. Set aside for 30 minutes, or until softened. Drain.

2 Split the pepper and discard the seeds, membranes, and stem. Chop the pepper finely and place in a medium bowl.

3 In a large no-stick skillet, combine the tomatoes, garlic, and jalapeño pepper. Cook over medium-high heat, turning occasionally, for 10 minutes, or until the tomato skins are blackened on all sides. Remove and set aside cool.

4 Add the oregano and cumin to the skillet. Cook over medium heat, tossing constantly, for 2 to 3 minutes, or until fragrant. Transfer to the bowl with the chipotle peppers.

5 Core and peel the tomatoes; discard the cores and skin. Chop the tomatoes coarsely. Add to the bowl.

6 Peel the garlic. Finely chop the garlic and the jalapeño pepper. Add to the bowl. Add the beans, onions, green peppers, lime juice, and parsley. Mix well. Season to taste with the salt (if using).

Makes about **2½** cups.

nutrition at a glance
per 2 tablespoons
0.1 g. total fat
0 g. saturated fat
19 calories
0 mg. cholesterol
22 mg. sodium
0.9 g. protein
3.7 g. carbohydrates
1 g. dietary fiber

Nectarine Salsa

quick and easy

Refreshing fruit salsas add terrific tastes to summer meals. Serve with fish, meat, poultry, pork, or bean dishes. Peaches can easily substitute for the nectarines. Just be sure that the fruit you use is ripe and sweet.

3	nectarines, diced
4	scallions, chopped
¼	cup freshly squeezed lime juice
1	teaspoon finely chopped jalapeño peppers (wear plastic gloves when handling)
1	small clove garlic, minced
1	teaspoon chopped fresh mint
1–2	teaspoons sugar (optional)

1 In a medium bowl, combine the nectarines, scallions, lime juice, peppers, garlic, and mint. Mix well. If the fruit is not sweet enough, add 1 to 2 teaspoons sugar. Cover and refrigerate for 30 minutes. Drain off excess liquid before serving.

Makes about **2½** cups.

Photograph on page 254

nutrition at a glance

per 2 tablespoons

0.1 g.	total fat
0 g.	saturated fat
12	calories
0 mg.	cholesterol
1 mg.	sodium
0.3 g.	protein
2.9 g.	carbohydrates
0.4 g.	dietary fiber

Roasted Garlic

Garlic that has been roasted has a mellow flavor and spreadable consistency. It can replace butter as a bread spread. Or it can be mixed with cooked rice or pasta or whisked into savory sauces. Be sure to use 4 whole bulbs garlic, not individual cloves.

4   large bulbs garlic, unpeeled

1   Preheat the oven to 350°F. Cut the tops from the garlic bulbs to expose just the tips of the garlic cloves. Place the garlic bulbs in the center of a large piece of foil. Mist with no-stick spray. Seal the foil tightly, leaving some air space around the garlic. Bake for 55 to 60 minutes, or until the garlic is tender.

2   Open the foil and set aside to cool slightly. One clove at a time, squeeze the roasted garlic out of its skin. Discard the foil and skins. Puree the garlic in a blender or food processor, adding 1 teaspoon water, if necessary, to facilitate blending. Refrigerate for up to 1 week.

Makes about ½ cup.

Photograph on page 322

Photograph on page 322

Lynn's Kitchen Tip

Here's an alternate way to roast garlic. Break the bulbs into individual cloves and peel them. Mist with no-stick spray and wrap in foil, as in the recipe. Bake at 350°F for 40 minutes, or until the garlic is tender.

nutrition at a glance

per 1 tablespoon

0.1 g.	total fat
0 g.	saturated fat
34	calories
0 mg.	cholesterol
4 mg.	sodium
1.4 g.	protein
7.5 g.	carbohydrates
0.5 g.	dietary fiber

Yogurt Cheese

Be sure to buy yogurt without added gelatin, which prevents the whey from separating from the curd to make cheese. To test your yogurt, remove a spoonful from the carton. If the space fills with liquid within a few minutes, you can make yogurt cheese from it.

2   cups fat-free plain yogurt

1   Line a fine mesh sieve with cheesecloth or use a plastic mesh-lined yogurt cone. Spoon the yogurt into the sieve or cone. Set over a large glass measuring cup or other tall container. Refrigerate for at least 4 hours, or until well-drained.

2   Remove the yogurt from the sieve or cone. Store, tightly covered, in the refrigerator.

Makes about **1** cup.

Lynn's Kitchen Tip

Save the whey left from making yogurt cheese to add to soups or pancake batters.

nutrition at a glance

per 2 tablespoons

0.1 g.	total fat
0 g.	saturated fat
34	calories
1 mg.	cholesterol
47 mg.	sodium
3.5 g.	protein
4.7 g.	carbohydrates
0 g.	dietary fiber

Breakfast, Brunch, and Lunch

Dinners are certainly important on a low-fat

eating plan, but there are only seven dinners in

a week.

Breakfasts, brunches, and lunches provide

many more opportunities to eat healthfully.

Too often, these meals are treated as an

afterthought. With some forethought, however, break-

fasts, brunches, and lunches can become important

occasions to incorporate nutrient- and fiber-packed

grains, vegetables, and fruits into your eating plan.

Breakfast

We Americans are from a farm heritage and think that the ideal breakfast is big and rich. Traditional offerings are oozing with butter or other animal fats. Bacon, ham, sausage, corned beef hash, hash brown potatoes, eggs, pancakes, waffles, French toast, biscuits and gravy, and dough-nuts are as much an anachronism as the horse and carriage.

An enlightened breakfast for modern lifestyles is whole-grain cereal, skim milk, and fruit juice or fresh fruit. Toasted bagels or English muffins are also good options. Serve with jam, preserves, honey, marmalade, or jelly—all of which are fat-free. Or drizzle with fat-free butter from a squeeze bottle.

For those on the go, a bag of my Orange Granola makes a handy desk companion. Or a banana smoothie is quick to whip up to sip on the way to the office. (Cut a frozen banana into chunks—store peeled overripe bananas in the freezer for just such occasions. Puree in a blender or food processor with a scoop of fat-free vanilla frozen yogurt, skim milk to thin, and a dash of cinnamon.)

Brunch

Weekends are more leisurely and can include brunch fare that tastes as luscious as it is nutritious.

Omelets, scrambled eggs, quiches, and French toast can all be made fat-free using egg substitutes. Fat-free egg substitutes, available refrigerated or frozen, are made mostly from egg whites. They are also pasteurized, which makes them safe to eat even when slightly undercooked.

My Spinach Quiche in Potato Crust, Salmon-Stuffed Mushrooms, Cranberry Biscotti, and assorted filled omelets will make any brunch special.

Lunch

Whether you're eating at home or at your office desk, lunch is the second-most important meal of the day. My lunch main dishes are based on vegetables, grains, and lean proteins to fuel your body and keep your energy high throughout the busy afternoon.

My Spaghetti with Fresh Vegetables and Baked Potatoes Italiano are the kinds of carbohydrate-rich dishes that stick to your ribs. My Hearty Vegetable Sauté, Malaysian Curried Rice, and Polenta with Roasted Ratatouille make great brown-bag lunches to heat in an office microwave. You might want to make double batches so that you have leftovers on hand for lunch.

Orange Granola

Orange juice and fresh ginger give this granola a spirited new flavor. For the fruit, use a mixture of dates, figs, tart cherries, apricots, and prunes—or whatever dried fruit you have on hand. Both old-fashioned rolled oats and the quick-cooking kind work fine in this recipe.

1½	cups finely chopped mixed dried fruit
2	tablespoons orange juice
1	teaspoon grated fresh ginger
½	cup maple syrup
2	cups rolled oats

1 Preheat the oven to 325°F.

2 In a medium microwaveable bowl, combine the fruit, orange juice, ginger, and ¼ cup of the maple syrup. Microwave on high power for 1½ to 2 minutes, or until hot.

3 Coat a jelly-roll pan with no-stick spray. Place the oats in the pan. Drizzle with the remaining ¼ cup maple syrup; toss lightly to coat. Spread the oats in an even layer and bake for 20 minutes, stirring once.

4 Pour the fruit mixture over the oats; stir well to mix. Spread in an even layer. Bake for 20 minutes, stirring every 5 minutes, or until the mixture is crisp and golden.

5 Allow to cool, then store in an airtight container in a cool spot.

Makes **4** cups.

Lynn's Kitchen Tip

If granola becomes soggy in humid weather, you can recrisp it by spreading it on a baking sheet coated with no-stick spray and baking at 200°F for 10 minutes. Turn off the oven and leave the granola in the oven for 1 hour.

nutrition at a glance

per ¼ cup

0.9 g.	total fat
0.1 g.	saturated fat
113	calories
0 mg.	cholesterol
2 mg.	sodium
2 g.	protein
26 g.	carbohydrates
1.9 g.	dietary fiber

Hot Porridge with Scalloped Apples

The scalloped apple topping makes this breakfast cereal even more special. Add dried cranberries, dried cherries, or chopped dried apricots to the scalloped apples instead of the raisins if you like. Serve with fat-free liquid creamer or skim milk.

Scalloped Apples

2	large Granny Smith apples, thinly sliced
2	tablespoons freshly squeezed lemon juice
2	tablespoons sugar
¼	teaspoon ground cinnamon
	Pinch of ground allspice
¼	cup raisins (optional)

Porridge

2	cups skim milk
1	cup farina
¼	cup water
1	tablespoon oat bran
¼	teaspoon salt (optional)

1 *To make the scalloped apples:* In a medium microwaveable bowl, combine the apples, lemon juice, sugar, cinnamon, and allspice. Cover loosely with wax paper. Microwave on high power, stirring occasionally, for 15 minutes, or until the apples are almost tender. Add the raisins (if using). Microwave on high power for 5 minutes more; set aside.

2 *To make the porridge:* In a medium microwaveable bowl, combine the milk, farina, water, oat bran, and salt (if using). Cover loosely with wax paper. Microwave on medium power, stirring frequently, for 10 to 12 minutes, or until the cereal is thick and smooth. Serve topped with the apples.

Makes **6** servings.

nutrition at a glance

per serving

0.9 g.	total fat
0.2 g.	saturated fat
196	calories
1 mg.	cholesterol
157 mg.	sodium
6 g.	protein
42 g.	carbohydrates
2.4 g.	dietary fiber

Pancakes with Nectarines

quick and easy

You can substitute other fruits for the nectarines in these light and fluffy pancakes. Try cherries, raspberries, blueberries, peaches, plums, strawberries, or bananas. If using bananas, be sure to toss the slices with a few teaspoons lemon juice to prevent discoloring.

½   cup fat-free cottage cheese
¼   cup fat-free egg substitute
3   tablespoons sugar
½   cup all-purpose flour
½   teaspoon baking soda
½   teaspoon baking powder
½   teaspoon ground cinnamon
4   egg whites
2   nectarines, chopped

1   Place the cottage cheese in a sieve. Set over a bowl and allow to drain for 10 minutes. Transfer to a blender or food processor. Blend, scraping the sides of the container occasionally, for 3 to 5 minutes, or until completely smooth. Add the egg substitute and sugar. Process briefly to mix. Set aside.

2   In a small bowl, combine the flour, baking soda, baking powder, and cinnamon. Mix well.

3   Place the egg whites in a large bowl. Beat with an electric mixer until stiff peaks form. Sift the flour mixture over the egg whites. Fold to combine. Add the cottage-cheese mixture. Fold to combine.

4   Coat a large no-stick skillet with no-stick spray. Warm over low heat. Spoon the batter in ¼-cup measures into the pan. Sprinkle 2 tablespoons of the nectarines over each pancake, pressing in lightly. Cook for 5 minutes, or until the bottoms are golden. Flip and cook for 4 minutes, or until golden. Remove to a platter. Cover to keep warm while cooking the remaining pancakes.

Makes **8** pancakes.

Photograph on page 325

Photograph on page 325

Lynn's Kitchen Tip

Plain pancakes freeze well for quick weekday breakfasts. Allow the cooked pancakes to cool, then stack with pieces of wax paper between the pancakes. Place in a plastic freezer bag and seal tightly. Freeze. Remove just the number of pancakes that you need. Allow to stand at room temperature for 15 minutes, then heat in a toaster, toaster oven, or conventional oven.

nutrition at a glance

per pancake

0.2 g.	total fat
0 g.	saturated fat
84	calories
1 mg.	cholesterol
189 mg.	sodium
5.2 g.	protein
15.6 g.	carbohydrates
0.9 g.	dietary fiber

Baked Winter Fruits

This luscious baked fruit compote is delicious as a topping for fat-free plain yogurt or as a sweet in its own right—drizzle it with some evaporated skim milk.

1	baking apple
1	ripe but firm pear
½	cup apple juice
¼	cup raisins
¼	cup chopped dates
1½	tablespoons cherry preserves
2	teaspoons freshly squeezed lemon juice
	Pinch of ground nutmeg
	Pinch of ground cinnamon

1   Preheat the oven to 375°F.

2   Cut the apple and pear into lengthwise quarters. Cut out the seeds and discard. Place in an 8" x 8" baking dish.

3   In a small bowl, combine the apple juice, raisins, dates, preserves, lemon juice, nutmeg, and cinnamon. Pour over the apples and pears. Stir to mix.

4   Cover with foil. Bake, basting occasionally with the sauce, for 35 to 40 minutes, or until the fruit is tender.

Makes **4** servings.

nutrition at a glance

per serving

0.5 g.	total fat
0.1 g.	saturated fat
141	calories
0 mg.	cholesterol
5 mg.	sodium
0.9 g.	protein
36.6 g.	carbohydrates
3.3 g.	dietary fiber

French Toast

quick and **easy**

This French toast is so easy to make that it's sure to become a weekend favorite. Let the bread slices sit out overnight to dry slightly so they keep their shape when dipped in the egg mixture. Serve with a dollop of fruit jam or a drizzle of warm maple syrup or honey. Using a large skillet to cook the French toast will allow you to do them in 2 batches.

¾ cup fat-free egg substitute
1 cup skim milk
¼ teaspoon vanilla
    Pinch of ground cinnamon
8 slices (40-calorie-per-slice) white bread
2 teaspoons confectioners' sugar

1 In a large shallow bowl, combine the egg substitute, milk, vanilla, and cinnamon. Whisk to combine.

2 Coat a large no-stick skillet with no-stick spray. Warm over medium heat. Dip one bread slice at a time into the egg mixture, turning to coat both sides and to soak up as much of the mixture as possible. Add to the skillet. Cook for 4 minutes, or until golden. Flip and cook for 4 minutes, or until golden. Remove and keep warm.

3 Wipe the skillet with a paper towel to remove any browned bits. Off the heat, coat the skillet with no-stick spray. Warm over medium heat. Dip and cook more bread slices. Repeat to cook all the bread slices.

4 Place the confectioners' sugar in a small fine sieve. Sprinkle over the French toast just before serving.

Makes **8** slices.

Lynn's Lore

The French call French toast *pain perdu*, or "lost bread," because the recipe was originally devised to use up old, dry bread.

nutrition at a glance

per slice

0.6 g.	total fat
0.1 g.	saturated fat
66	calories
1 mg.	cholesterol
144 mg.	sodium
5 g.	protein
11.4 g.	carbohydrates
1.9 g.	dietary fiber

Salmon-Stuffed Mushrooms

These savory stuffed mushrooms make a lovely addition to the brunch table. Serve with scrambled fat-free egg substitute and toasted English muffins.

8	large mushrooms (3" diameter)
1¼	cups diced French bread
1	clove garlic, minced
⅛	teaspoon dried thyme
⅛	teaspoon dried crumbled rosemary
1	cup fat-free egg substitute
1	egg white
2	tablespoons fat-free mayonnaise
1	teaspoon finely chopped fresh dill
3	scallions, chopped
¼	cup chopped smoked salmon
	Salt (optional)
3	tablespoons fat-free sour cream

1 Preheat oven to 375°F.

2 Remove the stems from the mushrooms. Set aside the caps. Chop the stems and set aside.

3 Coat a large no-stick skillet with no-stick spray. Warm over medium-high heat. Place the caps in the skillet, round side down. Reduce the heat to medium, cover, and cook for 4 minutes. Turn the mushrooms. Cover and cook for 4 minutes, or until the mushrooms are softened. Place the caps, round side down, in a 12" x 8" baking dish. Set aside.

4 Add the bread, garlic, thyme, and rosemary to the skillet. Mist with no-stick spray. Cook over medium heat, tossing frequently, for 4 minutes, or until golden. Add the mushroom stems. Cook, tossing, for 4 minutes, or until the stems soften.

5 In a small bowl, mix the egg substitute, egg white, mayonnaise, dill, and half of the scallions. Add to the skillet. Cook, stirring, for 3 to 5 minutes, or until the eggs start to set. Add the salmon and mix to combine. Season to taste with the salt (if using).

6 Remove from the heat. Divide the filling among the mushroom caps. Bake for 8 to 10 minutes, or until the stuffing is hot.

7 Top each cap with a dollop of the sour cream and sprinkle with the remaining scallions.

Makes **8** mushrooms.

Basic Omelet with Variations

quick and easy

Omelets are one of the easiest and most versatile dishes for breakfast or brunch. They can be made without fat just by using fat-free egg substitute and egg whites. After you master the basic omelet, try any my fillings below or create your own. For best results if doubling the recipe, don't increase the size of the pan. Instead, cook the omelets in two batches.

1 cup fat-free egg substitute
2 egg whites
  Pinch of ground black pepper
  Pinch of salt (optional)

1 In a medium bowl, combine the egg substitute, egg whites, pepper and salt (if using). Whisk until slightly frothy.

2 Coat a medium no-stick skillet or omelet pan with no-stick spray. Warm over medium-high heat. Add the egg mixture. Cook over high heat for 3 to 4 minutes, occasionally lifting the edges of the egg mixture to let the uncooked eggs run underneath. When the eggs are almost set, use a spatula to loosen the edges.

3 With the spatula, fold the eggs in half to create a half-moon. Reduce the heat to low and cook for 2 minutes, or until the eggs are cooked through. Cut in half.

nutrition at a glance
per serving
0 g. total fat
0 g. saturated fat
79 calories
0 mg. cholesterol
255 mg. sodium
15.5 g. protein
3 g. carbohydrates
0 g. dietary fiber

Makes **2** servings.

Cheese Omelet: Add a pinch of nutmeg to the egg mixture instead of the pepper. Just before folding the omelet, sprinkle with ¼ cup shredded fat-free Cheddar cheese or fat-free mozzarella cheese. Fold and cook for 2 minutes, or until the cheese melts. Sprinkle with finely chopped scallions.

Greek Omelet: Coat a large no-stick skillet with no-stick spray. Add 1 cup torn spinach leaves, 1 scallion (chopped), and ¼ teaspoon dried oregano. Cook over medium heat, stirring, for 2 to 3 minutes, or until the spinach wilts. Add 1 small tomato (chopped). Cook for 2 minutes. Set aside while preparing the omelet. Just before folding the omelet, spoon the mixture over the eggs. Sprinkle with 1 tablespoon crumbled low-fat feta cheese. Fold and cook for 2 minutes, or until the filling is hot. Sprinkle with chopped fresh dill.

Ham Omelet: Just before folding the omelet, sprinkle with 2 ounces diced fat-free ham or Canadian bacon. Fold and cook for 2 minutes, or until the filling is hot. Sprinkle with finely chopped fresh parsley.

Jelly Omelet: Add ½ teaspoon sugar to the egg mixture instead of the pepper. Just before folding the omelet, spoon 3 tablespoons jelly over the eggs. Fold and cook for 2 minutes, or until the filling is hot.

Mushroom Omelet: Coat a large no-stick skillet with no-stick spray. Add 4 ounces mushrooms, sliced. Cover and cook over medium heat for 3 to 4 minutes, or until the mushrooms start to release moisture. Uncover and cook, stirring occasionally, for 2 to 3 minutes, or until softened. Set aside while preparing the omelet. Just before folding the omelet, spoon the mushrooms over the eggs. Fold and cook for 2 minutes, or until the filling is hot. Sprinkle with fat-free Parmesan topping.

Onion Omelet: Coat a large no-stick skillet with no-stick spray. Add ½ cup chopped onions. Cover and cook over medium heat for 3 to 4 minutes, or until the onions start to release moisture. Uncover and cook, adding 1 to 2 teaspoons water if needed to prevent sticking, for 2 to 3 minutes, or until golden. Set aside while preparing the omelet. Just before folding the omelet, sprinkle the onions over the eggs. Fold and cook for 2 minutes, or until the filling is hot. Sprinkle with finely chopped fresh parsley.

Spanish Omelet: Coat a large no-stick skillet with no-stick spray. Add 1 small potato (diced), 1 small onion (diced), and 1 small clove garlic (minced). Mist with no-stick spray. Cook over medium-high heat, without stirring, for 3 to 4 minutes. Stir. Cook, stirring occasionally, for 8 to 10 minutes, or until the potatoes are tender. Set aside while preparing the omelet. Just before folding the omelet, spoon the potato mixture over the eggs. Fold and cook for 2 minutes, or until the filling is hot. Sprinkle with finely diced tomatoes.

Tex-Mex Omelet: Coat a large no-stick skillet with no-stick spray. Add ¼ cup finely diced onions, ¼ cup finely diced green peppers, ¼ cup finely diced tomatoes, and 1 clove garlic (minced). Mist with the no-stick spray. Cook over medium heat, stirring occasionally, for 4 to 6 minutes, or until the peppers are softened. Season with ¼ teaspoon chili powder, ¼ teaspoon ground cumin, and ¼ teaspoon dried oregano. Set aside while preparing the omelet. Just before folding the omelet, spoon the mixture over the eggs. Fold and cook for 2 minutes, or until the filling is hot. Sprinkle with chopped fresh cilantro.

Photograph on page 324

Creamy Banana Bowl

quick and easy

I sometimes sprinkle these bananas with a bit of toasted coconut or brown sugar just before serving. A sprig of fresh mint makes a lovely garnish.

½ cup fat-free plain yogurt
1 tablespoon sugar
2 ripe but firm bananas, sliced
 Ground cinnamon or nutmeg

1 In a medium bowl, combine the yogurt and sugar. Stir to dissolve the sugar. Add the bananas. Stir to combine. Sprinkle with the cinnamon or nutmeg.

Makes **4** servings.

nutrition at a glance
per serving
0.3 g. total fat
0.1 g. saturated fat
82 calories
1 mg. cholesterol
24 mg. sodium
2.4 g. protein
18.8 g. carbohydrates
1.2 g. dietary fiber

Spinach Quiche in Potato Crust

Using potato slices as a quiche crust eliminates the astronomically high amount of fat that comes with a traditional pastry crust. In fact, this recipe is so low in fat that I was able to use some real Parmesan cheese without raising the total fat above 1 gram per serving.

Potato Crust

2 medium baking potatoes, thinly sliced
 Salt (optional)

Spinach Filling

1 large onion, sliced
1 package (10 ounces) frozen chopped spinach, thawed
2 cups fat-free egg substitute
1½ cups fat-free liquid creamer
2 tablespoons all-purpose flour
¼ teaspoon ground nutmeg
2 ounces shredded fat-free Cheddar or mozzarella cheese
¼ teaspoon salt (optional)
2 tablespoons grated Parmesan cheese

1 *To make the potato crust:* Preheat the oven to 400°F.

2 Cover a large baking sheet with foil and coat with no-stick spray. Arrange the potatoes, slightly overlapping, in rows. Mist with no-stick spray. Sprinkle lightly with the salt (if using). Bake for 10 minutes, or until golden. Remove the potatoes from the oven.

3 Reduce the oven temperature to 350°F.

4 Coat a 10" deep-dish pie plate with no-stick spray. Arrange the potatoes in overlapping circles to cover the bottom. Overlap slices on the sides so that slices protrude above the edge of the pan. If you have extra potatoes, place them on the bottom. Set aside.

5 *To make the spinach filling:* Coat a large no-stick skillet with no-stick spray. Add the onions. Cover and cook over medium heat, stirring occasionally, for 6 minutes, or until golden. If necessary, add 1 to 2 teaspoons water to prevent sticking.

6 Add the spinach and cook for 2 minutes, or until the spinach is hot.

7 In a large bowl, combine the egg substitute, creamer, flour, and nutmeg. Whisk to combine. Add the Cheddar or mozzarella, onions, spinach, and salt (if using). Mix to combine. Pour into the prepared pie pan. Sprinkle with the Parmesan.

8 Bake for 40 minutes, or until a knife inserted in the center comes out clean.

Makes **8** servings.

Photograph on page 323

nutrition at a glance

per serving

0.6 g.	total fat
0.3 g.	saturated fat
128	calories
1.7 mg.	cholesterol
217 mg.	sodium
10.5 g.	protein
18.5 g.	carbohydrates
1.5 g.	dietary fiber

Quiche in Tomato Shells

On a chilly day, a piping hot quiche baked in a tomato shell makes a warm and inviting dish.

2   large firm tomatoes
1   cup fat-free egg substitute
2   tablespoons minced scallions
2   tablespoons chopped fresh parsley
1   tablespoon capers, rinsed and drained
¼   teaspoon ground black pepper
     Pinch of salt (optional)
4   teaspoons fresh bread crumbs (from 40-calorie-per-slice bread)
4   teaspoons fat-free Parmesan topping

1   Preheat the oven to 350°F.

2   Cut the tomatoes in half crosswise. Scoop out the pulp, leaving a ¼" shell. Set the shells, upside down, on paper towels to drain.

3   Chop the pulp and place in a medium bowl. Add the egg substitute, scallions, parsley, capers, pepper, and salt (if using). Stir to combine.

4   Place 4 custard cups in an 8" x 8" baking dish. Place a tomato shell, cut side up, in each cup. Divide the egg mixture among the shells. Sprinkle with the bread crumbs and Parmesan.

5   Bake for 40 minutes, or until a knife inserted in the filling comes out clean. If desired, broil for 2 minutes to brown the tops.

Makes **4** servings.

> **Lynn's Kitchen Tip**
>
> Try baking quiche in hollowed zucchini halves, baby eggplant halves, or acorn squash halves. Make sure to partially cook the vegetable so that it will be thoroughly cooked when the quiche filling is done.

nutrition at a glance
per serving
0.4 g. total fat
0 g. saturated fat
61 calories
0 mg. cholesterol
227 mg. sodium
8 g. protein
7.2 g. carbohydrates
1.4 g. dietary fiber

Thai Peanut Dressing (page 116) on mixed salad greens

Tomato Relish (page 299) and Black Bean and Rice Cakes (page 181)

Baked Potatoes Italiano (page 342)

Roasted Garlic (page 304)

Spinach Quiche in Potato Crust (page 316)

Tex-Mex Omelet (page 315)

Pancakes with Nectarines (page 309)

Stacked-High Apple Pie (page 359)

Pineapple-Caramel Cake (page 348)

Lemon Bars (page 369)

Key Lime Cheesecake (page 347)

Daffodil Cake with Lemon Sauce (page 354)

Almond Tapioca and Lime-Blackberry Parfaits (page 372)

Chocolate-Raspberry Cake (page 350)

332

Chocolate-Banana Pie (page 360)

Glazed Tropical Fruit Cake (page 356)

Cranberry Biscotti

For a fancy party or holiday treat, use a mixture of candied red and green cherries and coarsely chopped candied pineapple in place of the dried cranberries. These crunchy cookies are the perfect close for any brunch. Offer hot coffee or tea for dunking.

3	egg whites
½	teaspoon cream of tartar
½	cup sugar
½	teaspoon almond extract
1	cup all-purpose flour
½	cup sliced almonds
1	cup dried cranberries or tart cherries

1 Preheat the oven to 350°F.

2 Place the egg whites and cream of tartar in a large bowl. Beat with an electric mixer until soft peaks form. Continue beating, adding 1 tablespoon sugar at a time, until stiff peaks form. Add the almond extract and beat briefly. Sprinkle the flour over the egg-white mixture; fold to combine. Sprinkle the almonds and cranberries or cherries over the egg-white mixture; fold to combine.

3 Coat an 8" x 4" loaf pan with no-stick spray. Dust lightly with flour, shaking out the excess. Spread the dough evenly in the pan. Bake for 30 minutes, or until lightly browned. Remove from the oven and set aside to cool completely.

4 Reduce the oven temperature to 275°F.

5 Remove the biscotti loaf from the pan. Cut in half lengthwise into 2 strips. Cut each strip into 15 slices. Place the biscotti on a baking sheet. Bake for 35 minutes, or until golden and dry. Cool to room temperature before serving.

Makes **30** biscotti.

nutrition at a glance
per biscotto

0.9 g.	total fat
0 g.	saturated fat
53	calories
0 mg.	cholesterol
6 mg.	sodium
1.1 g.	protein
10 g.	carbohydrates
0.6 g.	dietary fiber

Mediterranean Stuffed Tomatoes

quick and easy

Best with summer-ripe tomatoes, this versatile luncheon dish can be served warm or hot from the oven. If you like, you can substitute cooked bulgur or orzo pasta for the rice. Serve with dollops of fat-free plain yogurt or sour cream. Cuke and Zuke Raita (page 105) makes a fine accompaniment.

2	large firm tomatoes
¼	cup chopped onions
½	teaspoon dried oregano
⅛	teaspoon ground cinnamon
¼	cup defatted chicken stock (page 94)
2	tablespoons chopped raisins
½	cup cooked rice
1	teaspoon chopped fresh mint
	Salt (optional)

1 Preheat the oven to 350°F.

2 Cut the tomatoes in half crosswise. Scoop out the pulp, leaving a ¼" shell. Set the shells, upside down, on paper towels to drain.

3 Chop the pulp and place in a medium bowl.

4 Coat a large no-stick skillet with no-stick spray. Add the onions, oregano, and cinnamon. Cover and cook over medium-low heat for 2 to 3 minutes. Add the chopped tomatoes, stock, and raisins.

5 Bring to a boil over medium heat. Reduce the heat to low and simmer, stirring often, for 3 to 4 minutes, or until the tomatoes start to soften. Remove from the heat. Stir in the rice and mint. Season to taste with the salt (if using).

6 Coat an 8" x 8" baking dish with no-stick spray. Place the tomatoes in the dish. Divide the tomato mixture among the shells. Bake for 15 minutes, or until the stuffing is hot.

Makes **4** servings.

nutrition at a glance
per serving
0.4 g. total fat
0.1 g. saturated fat
72 calories
0 mg. cholesterol
12 mg. sodium
2 g. protein
16 g. carbohydrates
2 g. dietary fiber

Spaghetti with Fresh Vegetables

quick and easy

I chop the vegetables while the pasta cooks, then toss them all, except the garlic, in a bowl so that the flavors blend for a few minutes. If you like, you can substitute finely chopped broccoli florets, fresh spinach, or fresh or thawed frozen peas for the sugar snap peas. Garnish with fat-free Parmesan topping and chopped fresh parsley.

8   ounces low-fat spaghetti (0.5 g. fat per 2-ounce serving)
2   cloves garlic, minced
4   ripe plum tomatoes, diced
4   scallions, finely chopped
1   stalk celery, finely chopped
1   cup sugar snap peas sliced ¼" thick
3   tablespoons capers, rinsed and drained
    Ground black pepper
    Salt (optional)
2   tablespoons thinly sliced fresh basil

1 Bring a large pot of water to a boil over high heat. Add the spaghetti and cook according to the package directions. Drain and let stand in the colander.

2 Coat the pot with no-stick spray. Add the garlic and cook over low heat, stirring, for 30 seconds. Add the tomatoes, scallions, celery, peas, and capers. Toss for 1 minute to heat. Season to taste with the pepper and salt (if using). Add the spaghetti and basil; toss.

Makes **4** servings.

Lynn's Kitchen Tip

Here's how to save on pot washing when making a pasta dish, such as pasta primavera, that requires cooked broccoli, asparagus, or other vegetables. Simply add the chopped vegetables to the pasta cooking water a few minutes before the pasta is done. Drain and add sauce according to the recipe.

nutrition at a glance
per serving
0.9 g. total fat
0.1 g. saturated fat
252 calories
0 mg. cholesterol
255 mg. sodium
10 g. protein
51 g. carbohydrates
5 g. dietary fiber

Hearty Vegetable Sauté

quick and easy

This dish offers big flavor. Serve it with grilled fish or turkey—or with cooked rice or quinoa as a vegetarian luncheon dish.

1	onion, thinly sliced
½	orange or sweet red pepper, cut into thin strips
2	cloves garlic, minced
1	small zucchini, sliced
6	ounces cremini or button mushrooms, sliced
½	teaspoon dried oregano
¼	teaspoon dried thyme
½	cup frozen peas, thawed
1	plum tomato, sliced
2	teaspoons white-wine Worcestershire sauce
2	tablespoons thinly sliced fresh basil
¼	cup fat-free Parmesan topping

1   Coat a large no-stick skillet or wok with no-stick spray. Add the onions, peppers, and garlic. Cover and cook over medium-high heat, stirring occasionally, for 3 to 4 minutes, or until the onions are golden. If necessary, add 1 to 2 teaspoons water to prevent sticking.

2   Add the zucchini, mushrooms, oregano, and thyme. Cover and cook for 3 to 4 minutes, or until the mushrooms give off liquid. Uncover and cook, stirring constantly, for 1 to 2 minutes, or until the liquid evaporates.

3   Add the peas, tomatoes, and Worcestershire sauce. Cook, stirring, for 3 to 4 minutes, or until the tomatoes soften. Stir in the basil. Sprinkle with the Parmesan. Toss to combine.

Makes **4** servings.

nutrition at a glance

per serving

0.9 g.	total fat
0.4 g.	saturated fat
78	calories
1 mg.	cholesterol
152 mg.	sodium
6 g.	protein
14 g.	carbohydrates
3 g.	dietary fiber

Garlicky Spinach Potatoes

Mellow roasted garlic makes these spinach-stuffed potatoes really special. If you don't have any roasted garlic on hand, simply bake a head of garlic at the same time you do the potatoes. Garnish with thin strips of pimentos.

4	large russet potatoes
10	ounces spinach leaves, chopped
½	cup water
1	cup fat-free ricotta cheese
½	cup fat-free liquid creamer or evaporated skim milk
2	tablespoons pureed Roasted Garlic (page 304)
¼	teaspoon ground black pepper
	Pinch of dried tarragon
	Salt (optional)

1 Preheat the oven to 350°F. Wash and gently scrub the potatoes, but don't dry. Place at least 4" apart on the oven rack and bake for 1 hour, or until tender. Remove from the oven. Do not turn off the oven.

2 Cut each potato in half lengthwise. Set aside for 10 minutes, or until cool enough to handle. Scoop the pulp from the potatoes, leaving ¼"-thick shells. Place the pulp in a large bowl. Set the shells aside.

3 Place the spinach and water in a large no-stick saucepan. Cover and cook for 3 to 4 minutes, or until the spinach is wilted. Drain well and press with paper towels to squeeze out excess moisture. Set aside.

4 Mash the potato pulp until smooth. Add the ricotta, creamer or milk, garlic, pepper, tarragon, and spinach. Season to taste with the salt (if using). Mix well. Spoon into the potato shells.

5 Place the potatoes in a single layer in a 13" x 9" baking dish. Cover loosely with foil. Bake for 10 minutes, or until the potatoes puff slightly. Remove the foil and bake for 3 to 5 minutes, or until lightly browned.

Makes **4** servings.

nutrition at a glance	
per serving	
0.5 g.	total fat
0.1 g.	saturated fat
303	calories
5 mg.	cholesterol
243 mg.	sodium
14 g.	protein
59.7 g.	carbohydrates
5.3 g.	dietary fiber

Malaysian Curried Rice

quick **and easy**

For a lovely luncheon main dish, top this aromatic rice with steamed shrimp or scallops, chopped scallions, shredded carrots, and sliced cucumbers. Add a pinch of ground red pepper for a hint of heat. For a slightly sweeter version, add a few tablespoons chopped dried aprictos, figs, raisins, or dates.

3	cups water
1½	cups long-grain white rice
	Pinch of salt (optional)
1	medium onion, thinly sliced
2	teaspoons minced fresh ginger
2	cloves garlic, minced
1½	teaspoons all-purpose flour
1	cup evaporated skim milk
⅓	cup peach or mango chutney
½	teaspoon coconut extract
½	teaspoon curry powder
½	teaspoon honey
1	tablespoon freshly squeezed lemon juice
1	tablespoon chopped fresh cilantro

1   In a medium no-stick saucepan, combine the water, rice, and salt (if using). Bring to a boil over medium-high heat. Reduce the heat to medium-low, cover, and cook for 20 minutes, or until the rice is tender and the liquid is absorbed.

2   Meanwhile, coat a large no-stick skillet with no-stick spray. Warm the skillet over medium heat. Add the onions, ginger, and garlic. Mist with no-stick spray. Cover and cook, stirring occasionally, for 2 to 3 minutes, or until the onions start to release moisture. Uncover and cook, stirring occasionally, for 3 to 4 minutes, or until golden. If necessary, add 1 to 2 teaspoons water to prevent sticking.

3 Place the flour in a small bowl. Gradually whisk in the milk until smooth. Add to the skillet. Cook, whisking constantly, for 2 to 3 minutes, or until thickened. Add the chutney, coconut, curry powder, and honey.

4 Remove from the heat. Add the lemon juice; whisk to combine.

5 Fluff the rice with a fork. Serve the sauce over the rice. Sprinkle with the cilantro.

Makes **4** servings.

nutrition at a glance
per serving
0.6 g. total fat
0.1 g. saturated fat
211 calories
0 mg. cholesterol
24 mg. sodium
5 g. protein
46 g. carbohydrates
2 g. dietary fiber

Baked Potatoes Italiano

I whipped up this easy oven dish one cold evening, and it's been a satisfying favorite ever since. The sauce cooks at the same time the potatoes are baking. Sprinkle with fat-free Parmesan topping just before serving.

4	large russet potatoes
2	medium tomatoes, diced
½	large onion, coarsely chopped
½	green pepper, cut into ½" chunks
¾	cup coarsely chopped fresh parsley
1	tablespoon finely chopped dry-pack sun-dried tomatoes
2	cloves garlic, minced
2	teaspoons dried oregano
3	tablespoons thinly sliced fresh basil
	Ground black pepper
	Salt (optional)

1 Preheat the oven to 350°F.

2 Wash and gently scrub the potatoes, but don't dry.

3 Coat a 12" x 8" baking dish with no-stick spray. Layer the fresh tomatoes, onions, green peppers, parsley, sun-dried tomatoes, garlic, and oregano in the dish. Cover tightly with foil.

4 Place the dish in the oven. Poke each potato several times with a fork. Place the potatoes directly on the oven rack next to the dish. Bake for 1 hour, or until the vegetables are tender and the potatoes can be easily pierced with a sharp knife.

5 Stir the basil into the vegetable sauce. Season to taste with the black pepper and salt (if using).

6 Cut a 1"-deep cross in each potato. Squeeze the ends to open the cut and push up the flesh slightly. Top with the vegetable sauce.

Makes **4** servings.

Photograph on page 321

nutrition at a glance
per serving
0.9 g. total fat
0.2 g. saturated fat
237 calories
0 mg. cholesterol
34 mg. sodium
5.8 g. protein
53.6 g. carbohydrates
6.3 g. dietary fiber

Poached Vegetables with Lemon-Horseradish Sauce

A sprightly horseradish-lemon sauce brings a fresh note to this satisfying cold-weather favorite.

1 small head green cabbage, cored and cut into 8 wedges
2 large potatoes, each cut into 4 wedges
2 medium carrots, cut into 2" lengths
1 large onion, cut into 8 wedges
2 cups defatted chicken stock (page 94)
½ teaspoon caraway seeds, crushed
¼ teaspoon ground black pepper
  Pinch of salt (optional)
2 tablespoons fat-free sour cream
1 tablespoon prepared horseradish
1 teaspoon grated lemon rind
¼ cup chopped fresh parsley

1   In a no-stick Dutch oven, combine the cabbage, potatoes, carrots, and onions. Add the stock, caraway seeds, pepper, and salt (if using). Cover and simmer over medium heat for 35 minutes, or until the carrots are tender. With a slotted spoon, carefully remove the vegetables to a serving platter.

2   Pour off all but ½ cup of the stock from the saucepan. (Reserve for another use.) Over low heat, whisk in the sour cream, horseradish, and lemon rind. Cook, stirring, just until hot. Pour over the vegetables. Sprinkle with the parsley.

Makes **4** servings.

Lynn's Fat-Free Flavor

To heighten the flavor of caraway and other seeds, toast them on a baking sheet in a 350°F oven for 10 minutes or in a heavy skillet over medium heat, stirring frequently, for 5 minutes, or until fragrant.

---

nutrition at a glance
per serving
0.9 g. total fat
0.1 g. saturated fat
176 calories
0 mg. cholesterol
52 mg. sodium
5 g. protein
40 g. carbohydrates
8 g. dietary fiber

Polenta with Roasted Ratatouille

Polenta, the Italian version of cornmeal mush, is easy to make from scratch. But if you're pressed for time, you can serve this quick-roasted ratatouille over slices of cooked fat-free polenta from a tube, which is available in most supermarkets.

Roasted Ratatouille

1	small eggplant, cut into 1" pieces
1	large onion, coarsely chopped
1	medium zucchini, cut into 1" pieces
1	small sweet red pepper, cut into 1" pieces
4	large cloves garlic, coarsely chopped
	Salt (optional)
2	cups canned tomatoes, coarsely chopped (with juice)
¼	cup balsamic vinegar
2	teaspoons dried oregano

Polenta

3	cups skim milk
1	cup yellow cornmeal
½	cup fat-free plain yogurt

1 *To make the roasted ratatouille:* Preheat the oven to 450°F.

2 Coat a no-stick roasting pan with no-stick spray. Add the eggplant, onions, zucchini, peppers, and garlic. Mist with no-stick spray. Season lightly with the salt (if using). Roast for 15 minutes.

3 Stir in the tomatoes (with juice), vinegar, and oregano. Mist with no-stick spray. Roast for 15 minutes, or until the vegetables are tender.

4 *To make the polenta:* Meanwhile, in a medium no-stick saucepan over medium heat, bring the milk to a boil. Add the cornmeal in a slow, steady stream, stirring constantly. Reduce the heat to medium-low. Cook, stirring constantly, for 8 to 10 minutes, or until the cornmeal is soft. Stir in the yogurt.

5 To serve, spoon the ratatouille over the polenta.

Makes **6** servings.

Lynn's Kitchen Tip

To remove any bitterness from eggplant, cut the eggplant into cubes and place in a colander. Sprinkle with salt and toss well. Let stand for 15 minutes, or until drops of liquid form on the eggplant. Rinse with cold running water to remove the salt and bitter juices. Pat dry with paper towels before cooking.

---

nutrition at a glance

per serving

0.9 g.	total fat
0.2 g.	saturated fat
160	calories
0 mg.	cholesterol
156 mg.	sodium
5 g.	protein
34 g.	carbohydrates
5 g.	dietary fiber

Cakes, Pies, and Other Sweets

Nutritionists tell us that a perfectly ripe piece of

fresh fruit is the healthful way to close a meal. We

know they're right, but in our hearts we long for

cheesecake.

So let it be cheesecake—as long as it's a wedge

of fabulous fat-free Key Lime Cheesecake. The

cheesecake and all the other desserts in this

chapter are crammed with satisfaction, yet none

contain more than 1 gram of fat per (generous)

serving. Occasional indulgences like this won't upset your nutritional apple cart.

Feast on Chocolate-Banana Pie, Pineapple-Caramel Cake, Stacked-High Apple Pie, Pumpkin Pudding, Lemon Bars, Raisin and Spice Oatmeal Cookies, and more.

My desserts are based on intensely flavored, naturally low fat ingredients—such as cocoa powder, citrus, ripe fruits, and spices. These old-fashioned ingredients deliver honest flavor. To these I add a host of fat-free versions of dairy products—cream cheese, sweetened condensed milk, buttermilk, plain yogurt, and sour cream. These products deliver excellent texture and flavor in baked and cooked desserts.

Occasionally, I call for prune puree, applesauce, or corn syrup to replace fat. They trap moisture in baked goods in much the same way that fat does.

For other cakes, cookies, and pies, I rely on fat-free egg-white meringues to lightly carry sweetness and flavors. And many of the low-fat and fat-free cookies now in supermarkets make delicious crumb pie crusts without all the fat that's needed in pastry crust.

Don't you dare tell your family and friends that these desserts are fat-free. Because otherwise, they'll never know.

A Note about Ingredients

I created these recipes using large eggs and all-purpose flour. Most of the recipes do not require sifting the flour before measuring. When it is necessary for a lighter result, for example, in the Daffodil Cake, I specify "sifted flour," which means that you should sift it and then measure the amount needed. If you have access to soft wheat flour or cake flour, you can substitute it for the all-purpose flour. It will produce a more tender crumb.

Be sure to use pure extracts—vanilla, maple, almond, and such—for the highest quality results.

For fruit desserts like Fresh Berry Angel Tart or Plum and Blueberry Tart, use the ripest berries available. Choose berries that are deeply colored with no soft spots.

For Glazed Tropical Fruit Cake, Rice Pudding with Nectarines, and Summer Fruits in Phyllo, select fruits with smooth skin and no blemishes or bruises. Ripe fruits yield slightly when gently pressed. To ripen hard plums, peaches, nectarines, papayas, or mangoes, store them at room temperature in a brown paper bag with some bananas. They'll ripen in one or two days and can then be stored in the refrigerator until you're ready to use them.

Key Lime Cheesecake

If you can't find Key lime juice, substitute regular lime juice. Low-fat graham crackers can be substituted for the low-fat gingersnaps. You can make the cheesecake 1 or 2 days in advance, but top it with the sliced kiwifruit just before serving.

Gingersnap Crust

30	low-fat gingersnaps
2	tablespoons sugar
1	egg white

Key Lime Cheesecake

2	tablespoons cold water
1	teaspoon unflavored gelatin
2	packages (8 ounces each) fat-free cream cheese, at room temperature
1	can (14 ounces) fat-free sweetened condensed milk
½	cup Key lime juice
2	egg whites
2	tablespoons cornstarch
1	teaspoon grated lime rind

Kiwifruit Topping

3	kiwifruit
1	tablespoon confectioners' sugar

1 *To make the gingersnap crust:* Preheat the oven to 350°F. Coat a 9" springform pan with no-stick spray.

2 Break the gingersnaps and place in a food processor. Process until the gingersnaps are broken into fine crumbs (there should be 1½ cups crumbs). Add the sugar and egg white; process until evenly blended and slightly moist. Press into the bottom and ½" up the sides of the pan.

3 Bake for 10 minutes, or until the crust is lightly browned. Set aside. Do not turn off the oven.

4 *To make the Key lime cheesecake:* Place the water in a cup. Sprinkle with the gelatin and set aside for 5 minutes to soften.

(continued)

5 Rinse out the bowl of the food processor. Add the cream cheese, condensed milk, lime juice, egg whites, cornstarch, and lime rind. Process until smooth. Add the gelatin mixture and process until completely incorporated.

6 Pour into the warm crust. Bake for 55 minutes, or until a knife inserted in the center comes out clean. Cool on a wire rack, then chill for at least 2 hours.

7 *To make the kiwifruit topping:* Peel and thinly slice the kiwifruit.

8 Remove the outer ring from the springform pan. Arrange the kiwifruit in a spiral pattern on top of the cheesecake. Dust with the confectioners' sugar.

Makes **10** servings.

Photograph on page 329

<table>
<tr><td colspan="2">nutrition at a glance</td></tr>
<tr><td colspan="2">per serving</td></tr>
<tr><td>0.7 g.</td><td>total fat</td></tr>
<tr><td>0 g.</td><td>saturated fat</td></tr>
<tr><td>235</td><td>calories</td></tr>
<tr><td>8 mg.</td><td>cholesterol</td></tr>
<tr><td>352 mg.</td><td>sodium</td></tr>
<tr><td>12 g.</td><td>protein</td></tr>
<tr><td>44.9 g.</td><td>carbohydrates</td></tr>
<tr><td>1.2 g.</td><td>dietary fiber</td></tr>
</table>

Pineapple-Caramel Cake

You won't find a more luscious version of the classic pineapple upside-down cake. Dried tart cherries also work beautifully in this cake in place of the dried cranberries.

½ cup packed brown sugar
¼ cup fat-free prepared caramel topping
6 canned pineapple slices (reserve the juice)
¼ cup dried cranberries
2 egg whites, at room temperature
¼ teaspoon salt
1 teaspoon vanilla
½ cup sugar
¾ cup all-purpose flour
¾ teaspoon baking powder

Lynn's Fun Food Fact
During the 1700s, fashionable Europeans cultivated pineapples in hothouses.

1   Preheat the oven to 350°F. Coat a 9" round cake pan with no-stick spray.

2   Spread the brown sugar evenly over the bottom of the pan and drizzle evenly with the caramel topping. Top with the pineapple in a decorative pattern. Sprinkle with the cranberries and 2 tablespoons of the reserved pineapple juice. Set aside.

3   Place the egg whites and salt in a large bowl. Beat with an electric mixer until soft peaks form. Beat in the vanilla. Gradually beat in the sugar until the whites are stiff but not dry.

4   In a small bowl, sift together the flour and baking powder. Sift half of the flour mixture over the egg whites. Gently fold in with a large rubber spatula.

5   Fold ¼ cup of the reserved pineapple juice into the egg-white mixture. Sift the remaining flour mixture over the egg-white mixture and fold in.

6   Spread the batter evenly over the pineapple mixture. Bake for 30 to 35 minutes, or until a wooden toothpick inserted in the center comes out clean. Cool in the pan for 2 minutes; invert onto a serving plate. Cool for at least 1 hour before serving.

Makes **8** servings.

Photograph on page 327

nutrition at a glance	
per serving	
0.2 g.	total fat
0 g.	saturated fat
219	calories
0 mg.	cholesterol
168 mg.	sodium
2.5 g.	protein
53.2 g.	carbohydrates
1.1 g.	dietary fiber

Chocolate-Raspberry Cake

This dark layer cake with a tender crumb will satisfy devil's-food longings. For a variation, frost the cake with marshmallow whip or fat-free whipped topping instead of the raspberry fruit spread.

1½   cups all-purpose flour
¾   cup cocoa powder
1½   teaspoons baking powder
½   teaspoon ground cinnamon
6   egg whites, at room temperature
½   teaspoon salt
2   teaspoons vanilla
1½   cups sugar
1   cup fat-free buttermilk
¼   cup raspberry all-fruit spread
     Confectioners' sugar
1½   cups fat-free whipped topping (optional)

1   Preheat the oven to 350°F. Coat two 9" round cake pans with no-stick spray. Dust with flour, shaking out the excess.

2   In a medium bowl, sift together the flour, cocoa, baking powder, and cinnamon. Set aside.

3   Place the egg whites and salt in a large bowl. Beat with an electric mixer until soft peaks form. Beat in the vanilla. Gradually beat in the sugar until the whites are stiff but not dry.

4   Sift about one-half of the cocoa mixture over the egg-white mixture; gently fold in with a large rubber spatula. Add ½ cup of the buttermilk and fold into the batter. Repeat with the remaining cocoa mixture and the remaining ½ cup buttermilk.

5   Divide the batter between the prepared pans and spread evenly. Bake for 20 to 25 minutes, or until a wooden toothpick inserted in the center comes out clean. Cool on a wire rack for 5 minutes. Turn the cakes out of the pans onto wire racks to cool completely.

Traditionally, buttermilk was the liquid left over after the fat portion of milk or cream was churned into butter. These days, commercial buttermilk is a thickened product cultured with bacteria. It's available in both low-fat and fat-free versions. Fat-free buttermilk is an excellent addition to fat-free baked goods, because its natural acidity acts as a tenderizing agent.

6 Place 1 cake layer on a serving plate. Cover with the raspberry spread. Top with the second cake layer. Dust the top with confectioners' sugar. Serve with dollops of the whipped topping (if using).

Makes **12** servings.

Photograph on page 332

Coffee Angel Food Cake

To prevent any specks of grease from inhibiting the foaming action of the egg whites, wash your mixing bowl, beaters, and the tube pan with hot, soapy water, then rinse thoroughly and dry before starting the recipe. And remember to use an ungreased tube pan so that the egg-white proteins can climb up the sides for a high rise. To make a vanilla angel food cake, omit the coffee and increase the vanilla to 1½ teaspoons.

1¼ cups sifted all-purpose flour
2½ teaspoons dry instant coffee
1¾ cups sugar
1¾ cups egg whites, at room temperature
1½ teaspoons cream of tartar
¼ teaspoon salt
1 teaspoon vanilla extract

1 Position an oven rack in the lower third of the oven. Preheat the oven to 375°F.

2 In a medium bowl, sift together the flour, coffee, and ¾ cup of the sugar; press the coffee granules through the mesh with a spoon if necessary. Sift 2 more times. Set aside.

3 Place the egg whites, cream of tartar, and salt in a large bowl. Beat with an electric mixer until soft peaks form. Beat in the vanilla. Gradually beat in the remaining 1 cup sugar until the egg whites are stiff but not dry.

Lynn's Lore

Several years ago, I inherited an angel food pan from my maternal grandmother, Ocean Irwin. Inscribed in the metal are the words "Swans Down Cake Pan 1/3/23." Although it has become blackened with time and rusts if I don't dry it by hand, it makes the best angel food cake. It has two cleverly designed slides on each side that open to reveal a hidden ½" space at the bottom of the pan. The slides are kept closed to trap heat during baking but are opened to allow air to circulate around the cake for faster cooling.

(continued)

4   Sift about one-third of the flour mixture over the egg-white mixture. Gently fold in with a large rubber spatula. Repeat with the remaining flour mixture, adding ¼ cup at a time.

5   Spoon the batter into an ungreased 10" tube pan. Run a knife gently through the batter in a swirling motion to remove air pockets.

6   Bake in the lower third of the oven for 40 to 50 minutes, or until a long wooden skewer inserted in the center comes out clean.

7   Remove from the oven. If the pan has feet on the rim, turn it upside down to cool. If the pan doesn't have feet on the rim, position the tube over a narrow-necked bottle. Let cool for several hours, or until no longer warm.

8   Stand the cake upright. Run a long, thin knife between the cake and pan to loosen. Invert onto a platter. Cut with a serrated knife.

Makes **10** servings.

nutrition at a glance	
per serving	
0.2 g.	total fat
0 g.	saturated fat
217	calories
0 mg.	cholesterol
125 mg.	sodium
6.1 g.	protein
48 g.	carbohydrates
0 g.	dietary fiber

Citrus-Glazed Carrot Cake

This moist cake has all the spicy savor of traditional carrot cake, without all the excess fat. A sprightly citrus glaze is an excellent substitute for traditional cream-cheese frosting.

Carrot Cake

2	cups all-purpose flour
2	teaspoons baking soda
2	teaspoons ground cinnamon
1	teaspoon ground ginger
½	cup sugar
3	cups shredded carrots
1	can (8 ounces) crushed pineapple (with juice)
½	cup pureed prunes
½	cup packed brown sugar
¼	cup light corn syrup
4	egg whites, at room temperature
1	teaspoon cream of tartar

Citrus Glaze

2	tablespoons fat-free sour cream
1½	teaspoons freshly squeezed lemon juice
1	teaspoon freshly squeezed orange juice
1	teaspoon grated lemon rind
¼	teaspoon grated orange rind
1½	cups sifted confectioners' sugar

1 *To make the carrot cake:* Preheat the oven to 350°F. Coat a 12-cup Bundt pan with no-stick spray. Dust with flour, shaking out the excess.

2 In a medium bowl, combine the flour, baking soda, cinnamon, ginger, and ¼ cup of the sugar. Mix well and set aside.

3 In a large bowl, combine the carrots, pineapple (with juice), prunes, brown sugar, and corn syrup. Mix well. Add the flour mixture and blend well.

4 Place the egg whites and cream of tartar in a large bowl. Beat with an electric mixer until soft peaks form. Gradually beat in the remaining ¼ cup sugar until the egg whites are stiff but not dry. Fold into the carrot mixture with a large rubber spatula. Pour into the Bund+pan.

5 Bake for 50 minutes, or until a wooden toothpick inserted in the center comes out clean. Cool on a wire rack for 10 minutes. Turn the cake out of the pan onto a wire rack to cool.

6 *To make the citrus glaze:* In a medium bowl, combine the sour cream, lemon juice, orange juice, lemon rind, and orange rind. Whisk well to combine. Whisk in 1 cup of the confectioners' sugar. With a spoon, blend in the remaining ½ cup confectioners' sugar until smooth. Drizzle over the cake.

Makes **10** servings.

nutrition at a glance

per serving

0.4 g.	total fat
0.1 g.	saturated fat
320	calories
0 mg.	cholesterol
304 mg.	sodium
4.7 g.	protein
76 g.	carbohydrates
2.4 g.	dietary fiber

Daffodil Cake with Lemon Sauce

This light and elegant cake is delightful for a wedding shower or other special occasion. If you like, you can make the lemon sauce and the cake a day before serving. Reheat the sauce gently in a saucepan or microwave it in a glass measuring cup just until warm. For a special touch, decorate with candied violets and tiny fresh mint leaves.

Daffodil Cake

1¼	cups + 2 tablespoons sifted all-purpose cake flour
1¾	cups + 2 tablespoons sugar
1¾	cups egg whites, at room temperature
1½	teaspoons cream of tartar
¼	teaspoon salt
1½	teaspoons vanilla
¼	cup fat-free egg substitute
1	tablespoon grated lemon rind

Warm Lemon Sauce

1	cup sugar
1	tablespoon cornstarch
½	cup water
3	tablespoons freshly squeezed lemon juice
1	tablespoon grated lemon rind

1 *To make the daffodil cake:* Position an oven rack in the lower third of the oven. Preheat the oven to 375°F.

2 Sift 1¼ cups of the flour and ¾ cup of the sugar together 3 times. Set aside.

3 Place the egg whites, cream of tartar, and salt in a large bowl. Beat with an electric mixer until soft peaks form. Beat in the vanilla. Gradually beat in 1 cup of the remaining sugar until the egg whites are stiff but not dry.

4 Sift about one-third of the flour mixture over the egg-white mixture. Gently fold in with a large rubber spatula. Repeat with the remaining flour mixture, adding ¼ cup at a time.

5 Transfer one-third of the batter to a medium bowl. Set aside.

Vanilla sugar is a wonderful way to sweeten fruit desserts and baked goods. To make it, slit 2 vanilla beans lengthwise with a sharp knife, then tuck the pieces into a pound of sugar. Let stand for a few weeks so that the sugar can absorb the delicate vanilla flavor.

6 In another medium bowl, combine the egg substitute, the remaining 2 tablespoons flour, and the remaining 2 tablespoons sugar. Beat with an electric mixer for 3 minutes, or until thickened. Stir in the lemon rind. Pour over the reserved batter in the medium bowl. Gently fold in with a large rubber spatula.

7 Spoon the white and yellow batters alternately into an ungreased 10" tube pan. Run a knife gently through the batter in a swirling motion to remove air pockets and to marbleize the batter slightly.

8 Bake in the lower third of the oven for 40 to 45 minutes, or until a long wooden skewer inserted in the center comes out clean.

9 Remove from the oven. If the pan has feet on the rim, turn it upside down to cool. If the pan doesn't have feet on the rim, position the tube over a narrow-necked bottle. Let cool for several hours, or until no longer warm.

10 *To make the warm lemon sauce:* In a small no-stick saucepan, combine the sugar and cornstarch. Stir in the water. Whisk over medium heat for 10 minutes, or until smooth and thickened. Add the lemon juice and lemon rind. Cook, whisking constantly, for 2 to 3 minutes, or until the mixture boils. Remove from the heat and set aside.

11 Stand the cake upright. Run a long, thin knife carefully around the edge, between the cake and pan, to loosen. Invert onto a platter. Cut with a serrated knife. Serve topped with the warm lemon sauce.

Makes **10** servings.

Photograph on page 330

nutrition at a glance	
per serving	
0.2 g.	total fat
0 g.	saturated fat
311	calories
0 mg.	cholesterol
135 mg.	sodium
6.7 g.	protein
71.5 g.	carbohydrates
1 g.	dietary fiber

Glazed Tropical Fruit Cake

This beautiful dessert is a sponge cake moistened with tropical fruit syrup and crowned with colorful fruits. You can use either bottled or reconstituted frozen mango, passion fruit, or other tropical fruit juice for the glaze.

Sponge Cake

6	egg whites, at room temperature
2	eggs, at room temperature
1	teaspoon vanilla
¼	teaspoon salt
1½	cups sugar
1½	cups all-purpose flour
1½	teaspoons baking powder

Tropical Fruit Glaze

¾	cup tropical fruit juice
½	cup sugar

Tropical Fruit Topping

½	cup sliced papayas
½	cup sliced mangoes
1	kiwifruit, sliced
1	banana, sliced
	Confectioners' sugar (optional)

1   *To make the sponge cake:* Preheat the oven to 350°F. Coat a 9" springform pan with no-stick spray. Dust with flour, shaking out the excess.

2   Place the egg whites, eggs, vanilla, and salt in a large bowl. Beat with an electric mixer until light and fluffy. Gradually beat in the sugar. Beat for 5 minutes, or until thick.

3   In a medium bowl, sift together the flour and baking powder. Sift over the egg mixture. Gently fold in with a large rubber spatula. Pour the batter into the prepared pan.

Store eggs in the carton in the refrigerator. The carton protects the fragile eggs from breaking and serves as a barrier, so the porous shells don't absorb unwanted odors.

4 Bake for 30 to 35 minutes, or until a wooden toothpick inserted in the center comes out clean. Cool on a wire rack.

5 *To make the tropical fruit glaze:* In a small no-stick saucepan, combine the fruit juice and sugar. Whisk over medium heat and bring to a boil. Boil for 3 minutes, or until the sugar dissolves.

6 Using a wooden toothpick or skewer, poke holes about 1" apart all over the cake. Spoon all but 2 tablespoons of the syrup over the cake. Set aside to cool.

7 *To make the tropical fruit topping:* Remove the outer ring from the springform pan. Place the cake on a serving plate. Top with the papayas, mangoes, kiwifruit, and bananas. Brush with the remaining 2 tablespoons syrup. Dust with the confectioners' sugar (if using) just before serving.

Makes **12** servings.

Photograph on page 334

nutrition at a glance	
per serving	
0.8 g.	total fat
0.2 g.	saturated fat
177	calories
27 mg.	cholesterol
109 mg.	sodium
3.5 g.	protein
39.7 g.	carbohydrates
1 g.	dietary fiber

Ripe summer berries—blueberries, strawberries, boysenberries, blackberries, and raspberries—make desserts that are as elegant as they are healthful. When the ice is on the berry vines, turn to loose-pack frozen berries to re-create summer memories. Whether you start with fresh or frozen, these quick desserts are the berry best.

Berry Berry. Intensify the berry bounty by stirring a handful of fresh berries into berry yogurt.

Blueberry Thrill. Top fresh blueberries with a sauce of pureed ripe mangoes or papayas seasoned to taste with freshly squeezed lime juice and sugar.

Citrus Twist. Any berries will benefit from a rich, tart sauce made from lemon yogurt mixed with a tablespoon of freshly squeezed lemon juice or lime juice. Use 1 tablespoon juice for each container (8 ounces) of yogurt.

Lickety Split. Line old-fashioned glass banana boats with 2 banana halves each. Top with scoops of fat-free vanilla, chocolate, and strawberry ice cream or frozen yogurt. Spoon on separate sauces: lightly mashed and sweetened strawberries, lightly mashed and sweetened raspberries, and blueberries that have been briefly cooked with a bit of sugar, then cooled. Top with dollops of marshmallow fluff and a generous drizzle of fat-free chocolate sauce. Sprinkle with finely chopped walnuts and a long-stem maraschino cherry for a real retro touch.

Parfait Perfection. In parfait glasses, layer blueberries, raspberries, or sliced strawberries with fat-free vanilla ice cream, frozen yogurt, citrus sorbet, or vanilla pudding. Crown with fat-free whipped topping, a berry, and a fresh mint sprig.

Short Cake—Tall Taste. For an instant fat-free strawberry shortcake, spoon sliced fresh strawberries over slices of angel food cake. Top with fat-free whipped cream or vanilla ice cream.

Strawberry Yields Forever. Choose the largest, reddest strawberries (on the stems, if possible) to serve with bowls of fat-free chocolate sauce, fat-free sour cream (sweetened with brown sugar), and fat-free whipped topping.

A Toast to Melba. Cover pitted ripe peach halves with fat-free vanilla ice cream and a sauce of pureed raspberries mixed with sugar, cinnamon, and freshly squeezed lemon juice.

Stacked-High Apple Pie

If you thought you'd never see a delicious fat-free apple pie, you will be delighted with this. Our testers loved it so much that it disappeared immediately. The secret to the crust is using fat-free cinnamon-and-honey cookies. Low-fat graham crackers or gingersnaps also work beautifully. Serve slightly warm from the oven—solo or accompanied by fat-free frozen yogurt, ice cream, or whipped topping.

6	tart apples, cut into quarters and sliced
¾	cup sugar
3	tablespoons freshly squeezed lemon juice
3	tablespoons quick-cooking tapioca
¾	teaspoon ground cinnamon
⅛	teaspoon ground allspice
1	egg white
1½	cups fat-free cinnamon-and-honey cookie crumbs

1   Preheat the oven to 350°F. Coat a 9" pie plate with no-stick spray.

2   In a large bowl, combine the apples, sugar, lemon juice, tapioca, cinnamon, and allspice. Mix well. Cover and let stand, stirring occasionally, for 15 minutes.

3   Place the egg white in a medium bowl and beat lightly with a fork. Add the cookie crumbs and mix well. Press into the bottom and up the sides of the prepared pie plate. Mist the crust with no-stick spray.

4   Spoon the apple mixture into the crust. Bake for 45 minutes, or until the filling bubbles and the apples are tender when tested with the tip of a sharp knife.

Makes **6** servings.

Photograph on page 326

Lynn's Fat-Free Flavor

The type of apple that you use in any cooked apple dessert makes a huge difference. So select cooking apples that are tart and aromatic, such as the Australian Braeburn, Rome, Winesap, Newton, Gravenstein, and Granny Smith.

nutrition at a glance

per serving

0.4 g.	total fat
0.1 g.	saturated fat
347	calories
0 mg.	cholesterol
196 mg.	sodium
2.4 g.	protein
86.2 g.	carbohydrates
4.2 g.	dietary fiber

Chocolate-Banana Pie

Your family and friends will never guess that this creamy dream of a pie is free of fat. The shell and chocolate filling can be made well in advance. Top with the bananas and fat-free whipped topping just before serving.

Meringue Shell

3	egg whites, at room temperature
¼	teaspoon cream of tartar
⅔	cup sugar
1	tablespoon cornstarch

Chocolate Filling

¼	cup cold water
1	envelope (¼ ounce) unflavored gelatin
1	can (14 ounces) fat-free sweetened condensed milk
¼	cup cocoa powder
1	teaspoon vanilla
2	cups fat-free sour cream
½	cup fat-free vanilla yogurt

Banana Topping

2	medium bananas, sliced
2	cups fat-free aerosol whipped topping or thawed frozen fat-free whipped topping

1   *To make the meringue shell*: Preheat the oven to 275°F. Coat a 10" pie plate with no-stick spray. Dust generously with flour, shaking out the excess.

2   Place the egg whites and cream of tartar in a large bowl. Beat with an electric mixer until foamy.

3   In a small bowl, combine the sugar and cornstarch. Add to the egg whites, 1 table-spoon at a time, beating until stiff peaks form and the sugar dissolves. Spread the meringue carefully into the bottom and up the sides of the pie plate.

4   Bake for 1 hour. Turn the oven off and leave the meringue in the oven for at least 2 hours, or until completely cooled.

5 *To make the chocolate filling*: Place the water in a cup. Sprinkle with the gelatin and set aside for 5 minutes to soften.

6 In a medium saucepan, combine the condensed milk and cocoa. Whisk over low heat for 2 to 3 minutes, or until the cocoa is completely blended into the milk. Add the vanilla. Remove from the heat and stir in the gelatin mixture until dissolved.

7 Cool to room temperature. Add the sour cream and yogurt; mix until blended. Pour into the meringue shell. Chill for several hours, or until firm.

8 *To make the banana topping*: Just before serving, arrange the bananas in a single layer over the chocolate filling. Cover with the whipped topping.

Makes **8** servings.

Photograph on page 333

nutrition at a glance
per serving
0.5 g. total fat
0.3 g. saturated fat
357 calories
5 mg. cholesterol
149 mg. sodium
11 g. protein
73.6 g. carbohydrates
1.5 g. dietary fiber

Fresh Berry Angel Tart

When early summer berries are in their prime, you won't find a more heavenly dessert.

Angel Tart

3	egg whites, at room temperature
½	teaspoon cream of tartar
	Pinch of salt
½	teaspoon vanilla
¾	cup sugar
¾	cup all-purpose flour

Fresh Berry Topping

2	cups sliced strawberries or raspberries
¼	cup red currant jelly
1	cup fat-free aerosol whipped topping or thawed frozen fat-free whipped topping

1 *To make the angel tart*: Preheat the oven to 375°F. Coat a 10" pie plate with no-stick spray. Dust generously with flour, shaking out the excess.

2 Place the egg whites, cream of tartar, and salt in a large bowl. Beat with an electric mixer until soft peaks form. Beat in the vanilla. Gradually beat in ¼ cup of the sugar until the whites are stiff but not dry.

3 In a medium bowl, sift together the flour and the remaining ½ cup sugar. Sift over the egg whites. Gently fold in with a large rubber spatula.

4 Spread the batter in the pie plate. Bake for 20 to 25 minutes, or until a wooden pick inserted in the center comes out clean. Cool on a wire rack.

5 With a sharp knife, gently loosen the edges of the tart and place on a serving plate.

6 *To make the fresh berry topping*: Arrange the strawberries or raspberries over the top of the tart.

7 Place the jelly in a small microwaveable dish. Microwave on high power for 30 to 60 seconds, or until liquid. Spoon over the berries.

8 Top with the whipped topping just before serving.

Makes **8** servings.

Plum and Blueberry Tart

Top this luscious fruit tart with fat-free whipped topping, vanilla ice cream, or frozen yogurt.

½   cup sugar
3   tablespoons freshly squeezed lemon juice
1   tablespoon quick-cooking tapioca
½   teaspoon ground cinnamon
1½   cups fat-free lemon cookie crumbs
4   medium purple plums, cut into quarters
1   cup blueberries

1 Preheat the oven to 350°F.

2 In a small bowl, combine the sugar, lemon juice, tapioca, and cinnamon. Cover and let stand, stirring occasionally, for 5 minutes.

3 Coat an 9" springform pan with no-stick spray. Press the cookie crumbs over the bottom and ¾" up the sides of the pan. Mist with no-stick spray. Bake for 7 minutes.

4 Remove the pan from the oven. Arrange the plums in concentric circles over the bottom of the pan. Spoon the tapioca mixture evenly over the plums. Sprinkle with the blueberries.

5 Bake for 45 to 50 minutes, or until the filling bubbles and the plums are soft. Cool on a wire rack. Remove the outer ring from the springform pan.

Makes **8** servings.

Lynn's Lore

Should we all be saying, "as American as blueberry pie"? Blueberries are native plants of North America, and apples are not.

Summer Fruits in Phyllo

These flaky pastry bundles are best served warm and crisp from the oven. You can assemble them and hold them at room temperature for up to 2 hours before baking.

3   large peaches or nectarines, peeled and diced
1   cup raspberries
1   package (3.4 ounces) fat-free instant vanilla pudding and pie filling mix
6   sheets frozen phyllo dough, thawed
     Confectioners' sugar
¾   cup fat-free aerosol whipped topping or thawed frozen fat-free whipped topping

1   Preheat the oven to 375°F. Coat a baking sheet with no-stick spray.

2   In a large bowl, combine the peaches or nectarines, raspberries, and pudding mix. Fold with a rubber spatula until all the fruit is evenly coated with the dry pudding.

3   Unwrap the phyllo dough and cover it with a damp kitchen towel.

4   Remove 1 sheet from the stack and lay it on the work surface. Mist it with no-stick spray. Scoop out about ¾ cup of the fruit mixture and place it on one end of the phyllo sheet. Fold the lengthwise sides of the phyllo over the filling, then roll up, enclosing the filling. Place the bundle, seam side down, on the prepared baking sheet.

5   Repeat with the remaining phyllo dough and filling to make a total of 6 individual pastry packets.

6   Bake for 25 to 35 minutes, or until the pastry is lightly browned. Dust with the confectioners' sugar. Serve hot, topped with the whipped topping.

Makes **6** servings.

nutrition at a glance
per serving
0.7 g. total fat
0.1 g. saturated fat
92 calories
0 mg. cholesterol
170 mg. sodium
1 g. protein
20.2 g. carbohydrates
1.3 g. dietary fiber

Raisin and Spice Oatmeal Cookies

Stored in a tin in a cool spot, these wholesome cookies keep beautifully. They're wonderful for brown-bag lunches and snacks—try dunking them in a glass of cold fat-free milk.

1	cup all-purpose flour
1	teaspoon baking powder
½	teaspoon baking soda
½	teaspoon salt
½	teaspoon ground cinnamon
1	cup packed brown sugar
¼	cup unsweetened applesauce
1	egg white
2	tablespoons water
2	tablespoons canola oil
1	teaspoon vanilla
1⅓	cups regular or quick-cooking rolled oats
1	cup raisins

1   Preheat the oven to 375°F. Coat 2 or 3 large baking sheets with no-stick spray.

2   In a small bowl, combine the flour, baking powder, baking soda, salt, and cinnamon. Mix well.

3   In a large bowl, combine the brown sugar, applesauce, egg white, water, oil, and vanilla. Mix well.

4   Stir in the flour mixture. Add the oats and raisins; mix well. (The mixture will look thinner than most cookie doughs.)

5   Drop by rounded teaspoonfuls, 2" apart, on the prepared baking sheets. Bake one sheet at a time for 10 to 12 minutes, or until lightly browned.

6   Place the baking sheet on a wire rack and let stand for 5 minutes. Remove the cookies from the baking sheet and let cool on the rack.

Makes **42** cookies.

---

nutrition at a glance

per cookie

0.9 g.	total fat
0.1 g.	saturated fat
58	calories
0 mg.	cholesterol
56 mg.	sodium
0.9 g.	protein
12 g.	carbohydrates
0.5 g.	dietary fiber

Chocolate-Cherry Cookies

Glazed chocolate-and-fruit drops make a terrific snack or dessert. Be sure not to overbake to keep them tender. Kids love these. You can add ½ cup chopped walnuts or pecans. The fat will rise—to slightly less than 2 grams per cookie—but so will the nutrients and fiber.

Chocolate-Cherry Cookies

½	cup dried cherries
¼	cup water
¼	cup skim milk
1½	teaspoons vanilla
1¼	cups all-purpose flour
1	cup packed brown sugar
⅓	cup cocoa powder
2	teaspoons baking powder
½	teaspoon salt
1	cup sugar
4	egg whites, at room temperature
½	teaspoon cream of tartar

Chocolate Glaze

1	cup confectioners' sugar
1	teaspoon cocoa powder
1	teaspoon vanilla
2–3	teaspoons skim milk

1 *To make the chocolate-cherry cookies*: Preheat the oven to 350°F. Coat a large baking sheet with no-stick spray.

2 In a small no-stick saucepan, combine the cherries and water. Bring to a boil over medium-high heat. Reduce the heat and simmer for 15 minutes, or until all the water is absorbed. Cover and set aside for 30 minutes.

3 Pour the cherries into a blender or food processor. Process until pureed. (The cherries can also be pureed in the saucepan with a hand blender.) Add the milk and vanilla; blend to combine. Set aside.

4 In a medium bowl, sift together the flour, brown sugar, cocoa, baking powder, salt, and ½ cup of the sugar.

5 Place the egg whites and cream of tartar in a large bowl. Beat with an electric mixer until soft peaks form. Gradually beat in the remaining ½ cup sugar until the egg whites are stiff but not dry.

6 Fold a third of the flour mixture and a third of the cherry mixture into the egg-white mixture. Repeat twice to use all the flour and cherries. The mixture will be thick.

7 Drop by level tablespoonfuls, 1" apart, on the prepared baking sheet. Bake for 10 to 12 minutes, or until the edges are set (the centers will look moist).

8 Place the baking sheet on a wire rack and let stand for 5 minutes. Remove the cookies from the baking sheet and let cool on the rack.

9 *To make the chocolate glaze*: In a small bowl, combine the confectioners' sugar and cocoa. Add the vanilla and 2 teaspoons of the milk. Whisk until smooth. Add more milk if a thinner consistency is desired. Drizzle the glaze over the cooled cookies.

Makes **24** cookies.

nutrition at a glance
per cookie
0.3 g. total fat
0.1 g. saturated fat
147 calories
0 mg. cholesterol
100 mg. sodium
2.9 g. protein
34.6 g. carbohydrates
0.9 g. dietary fiber

Peppermint Stick Meringues

A properly baked meringue is crisp on the outside with an interior that literally melts on your tongue. The key ingredient is patience. Bake meringues slowly at a very low temperature. Bake on sheets without sides to allow air to circulate around the cookies. If you have only baking sheets with sides, turn them upside down and bake the cookies on the bottom. For best results, make meringues on a dry day. After baking, store in an airtight tin.

1   cup sugar
1   tablespoon cornstarch
3   egg whites, at room temperature
⅛   teaspoon salt
1   teaspoon vanilla
1   cup crushed peppermint sticks

1   Preheat the oven to 200°F. Coat 2 large baking sheets with no-stick spray. Dust with flour, shaking off the excess.

2   In a small bowl, combine the sugar and cornstarch. Set aside.

3   Place the egg whites and salt in a large bowl. Beat with an electric mixer until soft peaks form. Beat in the vanilla. Beat in the sugar mixture, 1 tablespoon at a time, until the whites are stiff but not dry. Fold in the peppermint.

4   Drop by rounded teaspoonfuls on the prepared baking sheets. Place in the oven on two shelves.

5   Bake for 2½ hours, or until the meringues are dry. Turn the oven off and leave the meringues in the oven for several hours or overnight. Store in an airtight container.

Makes **72** meringues.

nutrition at a glance
per meringue
0 g. total fat
0 g. saturated fat
24 calories
0 mg. cholesterol
7 mg. sodium
0.1 g. protein
6 g. carbohydrates
0 g. dietary fiber

Lemon Bars

Lemon yogurt adds a creamy texture and a pleasing tartness to these bars. For an even tangier filling, add an extra teaspoon of grated lemon rind. For best results, partially freeze these delicate bars before cutting.

Cookie Crust

24	low-fat vanilla wafers
⅓	cup confectioners' sugar
1	teaspoon grated lemon rind
3	tablespoons applesauce

Lemon Filling

¾	cup sugar
2	egg whites
1	egg
¾	cup fat-free lemon yogurt
3	tablespoons all-purpose flour
2	tablespoons freshly squeezed lemon juice
1	teaspoon grated lemon rind
½	teaspoon baking powder
	Confectioners' sugar

1   *To make the cookie crust*: Preheat the oven to 350°F. Coat an 8" x 8" baking dish with no-stick spray.

2   Break the wafers into pieces; place in a food processor or blender. Process to make crumbs. Add the confectioners' sugar, lemon rind, and applesauce; process to make a moist dough. Flour your fingers, then press the dough evenly into the prepared dish. Bake for 15 to 20 minutes, or until the crust feels firm and is lightly browned. Set aside. Do not turn off the oven.

3   *To make the lemon filling*: Place the sugar, egg whites, and egg in a medium bowl. Beat with an electric mixer until thick and smooth. Add the yogurt, flour, lemon juice, lemon rind, and baking powder. Mix until smooth. Spread over the baked crust.

(continued)

4   Bake for 25 to 30 minutes, or until set and lightly browned. Cool completely on a wire rack.

5   Place in the freezer for 1 hour before cutting into 16 bars. Refrigerate if not serving right away.

6   Sprinkle with the confectioners' sugar just before serving.

Makes **16** bars.

Photograph on page 328

nutrition at a glance	
per bar	
0.9 g.	total fat
0.2 g.	saturated fat
91	calories
13 mg.	cholesterol
58 mg.	sodium
1.8 g.	protein
19.6 g.	carbohydrates
0.2 g.	dietary fiber

Pumpkin Pudding

Made for my 7-year-old friend Haley, this luscious dessert has all the comfort of pumpkin pie without the fatty crust. A dollop of fat-free topping makes it extra special. For autumn holidays, garnish with candy corn or candy pumpkins.

2	cups canned pumpkin
1½	cups fat-free liquid creamer
¾	cup fat-free egg substitute
½	cup packed brown sugar
1½	teaspoons ground cinnamon
½	teaspoon ground ginger
¼	teaspoon ground nutmeg
⅛	teaspoon ground allspice
⅛	teaspoon ground cloves

Lynn's Nutrition Note

Canned pumpkin is a convenience product with class. It contains only cooked pureed pumpkin (not even sodium is added) and is an outstanding source of vitamin A.

1   Preheat the oven to 350°F.

2   In a large bowl, combine the pumpkin, creamer, egg substitute, brown sugar, cinnamon, ginger, nutmeg, allspice, and cloves.

3   Pour the mixture into six 1-cup baking dishes or custard cups. Bake for 35 to 40 minutes, or until a knife inserted in the center of a pudding comes out clean. Cool on a wire rack. Chill before serving.

Makes **6** servings.

nutrition at a glance	
per serving	
0.4 g.	total fat
0 g.	saturated fat
191	calories
3 mg.	cholesterol
82 mg.	sodium
6.4 g.	protein
47 g.	carbohydrates
3.8 g.	dietary fiber

Rice Pudding with Nectarines

Sliced ripe peaches or mangoes are also delicious with this pudding.

2   cups water
¾   cup long-grain white rice
1   can (14 ounces) fat-free sweetened condensed milk
2   egg whites
½   teaspoon ground cinnamon
3   nectarines, sliced

1   In a medium no-stick saucepan over medium-high heat, bring 1¾ cups of the water to a boil. Add the rice. Return to a boil. Reduce the heat to medium-low, cover, and simmer for 15 to 20 minutes, or until the rice is tender and the water is absorbed.

2   Meanwhile, in a large no-stick saucepan, combine the condensed milk, egg whites, cinnamon, and the remaining ¼ cup water. Cook over medium heat, stirring constantly, for 10 to 12 minutes, or until the mixture thickens slightly. Remove from the heat; stir in the rice. Refrigerate to chill completely.

3   Spoon the pudding into 8 dessert dishes. Top with the nectarines.

Makes **8** servings.

nutrition at a glance

per serving

0.4 g.	total fat
0.1 g.	saturated fat
239	calories
5 mg.	cholesterol
67 mg.	sodium
6.6 g.	protein
51.8 g.	carbohydrates
1.2 g.	dietary fiber

Almond Tapioca and Lime-Blackberry Parfaits

Childhood favorite tapioca pudding grows up in these lovely parfaits. You can hold the parfaits for several hours in the refrigerator after assembling them.

2   cups fat-free liquid creamer
3   tablespoons quick-cooking tapioca
6   tablespoons + ¼ cup sugar
½   cup fat-free egg substitute
½   teaspoon almond extract
1   pint blackberries
2   tablespoons freshly squeezed lime juice
½   teaspoon grated lime rind
    Pinch of ground cinnamon
1   tablespoon cornstarch
1   tablespoon water

1   In a medium no-stick saucepan, combine the creamer, tapioca, and 6 tablespoons of the sugar. Let stand for 5 minutes. Bring to the boiling point over medium heat. Cook, stirring constantly, for 5 minutes. Remove from the heat.

2   Place the egg substitute in a large bowl. Add a large spoonful of the hot tapioca; mix well. Continue adding tapioca by large spoonfuls until the mixture measures about 1 cup. Pour the egg mixture slowly into the saucepan and mix well. Cook over medium-low heat, stirring, for 2 minutes, or until thickened.

3   Cool to lukewarm. Stir in the almond extract. Cover and chill for several hours, or until thickened.

4   Meanwhile, in another medium no-stick saucepan, combine the blackberries, lime juice, lime rind, cinnamon, and the remaining ¼ cup sugar. Cook over medium-low heat, stirring often, for 7 to 8 minutes, or until a sauce forms but the berries hold their shape.

5   Place the cornstarch in a cup. Add the water and stir to dissolve the cornstarch. Add to the blackberry mixture and cook over medium heat, stirring, for 1 minute, or until thickened.

6   Cool to lukewarm. Cover and chill for several hours.

7   To serve, spoon the tapioca and blackberry mixture alternately into 6 parfait dishes.

Makes **6** servings.

Photograph on page 331

nutrition at a glance	
per serving	
0.2 g.	total fat
0.1 g.	saturated fat
192	calories
0 mg.	cholesterol
34 mg.	sodium
2.4 g.	protein
43.6 g.	carbohydrates
2.1 g.	dietary fiber

Lemon-Ginger Figs with Ice Cream

quick and easy

Poaching figs with ginger and lemon provides a counterpoint to the intense sweetness of the fruit. This sauce can be served warm or chilled. For a variation, serve the figs topped with fat-free whipped topping or custard sauce.

1	pound dried figs (stems removed), cut into quarters
1½	cups water
¼	cup sugar
	Juice of 1 lemon
2	teaspoons thin lemon rind strips
1	tablespoon thinly sliced candied ginger
1	quart fat-free vanilla ice cream or fat-free vanilla frozen yogurt

1   In a large saucepan, combine the figs, water, sugar, lemon juice, lemon rind, and ginger. Cover and simmer over low heat for 10 minutes. Remove the cover and simmer for 5 minutes, or until the figs are tender. Serve over the ice cream or frozen yogurt.

Makes **6** servings.

Lynn's Lore
Most figs consumed in this country are grown in California, where production of the sweet fruit dates from the establishment of the Spanish mission in San Diego in 1769.

nutrition at a glance	
per serving	
0.9 g.	total fat
0.2 g.	saturated fat
361	calories
5 mg.	cholesterol
75 mg.	sodium
6.4 g.	protein
86.5 g.	carbohydrates
7.1 g.	dietary fiber

373   Cakes, Pies, and Other Sweets

Orange and Cinnamon Rhubarb

I like rhubarb plain and simple, not in a fatty crust or diluted with strawberries. I enjoy this easy dessert all by itself, but it's also terrific spooned over fat-free vanilla pudding, tapioca, vanilla ice cream, or frozen yogurt.

1	pound fresh rhubarb stalks, cut into 1" lengths, or 1 pound frozen rhubarb pieces
¼	cup freshly squeezed orange juice
2	tablespoons freshly squeezed lemon juice (optional)
1	teaspoon grated orange rind
¼	teaspoon ground cinnamon
	Pinch of ground cloves (optional)
¾–1¼	cups sugar

1 In a large no-stick saucepan, combine the rhubarb, orange juice, lemon juice (if using), orange rind, cinnamon, cloves (if using), and ¾ cup of the sugar. Stir to combine. Bring to a boil over medium-high heat.

2 Reduce the heat to low, cover, and simmer, stirring occasionally, for 25 to 30 minutes, or until the rhubarb is tender. Taste for sweetness. Add up to ½ cup more sugar, if needed. Cook over low heat, stirring, for 2 to 3 minutes, or until the sugar dissolves. Serve warm or cold.

Makes **4** servings.

nutrition at a glance

per serving

0.3 g.	total fat
0.1 g.	saturated fat
178	calories
0 mg.	cholesterol
5 mg.	sodium
1.2 g.	protein
45 g.	carbohydrates
2.2 g.	dietary fiber

Menus for All Occasions

My fabulous fat-free dishes are made for feasting,

because they're a celebration of good health.

Although my recipes are intended as fat-free

accompaniments to the foods that you normally

serve—to help reduce your overall fat intake—they

can also be paired to create whole meals that are

hearty yet super-lean. So whether you're planning for

a holiday dinner, a seasonal meal with friends, an

exotic ethnic affair, or daily suppers, you'll find a

meal here to suit the occasion deliciously.

Unless otherwise noted, the portion size for

recipes featured in these menus is one serving.

Easter Brunch

Springtime
Asparagus Soup
(page 65)

Salmon-Stuffed
Mushrooms
(page 312)

Spinach Quiche
in Potato Crust
(page 316)

Daffodil Cake
with Lemon
Sauce (page
354)

For each serving, plan on 2
Salmon-Stuffed Mushrooms.

nutrition at a glance

per serving

2 g.	total fat
0.6 g.	saturated fat
607	calories
4 mg.	cholesterol
958 mg.	sodium
31 g.	protein
116 g.	carbohydrates
6 g.	dietary fiber

Fourth of July Block Party

Grilled halibut
steaks

All-American
Barbecue Sauce
(page 292)

Potato Salad
with Caramelized
Onions (page
108)

Fresh Berry
Angel Tart (page
362)

For each serving, plan on **4**
ounces grilled halibut and ¼ cup
All-American Barbecue Sauce.

nutrition at a glance

per serving

4.4 g.	total fat
0.6 g.	saturated fat
636	calories
47 mg.	cholesterol
526 mg.	sodium
40 g.	protein
109 g.	carbohydrates
8 g.	dietary fiber

Thanksgiving Dinner

Mushroom and
Wild Rice Soup
(page 77)

Roast turkey
breast

Chicken Gravy
(page 293)

Potato-Carrot
Mash (page 222)

Creamed Pearl
Onions (page
215)

Brussels Sprouts
with Apples
(page 234)

Cran-Blackberry
Gelatin Salad
(page 110)

Pumpkin Pudding
(page 370)

For each serving, plan on 1 cup
Mushroom and Wild Rice Soup, 3
ounces roast turkey breast, and
¼ cup Chicken Gravy.

nutrition at a glance

per serving

4.3 g.	total fat
0.9 g.	saturated fat
978	calories
77 mg.	cholesterol
650 mg.	sodium
49 g.	protein
191 g.	carbohydrates
23 g.	dietary fiber

Super-Bowl Bash

Turkey and Black
Bean Stew (page
168)

Asian Coleslaw
(page 107)

Citrus-Glazed
Carrot Cake
(page 352)

nutrition at a glance

per serving

2.1 g.	total fat
0.4 g.	saturated fat
518	calories
19 mg.	cholesterol
401 mg.	sodium
20 g.	protein
108 g.	carbohydrates
11 g.	dietary fiber

Mardi Gras Mirth

Assorted raw vegetables

Rémoulade Sauce (page 300)

Cajun Red Beans and Rice (page 278)

Pineapple-Caramel Cake (page 348)

For each serving, plan on 2 ounces mixed raw vegetable chunks or strips—such as carrots, broccoli, celery, or sweet red peppers—to dip in the Rémoulade Sauce, as well as 2 servings Cajun Red Beans and Rice.

nutrition at a glance

per serving

2.6 g.	total fat
0.2 g.	saturated fat
680	calories
6 mg.	cholesterol
1,066 mg.	sodium
22 g.	protein
144 g.	carbohydrates
13 g.	dietary fiber

Salute to Spring

Parsleyed Bay Scallops (page 32)

Soufflé Primavera (page 174)

Dill Sauce (page 294)

Artichoke Salad (page 103)

For each serving, plan on ¼ cup Dill Sauce.

nutrition at a glance

per serving

2.5 g.	total fat
0.6 g.	saturated fat
451	calories
14 mg.	cholesterol
843 mg.	sodium
42 g.	protein
65 g.	carbohydrates
14 g.	dietary fiber

Summer Luncheon

Gazpacho with Shrimp and Avocado (page 66)

Turkey Salad with Orange Dressing (page 100)

Lemon Bars (page 369)

For each serving, plan on 1 cup Gazpacho with Shrimp and Avocado and 2 Lemon Bars.

nutrition at a glance

per serving

3.6 g.	total fat
0.8 g.	saturated fat
363	calories
57 mg.	cholesterol
448 mg.	sodium
21 g.	protein
66 g.	carbohydrates
5 g.	dietary fiber

Harvest Garden Fest

Fresh Tomato Soup (page 67)

Garden and Grain Loaf (page 182)

Roasted Pepper Sauce (page 291)

Oven-Glazed Rutabagas (page 235)

Stacked-High Apple Pie (page 359)

For each serving, plan on 1 cup Fresh Tomato Soup and ½ cup Roasted Pepper Sauce.

nutrition at a glance

per serving

2.4 g.	total fat
0.4 g.	saturated fat
624	calories
0 mg.	cholesterol
481 mg.	sodium
150 g.	protein
145 g.	carbohydrates
15 g.	dietary fiber

Fireside Supper

Vegetable Stew with Beef (page 172)

Spinach-Orange Salad (page 109)

French bread

Baked Winter Fruits (page 310)

For each serving, plan on 2 slices (1" wide) French baguette.

nutrition at a glance

per serving

3.6 g.	total fat
1 g.	saturated fat
494	calories
13 mg.	cholesterol
706 mg.	sodium
17 g.	protein
104 g.	carbohydrates
11 g.	dietary fiber

Southwestern Sampler

Pinto Bean Dip (page 43)

Baked tortilla chips

Beef and Mushroom Fajitas (page 171)

Fruit Salad with Cantaloupe Dressing (page 112)

For each serving, plan on ½ cup Pinto Bean Dip, 14 tortilla chips (1 ounce), and 2 Beef and Mushroom Fajitas.

nutrition at a glance

per serving

4.2 g.	total fat
0.7 g.	saturated fat
640	calories
36 mg.	cholesterol
817 mg.	sodium
33 g.	protein
124 g.	carbohydrates
18 g.	dietary fiber

Florida Feast

Spicy Shrimp (page 131)

Lemon-Dill Rice (page 277)

Baked Citrus Carrots (page 212)

Key Lime Cheesecake (page 347)

nutrition at a glance

per serving

2.2 g.	total fat
0.3 g.	saturated fat
552	calories
129 mg.	cholesterol
696 mg.	sodium
31 g.	protein
100 g.	carbohydrates
5 g.	dietary fiber

French Bistro Supper

Better-Than-French Onion Soup (page 72)

Turkey Cutlets Tarragon (page 165)

Scalloped Potatoes and Fennel (page 220)

Chocolate-Raspberry Cake (page 350)

For each serving, plan on 1 cup Better-Than-French Onion Soup.

nutrition at a glance

per serving

2.1 g.	total fat
0.8 g.	saturated fat
443	calories
58 mg.	cholesterol
564 mg.	sodium
30 g.	protein
78 g.	carbohydrates
6 g.	dietary fiber

Alfresco Italian

Mediterranean Shrimp (page 37)

Orange-Rosemary Turkey (page 162)

Orzo with Asparagus (page 271)

Tomato, Basil, and Mozzarella Salad (page 106)

nutrition at a glance

per serving

3.3 g.	total fat
0.5 g.	saturated fat
461	calories
142 mg.	cholesterol
445 mg.	sodium
49 g.	protein
62 g.	carbohydrates
7 g.	dietary fiber

Moroccan Magic

Couscous-Stuffed Peppers (page 188)

Mediterranean Vegetables (page 230)

Summer Fruits in Phyllo (page 364)

nutrition at a glance

per serving

2.4 g.	total fat
0.3 g.	saturated fat
439	calories
0 mg.	cholesterol
527 mg.	sodium
13 g.	protein
95 g.	carbohydrates
12 g.	dietary fiber

Greek Get-Away

Wild Mushroom Moussaka (page 194)

Greek Salad (page 104)

Lemon-Ginger Figs with Ice Cream (page 373)

nutrition at a glance

per serving

2.6 g.	total fat
0.8 g.	saturated fat
562	calories
7 mg.	cholesterol
546 mg.	sodium
20 g.	protein
122 g.	carbohydrates
13 g.	dietary fiber

Escape to the Islands

Hawaiian Mahimahi-Shrimp Kabobs (page 130)

White rice

Sweet-and-Spicy Carrots (page 208)

Glazed Tropical Fruit Cake (page 356)

For each serving, plan on 2 Hawaiian Mahimahi-Shrimp Kabobs and ½ cup cooked white rice.

nutrition at a glance

per serving

3.3 g.	total fat
0.8 g.	saturated fat
600	calories
163 mg.	cholesterol
362 mg.	sodium
38 g.	protein
107 g.	carbohydrates
7 g.	dietary fiber

China Time

Lemongrass Egg-
Drop Soup (page
73)

Peking Turkey
and Vegetables
(page 166)

White rice

Orange and Cin-
namon Rhubarb
(page 374)

For each serving, plan on 1 cup
Lemongrass Egg-Drop Soup and
½ cup cooked white rice.

nutrition at a glance

per serving

2.4 g.	total fat
0.5 g.	saturated fat
516	calories
34 mg.	cholesterol
437 mg.	sodium
23 g.	protein
104 g.	carbohydrates
8 g.	dietary fiber

Soup for Supper

Winter Potato
and Fish
Chowder
(page 90)

Multigrain bread

Creamy Banana
Bowl (page 316)

For each serving, plan on 2
cups Winter Potato and Fish
Chowder and 1 slice multigrain
bread.

nutrition at a glance

per serving

3 g.	total fat
0.9 g.	saturated fat
483	calories
19 mg.	cholesterol
324 mg.	sodium
24 g.	protein
88 g.	carbohydrates
6 g.	dietary fiber

Dinner for a Busy Weeknight

Garden Pita
Pizza (page 177)

Tossed Antipasto
Salad (page 97)

For each serving, plan on 2
servings Tossed Antipasto
Salad.

nutrition at a glance

per serving

2.5 g.	total fat
0.3 g.	saturated fat
325	calories
1 mg.	cholesterol
528 mg.	sodium
21 g.	protein
62 g.	carbohydrates
11 g.	dietary fiber

Kids' Choice

Crispy Fish with
Tartar Sauce
(page 129)

Baby carrots

Western Fries
(page 223)

Rice Pudding
with Nectarines
(page 371)

For each serving, plan on 3 baby
carrots.

nutrition at a glance

per serving

1.9 g.	total fat
0.4 g.	saturated fat
602	calories
28 mg.	cholesterol
989 mg.	sodium
24 g.	protein
121 g.	carbohydrates
8 g.	dietary fiber

Index

Underscored page references indicate boxed text. **Boldface** page references indicate photographs. *Italic* page references indicate tables.